Harry Northwood
The Early Years
1881-1900

William Heacock
James Measell
Berry Wiggins

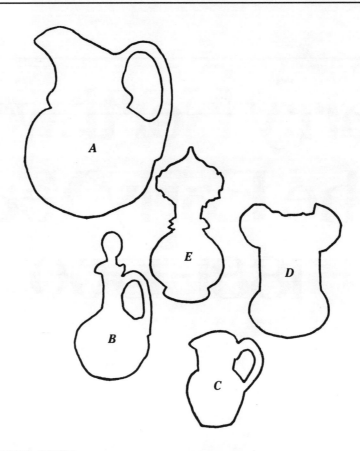

ON THE COVER:

A Leaf Umbrella pitcher in rose agate (Martins Ferry).

B Royal Ivy rubina cruet (Martins Ferry).

C Royal Art creamer (Martins Ferry).

D Opaline Brocade (Spanish Lace) cranberry opalescent vase with crimped and ruffled top (Indiana).

E Striped blue opalescent vase with applied rigaree on neck, embossed "Pan American 1901" (National Glass Company's Northwood Glass Works, Indiana).

Hardbound I.S.B.N. #0-915410-38-9

Softbound I.S.B.N. #0-915410-39-7

Additional copies may be ordered from:
ANTIQUE PUBLICATIONS
P.O. Box 553
Marietta, Ohio 45750

TABLE OF CONTENTS

William R. Heacock
1947-1988

Publisher's Introduction
By David E. Richardson

It all began in the summer of 1974, when a tall, skinny, redheaded "kid" came to see my father about a printing job. In the years since, I have recalled and chuckled many times over the letter my dad wrote to me describing this incident.

"Well, son, I just have to take a couple of minutes to tell you about this kid who came to see me today. I was having one of my typical Mondays when my receptionist came in to announce that there was a young man from Michigan here to see me about printing a book on toothpicks.

"I immediately thought to myself, here's one of those people we get from time to time who live in a dream world and who have some crazy idea that they think is going to make them a million dollars. Imagine, Dave, a book about toothpicks! Some are round and some are flat; some are wooden and some are plastic. What more can you say about toothpicks and who'd be interested anyway?

"It wasn't very long after he came into my office that I realized that the book he wanted us to print wasn't about toothpicks but about toothpick **holders**! I guess everybody in the glass world calls them 'toothpicks' for short. I told him quite frankly that the idea stank! 'No way am I going to print a book like that. ' 'Why not?' he wanted to know. And I told him—'because every time somebody has a great idea that doesn't work, the printer gets left holding the bag for the cost of the book.'

"That's when he offered to sell his collection if the book didn't make enough money to pay for the printing. I was impressed with his attitude. He thought it was a good idea and nothing I could do could shake him from that position. Well, Dave, I figured we're in the the printing business, and if this kid wants to waste his money on doing a book that only his grandmother will buy, who am I to stop him?"

My father is great at making predictions. (He's the one who said in 1960 that America wasn't ready to elect a Catholic President!) Though he thought it was a bad idea, he printed the book. A year and a half later, in 1975, when I got home from the Service, I finally got to meet this "kid" and judge his book for myself. The book was called *The Encyclopedia of Victorian Pattern Glass, Book 1, Toothpick Holders from A to Z*, and this "kid," I discovered much to my surprise, was a young man about my own age. His name was Bill Heacock.

Not long after that first book came out, it became obvious that my father was wrong and Bill was right. There <u>was</u> a market for good research and excellent color pictures of antique glass. So, he did a book on opalescent glass and then one on syrups, cruets and sugar shakers. Then came one on custard glass, and another in collaboration with Fred Bickenheuser on the companies of the U. S. Glass conglomerate.

The *Encyclopedia of Victorian Pattern Glass* series became the main focus of his writing life. Soon after the fifth book came out, Bill confided in me his "grand plan." He would do a book on cruets as number six in the series, then one, or possibly two books on stained glass, and the last three books in the series would be his crowning achievement, a trilogy on Harry Northwood. Bill's research and writings on Mr. Northwood would be the accomplishment of his life, for which he wished everyone to remember him.

As the years rolled by, Bill spent a lot of time accumulating information on Northwood. His computer and manila file folders bulged with tidbits of information. As he was researching and writing his other books, every time he came across something pertinent to Harry Northwood or a Northwood pattern, he would add it to his data banks. When he started to publish his journals—*The Glass Collector* and, later, *Collecting Glass*—he was so excited about some of the Northwood information he had found that he decided to share it with his readers in short articles instead of waiting until the trilogy was completed.

In early 1986, Bill began to have health problems which greatly reduced his strength and his ability to write. A deadly debilitating disease was already at work. He was having great difficulty meeting his deadlines and public appearances. By the spring of 1987, Bill's illness was wreaking havoc with his ability to concentrate and to organize data. Each time he would sit down at his computer to work on the book, his thoughts would be so jumbled that he could never get much accomplished. None of us knew it at the time, but Bill would have a little more than twelve months to live, during which time he was unable to do anything on his manuscripts.

Shortly before he passed away, Bill finally realized that he was unable to finish this book. He asked me what was going to happen to his incomplete manuscripts. I told him that I would do whatever was necessary to see that they were completed and published and that they would be under his name as author. At that time, he was working on <u>Fenton: The Third Twenty-Five Years,</u> <u>More Stained Glass from A to Z,</u> (Book 8 in his Encyclopedia Series), and the trilogy on Northwood, tentatively called <u>Northwood—The Early Years,</u> <u>Northwood—The Wheeling Years</u> and <u>Dugan -Diamond.</u>

He passed away on August 14, 1988.

We began to complete his unfinished projects in the same sequence in which he had been working on them. First came the third Fenton book, which was published in the spring of 1989. But when we turned our attention to the proposed book on ruby and amber stained glass, we discovered that it was not as well developed as Bill's work on Harry Northwood, so we decided to do the Northwood series next.

The "we" to whom I refer in the above paragraph is actually Dr. James Measell, noted glass historian and author, glass researcher Berry Wiggins, and my staff here at Antique Publications. Berry was working behind the scenes with Bill for many years, visiting libraries, museums and newspaper archives, digging up as much information as possible on molds, factory histories and Northwood/Dugan glass. Jim has accepted the job as Director of Glass History Reasearch with our publishing company and is doing an excellent job bringing Mr. Heacock's unfinished works to completion.

Here I would like to issue a public thank you to both Jim and Berry for their efforts in completing this first book in Bill's trilogy. I believe that Northwood admirers are deeply indebted.

Through my personal involvement in this book and with Jim and Berry's tutoring, I have come to recognize some Northwood patterns and to appreciate this great man's works. I am trying to collect as many pieces of Northwood Carnival as I can find, enjoying every one of them. Each piece reminds me not only Harry Northwood, but of the man who hoped the world would remember him for his Northwood research. As you read this book and study and collect the glass, it is my hope that Bill's dream will be realized. He will be remembered not only as a great researcher and Victorian Pattern Glass historian but also as the man who helped educate us on Harry Northwood and his glass.

INTRODUCTION

Publication of this book was one of William Heacock's dreams. Bill had become intensely interested in Harry Northwood, and he sought to document the patterns and articles made at various glass factories where Harry Northwood worked.

When Bill passed away on August 14, 1988, he left a wealth of research materials on Harry Northwood. With the aid of other researchers, chiefly Tom Klopp and Berry Wiggins, Bill had assembled data from two major glass tableware trade publications: *Pottery and Glassware Reporter* and *China, Glass and Lamps*. Quotes relating to Harry Northwood from the trade Journals and a few local newspapers, such as the Indiana (PA) *Gazette*, had been recorded in Bill's computer, and other material had been gathered — legal records such as land transfers and wills. Many glass fragments from the old Northwood factory site in Indiana, Pa., were carefully sorted and identified. A picture of Harry Northwood the glassmaker was just beginning to emerge.

As I began to read Bill's computer files on Harry Northwood in the fall of 1988, I was amazed at the information Bill had assembled about him. But I also recognized that much more research needed to be done — primarily with local history records such as city directories from the 1880s-90s and with lawsuits in several Ohio and Pennsylvania counties. Two other important trade publications — *Crockery and Glass Journal* and *Housefurnisher: China, Glass and Pottery Review* — needed to be examined in detail.

When Dave Richardson asked me in August, 1988, if I thought this book could be completed, my answer was a hesitant "Yes." Dave's desire to see this project through as a memorial to Bill removed the hesitation. I read all of Bill's computer files over the early months of 1989, and, with Dave's blessing and financial support, I spent

four months (May-August, 1989) in Marietta working full-time on this book.

On May 16, 1989, I first visited Miss Elizabeth Northwood Robb, Harry Northwood's granddaughter. Her warm memories of Harry Northwood and her vibrant personality had the same effect on me that they had had on Bill. The next day, a trip to the Ohio County Public Library in Wheeling yielded new information about Harry Northwood's whereabouts during the 1880s.

Bill's dream became my dream — produce a definitive book on Harry Northwood. Bill knew that a book on Harry Northwood would be difficult and even controversial, simply because several other authors (Kamm, Revi, Hartung, Olson and others) have offered accounts of Northwood's life and glassmaking career. Bill had encountered controversy when he published several articles about Dugan/Diamond carnival glass in *The Antique Trader* during 1981. The research reported here will contradict some assertions made in works by other authors. Unlike some of those earlier studies, however, this book on Harry Northwood will offer clear documentation — such as attributions of patterns based upon trade journals and other published sources. Harry Northwood's frequent changes of locale and/or factory affiliation will be traced through a variety of public records, ranging from city directories and newspapers to deeds and lawsuits. As you read this book, the kind of record consulted and used as evidence (newspapers, trade journals, deeds, etc.) should be clear every step of the way.

For instance, depending upon the author one reads, Harry Northwood arrived first in the United States as early as 1879 or as late as 1886. Obviously, only one date can be correct! And no author specifies the month/day of Northwood's arrival. Most of the time, other writers on Northwood present their conclusions without a clear indication of the evidence used to reach those conclusions. The first few sentences of the first chapter of this book take up the question of the date of Northwood's entry into this country. As you read these sentences in a few moments, you'll be aware of both the conclusion and the evidence used to reach it.

Every research project has its own successes and frustrations along the way. The wealth of material about Northwood in the glass trade press was sometimes amazingly clear and, on other occasions, dismayingly vague. Among the revelations of this book are the dates of introduction for many patterns and/or colors developed by Northwood and used at one or more of his plants. This book details Harry Northwood's glassmaking career from his immigration to America until his return to England in late 1899. During this time, Northwood was affiliated with some of the most significant glass factories in the United States — Hobbs, Brockunier at Wheeling and the La Belle at Bridgeport — and he founded and managed several plants of his own.

A second volume, *Harry Northwood: The Wheeling Years*, is already under way. It will cover Northwood's return to the United States in 1902, his purchase of the old Hobbs plant in Wheeling, and the products of that factory until its closure in the mid-1920s. Harry Northwood died in 1919, but his artistic genius and glassmaking knowledge live on in the design innovations and distinctive colors produced by his glassmaking firms.

James Measell

ACKNOWLEDGEMENTS

Many people and institutions deserve a hearty "thanks" for their assistance in the research and production of this book. First and foremost is David Richardson, president of Richardson Printing Corporation and of Antique Publications, Dave was determined that a decade of William Heacock's research not be lost. He provided the financial support and the measure of time necessary to complete this book. His enthusiasm for glass, tempered with his demanding standards for printing and photography, made this project a reality. Staff photographer Deana Wynn captured the beauty of much Northwood glass. Ronda Ludwig and Theresa Sauer performed the design and layout work. Their patience and care are reflected in the quality of the final product.

A particularly large gesture of appreciation must go to Berry Wiggins and Tom Klopp. Berry's trade publication research on Harry Northwood goes back many years, and much of the material on Harry Northwood in William Heacock's computer files came from Berry's patient examination of old journals. Tom Klopp put every word of this book through the "wringer" of his remarkable command of the literature on American pattern glass. He also pored over the Martins Ferry *Evening Times* and many other primary sources, seeking information on Harry Northwood, his glass and his personal life. Tom's research and insights helped get the Northwood story straight.

Miss Elizabeth Northwood Robb, the granddaughter of Harry Northwood, allowed complete access to family photographs, clippings and glass heirlooms. She also shared her vivid memories of her grandfather and grandmother, and she provided leads to other Northwood family members. Much of her contribution to this book can be readily seen in the credit lines (whenever *Courtesy of Miss Robb* appears), but her warm support is much appreciated, too. Welcome encouragement came from others in the Northwood families: Robert Hamilton; David McKinley; Karen McKinley; and Ken Northwood. Members of the Beaumont and the Dugan families also aided in this research. Special thanks go to Arthur J. Beaumont, Sr., Arthur J. Beaumont, Jr., Ernest R. Dugan and Mrs. Frances Dugan.

Frank M. Fenton willingly shared his knowledge of glass history and glassmaking technology as well as allowing photographic reproduction of materials in the Fenton Museum. He also provided access to the files of the National Association of Manufacturers of Pressed and Blown Glassware, a treasury of information that will be mined in future projects.

William Gamble's long-time acquaintance with Northwood glass proved valuable in compiling lists of items and colors, and his assistance in securing items to be photographed extended over several years. Among the collections visited were those assembled by Larry Loxterman and Tom and Betty Laney. Both were valuable learning experiences, as Northwood items could be closely compared. Bob and Carole Bruce contributed their knowledge of Northwood colors and loaned items to be photographed.

Raymond Notley of Sotheby's in London, who first provided William Heacock with Northwood material from England over a decade ago, shared both a knowledge of glassmaking techniques and his expertise in the history of art and design.

Paul Miller and Jabe Tarter loaned a jar of interesting glass fragments from Indiana, Pa., as well as tape-recorded interviews with Mildred Northwood Gilleland and Blanche Mock Dugan, both of whom are now deceased. Many fragments were provided to Bill Heacock by Del Helman of Indiana, Pa., and these proved valuable in this study.

The Mansion Museum at the Oglebay Institute in Wheeling has had an enduring interest in Northwood glass. Director John Artzberger and curator Holly Hoover supported this project and stand ready to assist with subsequent volumes.

Norma P. H. Jenkins, Head Librarian at the Rakow Library in the Corning Museum of Glass, was always quick to respond to inquiries. Jane Shadel Spillman, Curator of American Glass at the Corning Museum of Glass, shared her expertise on pattern attributions.

The Martins Ferry Historical Society, through president Ron Wrixon and Miss Annie Tanks, provided valuable information and photographs. Mr. Wrixon also loaned photos from his personal collection. Mrs. Jane Thiel Boddorf contributed important information about her great-grandfather, Henry Helling.

Among the libraries visited during this project were the Carnegie Library in Pittsburgh and the Ohio County Public Library in Wheeling, as well as libraries in Martins Ferry and Bellaire, Ohio; and New Castle, and Indiana, Pa. The archives at the American Flint Glass Workers Union in Toledo were also utilized. The American Kennel Club's library director, Roberta Vesley, provided valuable assistance.

Many elected representatives and municipal employees were co-operative when research was needed in these valuable public records. Gratitude is extended to the offices of the Secretary of State in Ohio, Pennsylvania, and West Virginia, as well as to officials and staff members in courthouses in Belmont County, Ohio; Indiana County and Lawrence County, Pa.; and Ohio County, West Virginia.

William Heacock's files contained many snapshots of unusual Northwood pieces, often without information as to the owner of the glass. To those who sent photos to Bill over the years: Thanks!

James Measell
Berkley, Michigan
June, 1990

CHAPTER ONE
LEARNING THE TRADE, 1881-1887

When he appeared before Probate Court Judge Isaac H. Gaston in Belmont County, Ohio, to apply for American citizenship on October 8, 1889, Harry Northwood stated that he had entered the United States "on or about" November 1, 1881. His memory of the trip to New York nearly eight years earlier on the *S. S. England* was accurate.

On November 1, 1881, Captain T. P. Heeley signed the passenger list on which the entry "Hy. Northwood" appears. At 21, Northwood's feelings upon immigration to this country must have been mixed. On the one hand, he felt the challenge and excitement of joining the American glass tableware industry. On the other, he must have had some pangs of homesickness, for he left three younger brothers (Fred, Carl, and John Northwood II) as well as six sisters. The Northwood family was close-knit, and Harry had especially strong associations with the uncles and cousins from his mother's side. Her maiden name is recorded as Duggin (or perhaps Duggins), but her brothers used the name Duggan (according to Blanche Mock Dugan, who compiled an extensive family history in 1960, the surname was shortened from Duggan to Dugan upon immigration).

Harry Northwood was born June 30, 1860, at Wordsley, Kingswinford, County of Stafford, in the Stourbridge district of England. His father, John Northwood, appeared before the Registrar on July 13, and he declared the newborn's mother as "Elizabeth Northwood formerly Duggin." John Northwood's occupation, "glass ornamenter," was to prove prophetic for Harry Northwood and two of his brothers, Carl and John II. Each followed in his father's footsteps by entering the glass trade, although each did so in his own way. This book (and a projected second volume, *Harry Northwood: The Wheeling Years*) will discuss the glassmaking careers of Harry and Carl Northwood.

The Northwood Patriarch

The career of John Northwood has been well-detailed by several writers, most notably John Northwood II, who published *John Northwood: His Contribution to the Stourbridge Flint Glass Industry, 1850-1902* in 1958, so only a brief recapitulation is necessary here. John Northwood first gained fame about 1873 with his creation of the Elgin Vase. Northwood's forte was "cameo glass," a nineteenth century re-creation of an ancient technique. In 1876, he completed a three year effort to carve a replica of the Portland vase, and this project assured his everlasting fame and international reputation. Within the next several years, John Northwood completed other cameo pieces, including the Milton Vase (1878) and the Pegasus or Dennis Vase (1882), which is

---

CERTIFIED COPY OF AN ENTRY OF BIRTH

GIVEN AT THE GENERAL REGISTER OFFICE, LONDON

Application Number........6884D..........

REGISTRATION DISTRICT		Stourbridge		
1860 BIRTH in the Sub-district of *Kingswinford* in the *County of Stafford*				

Columns:— 1	2	3	4	5	6	7	8	9	10*
No. When and where born	Name, if any	Sex	Name and surname of father	Name, surname and maiden surname of mother	Occupation of father	Signature, description and residence of informant	When registered	Signature of registrar	Name entered after registration
1,85 *Thirtieth June 1860 Wordsley Kingswinford*	*Harry*	*Boy*	*John Northwood*	*Elizabeth Northwood formerly Duggin*	*Glass ornamenter*	*John Northwood Father Wordsley Kingswinford*	*Thirteenth July 1860*	*James Whitehouse Registrar*	

CERTIFIED to be a true copy of an entry in the certified copy of a Register of Births in the District above mentioned. Given at the GENERAL REGISTER OFFICE, LONDON, under the Seal of the said Office, the *5th* day of *June* 19 79

*See note overleaf

BXA 466782

This certificate is issued in pursuance of the Births and Deaths Registration Act 1953. Section 34 provides that any certified copy of an entry purporting to be sealed or stamped with the seal of the General Register Office shall be received as evidence of the birth or death to which it relates without any further or other proof of the entry, and no certified copy purporting to have been given in the said Office shall be of any force or effect unless it is sealed or stamped as aforesaid.

English carved cameo vases. Courtesy of Miss Robb and the Oglebay Institute, Wheeling, WV.

now in the Smithsonian Institution. The Northwood cameos were brought together for the first time, along with many cameo articles created by others, in a major exhibition at the Corning Museum of Glass in 1982. The catalog for this exhibit, *Cameo Glass: Masterpieces from 2000 Years of Glassmaking*, is both an excellent reference book and an aesthetlc treat.

In addition to his expertise in cameo carving, John Northwood I was also an innovator in using various acids for etching glass, and he invented a template machine for decorating which produced precise geometric patterns, enabling etched glass to rival engraved glass (light cutting with a thin copper wheel) for its intricacy of design and regularity of execution. John Northwood also invented a glass crimping device and designed motifs to be made with hot glass, such as Acanthus decoration, Matsu-No-Kee decoration and Blackthorn spray. When the commercial demand for cameo glass was strong, John Northwood I developed designs and colors which allowed cameo-like effects to be produced more rapidly (and far less expensively) by a staff of glassworkers. He also invented a glass expansion testing machine which facilitated research into the physical characteris-

English commercial cameo pieces. Courtesy of Miss Robb.

tics of the cased glasses necessary for the production of commercial cameo pieces, and he pioneered intaglio processes which, according to John Northwood II, "combine the efforts" of cutters and engravers.

There can be no doubt that John Northwood the glass cameo artist exerted great influence

John Northwood I, his wife Elizabeth and five of the six daughters, ca. 1900. Ethel is standing at left, and Mabel and Ina (her long skirt is visible) are standing on the right. Eva is seated (closest to her father, with Mabel's hand on her shoulder), and Winifred is seated next to her (daughter Amy is not present). This photo was probably taken by George Woodall, a famous glass cameo carver who was also an avid photographer, for the negative used to make this print came from one of Woodall's descendants. Courtesy of the Fenton Museum, Williamstown, WV.

upon the young Harry Northwood. In addition to inheriting a measure of his father's natural talent for drawing, Harry attended a provincial art school while working at the Stevens and Williams glass works. *Pottery and Glassware Reporter* (August 11, 1887) associated Harry Northwood with the "South Kensington Art School," which was actually a comprehensive curriculum of design studies followed in various government schools. Harry Northwood likely attended a government design school in nearby Birmingham or Dudley. According to an obituary published at Harry Northwood's death in 1919, he was an apprentice at age 14 and "received specially careful instruction under his distinguished father" (*National Glass Budget*, February 8, 1919). John Northwood II recalls that his father filled many sketchbooks with drawings made during visits to museums in England and France, while he accompanied him and made his own sketches. Since

Harry Northwood was a decade older than John II, it is easy to imagine the young Harry trailing in his father's wake during earlier visits to these or other museums. The emphasis in Northwood's art and design training was decidedly classical, and Harry Northwood, perhaps more so than other graduates of the government schools, was prepared to use the principles of art in designing manufactured goods.

Harry Northwood at Hobbs, Brockunier

Among the earliest records of Harry Northwood's presence in the United States is a line in *Callin's Wheeling Directory* for 1882-83: "Northwood Harry, glassetcher, boards 3912 Jacob." Interestingly, Harry Northwood was not alone; the same city directory contains this entry: "Dugan, Thomas, glass etcher, boards 3912 Jacob." Northwood and the sixteen year old Dugan, who were cousins, probably came to the

Exterior and interior views of the Hobbs, Brockunier plant from Hayes' <u>Atlas</u> *(1877).* **Courtesy of the Fenton Museum, Williamstown, WV.**

United States at about the same time and found jobs at the Hobbs, Brockunier plant in Wheeling.

Their work as glass etchers consisted of preparing glass articles for the action of hydrofluoric acid fumes, which attack the unprotected surfaces of the ware and produce a satin finish. Wax was used to protect glass from the acid, and glass etchers first worked out the application of wax to achieve the desired decorative effects in various designs.

Why Northwood and Dugan came to Wheeling instead of other glass manufacturing centers (Philadelphia, Pittsburgh or the New England area) is not certain. One possible explanation stems from Harry Northwood's relationship with the Dugan family. Harry Northwood's uncle, Thomas Dugan, who was born in 1834, came to the United States, probably before the Civil War. After working in a steel mill in Cleveland, Dugan settled in Pittsburgh in the 1860s. About 1870, he "took charge of the old English Hotel ... becoming widely known to the travelling public as a genial and capable host" (Hazen's *History of Lawrence County and Representative Citizens*, p. 853). Obituaries for another Northwood uncle (Samuel Dugan, Sr., b. 1839), and a cousin (Samuel Dugan, Jr., b. 1870) indicate that the elder Samuel Dugan brought his family to the United States in 1881, taking up residence in Pittsburgh, perhaps on the advice of his brother Thomas. According to various Pittsburgh city directories, Dugan's English Hotel was at 445 Liberty Avenue in the 1870s and early 1880s. About 1885, he had a hotel at 1223 Liberty; from 1889 to 1892, it was known as the Dugan House.

Jobs for young glassworkers may have been hard to come by in Pittsburgh in 1881, or perhaps Harry Northwood and his young cousin simply wanted to be on their own in the country they had adopted. In any event, they found employment at Hobbs, Brockunier and Co., which was also known as the South Wheeling Glass Works. Their address on Jacob Street was just two short blocks west and two blocks south of the factory.

Virtually every Northwood researcher has said that Harry Northwood began his career at Hobbs, Brockunier and Company, and it is tempting indeed to credit the young Englishman with all sorts of innovative, distinctive colored glassware made there in the 1880s. One must bear in mind, however, that the Hobbs, Brockunier firm already had an established tradition of employing the best among American glassmakers. William Leighton, Sr., is generally credited with the development of "soda lime" glass formulas which greatly reduced the cost of manufacturing glass tableware in comparison to the earlier "flint" glass batches. William Leighton, Jr., took over at Hobbs, Brockunier after his father's retirement about 1869, and he and William F. Russell obtained a number of patents during the 1870s and 80s. Among them were procedures for opalescent glassware and spangled glassware (see Revi's *American Pressed Glass and Figure Bottles*). The son of William Leighton, Jr., George W. Leighton, was also on hand at Hobbs, Brockunier, and he was likely learning glass chemistry as well, for he became an established glassmaker with such later creations as Findlay Onyx. Harry Northwood was probably employed at Hobbs, Brockunier in 1881-84, to be sure, but he, like Thomas Dugan, was far more likely to have been observing and learning rather than at the forefront of any innovations.

In late February, 1882, a fire destroyed portions of the company, and newspaper reports of this calamity provide some information regarding the glass etching operation. The *Wheeling Register* (February 25, 1882) mentioned a "large new etching building," which was spared by the flames, and Baker has concluded that this building was

Portrait of the Harry Northwood family, ca. 1885.
Courtesy of Miss Robb.

erected in 1880 or shortly thereafter ("Hobbs, Brockunier & Co.'s Glass Factory Burned," *The Glass Club Bulletin*, Fall, 1987, pp. 14-16). The firm's apparently growing interest in etching glass may have required additional workers with the requisite skills, thus attracting Northwood and Dugan to Wheeling.

On May 27, 1882, Harry Northwood married Clara Elizabeth Beaumont at the residence of John Walford (3529 Jacob). The ceremony was performed by the Rev. J. W. Griffith of the North Street Methodist Episcopal Church in Wheeling (Ohio County, WV, *Marriage Book* 15, p. 94). A native of Staffordshire, England, nineteen year old "Lil" or "Lilly," as she was called, had embarked for the United States on May 10, accompanied by her younger brother, Percy J. Beaumont. Many years later, the *Morgantown Post* (May 3, 1947) recalled his immigration: "Mr. Beaumont accompanied a sister to this country in 1882. She was to be married to a glass designer in Wheeling. Mr. Beaumont learned the glassmaking and decorating business from this brother-in-law...." The long relationship between the Northwoods and the Beaumonts, like that of the Northwoods and the Dugans, will be an important feature of this book.

The Northwoods' first child, listed as H. C. [for Harry Clarence] Northwood in the Ohio County, West Virginia, birth records, was born on March 13, 1883. The young couple lived at 42 North York on Wheeling Island, and *Callin's Wheeling Directory* for 1884 reveals another member of the Northwood household: "Beaumont, Percy, glassetcher, boards 42 N. York." The Northwoods' second and last child, Mabel Virginia Northwood, was born on September 3, 1884. Miss Elizabeth Northwood Robb, who assisted greatly in the research for this book, is the only child from Mabel Virginia Northwood's marriage to Harry Melvin Robb on November 10, 1909.

The first mention of Harry Northwood to be found in the trade periodicals was this long report from Wheeling on glassware exhibited at the state fair (Crockery and Glass Journal, September 21, 1882):

"WHEELING — The past week has been one of a rather exciting nature. The West Virginia State Fair in progress drew thousands of strangers from far and near into our city. ... In our rounds in the main building at the Exposition on Saturday, we gleaned a few notes which we think will be of interest to the readers of the CROCKERY AND GLASS JOURNAL. Mr. Harry Northwood, of the etching department of Hobbs, Brockunier & Co. had on exhibition some fine designs of workmanship which arrested the attention of all of artistic taste. The glass is not engraved as many supposed, nor is it etched by the ordinary process now in vogue in this country. It surpasses in artistic design, fine workmanship and beauty of effect any work by any other process. Mr. Northwood came from England less than a year ago, and brought this new idea with him. Among the wares shown is a pair of pitchers, one having a representation of "Lampetia complaining to Apollo" from the *Odyssey*, and the other "Neptune Rising from the Sea" from the *Iliad*, which show that they are produced by an artist. Another "Rebecca" pitcher is surrounded with a wreath of roses, and for delicacy of work and beauty of design rivals anything we have ever seen. There is also a pitcher having an aquarium with fishes etched on the side, the effect being peculiarly beautiful when it is filled with water, and another with stags under trees shows three distinct processes of etching. A novel and attractive set of ware called "Vermicelli" set also attracted comment. He had also on display some genuine Wedgewood Rockingham ware, and etched by himself with an ornamental design on the edge. The difference between this work and the etching produced by the ordinary process consists not simply in the superior artistic work, but in the peculiar bright outlines which surround all the figures. In the stag scene and in some of the other pieces three effects, one a sort of mottled, one gray, and one bright rounded line, appear. Some of the wine glasses and other small pieces are perfect gems. This gentleman has carved a cameo by hand with chisels on dark blue glass that is wonderful, having taken six weeks' continuous labor."

Courtesy of Miss Robb.

The last sentence above probably refers to a cameo now owned by Miss Elizabeth Northwood Robb, Harry Northwood's granddaughter. The cameo is inscribed on the reverse: "Hy. Northwood 1882". This rendering of Shakespeare resembles John Northwood's cameo glass studies produced between 1877 and 1880. Corning's *Cameo Glass* (pp. 44-48) shows a series of tazzas devoted to Art, Literature, and Science as well as a Shakespeare pendant (see also William Heacock, GC-2, pp. 6-10 and GC-3, p. 61 and outside back cover).

The article in *Crockery and Glass Journal* went on to discuss some innovative engraved ware made by Otto Jaeger, who is listed in *Callin's*

Oil painting by Harry Northwood. **Courtesy of Miss Robb.**

Wheeling Directory (1882-83) as "manager, engraving room" of Hobbs, Brockunier. Jaeger went to Fostoria, Ohio, in the late 1880s (see Murray's *History of Fostoria, Ohio, Glass*). Later, he was manager of the Bonita Glass Company at Cicero, Indiana. *China, Glass and Lamps* (May 18, 1899) recalled his days at Hobbs, Brockunier, dubbing them "the palmy days when that high class firm got out the famous blown and pressed amberina, peachblow and fine flashed glass specialties and had such a glorious run on the old Hob-nail pattern."

Shortly after the fair closed, *Crockery and Glass Journal* (September 28, 1882) wrote once more about the young man from England: "Harry Northwood, etcher at Hobbs, Brockunier and Co.'s, took three first premiums at the State Fair: first for etched glass, second for best display of glassware, and third for oil painting from nature." At least one oil by Harry Northwood — a scene in Wales—survives.

In early October, 1882, the Hobbs, Brockunier firm began to advertise its new lines with a full page ad in *Crockery and Glass Journal*. No items

are pictured, and Northwood is not mentioned by name, but the reference to "engraved and etched ware" probably reflects his growing influence on the firm's products. This ad ran throughout the fall of 1882.

Throughout 1883, *Crockery and Glass Journal* mentioned Hobbs, Brockunier products, such as a "crackled ware" [called "Craquelle"] as well as pitchers in "white and old gold" and a 126 line described as "diamond and waterfall" (June 14, July 5 and September 6, 1883).

In its October 11, 1883, issue, *Crockery and Glass Journal* featured an interesting quote, which might have come from Harry Northwood: "Every pot in the factory is in operation and that to its fullest capacity. ... Orders are abundant for all classes of ware made by this factory. ... [quoting a gentleman at the factory] All that a designer has to do is to furnish an idea, and that idea is made tangible in a moment. There is nothing susceptible of so many and such wondrous changes, and this very quality will always make glass popular. ... The educated designer is the man who is always in demand about a factory, for by the

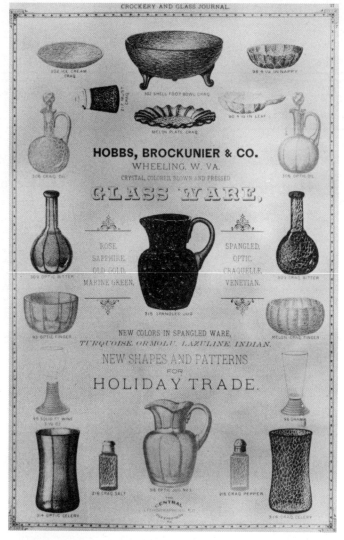

Full page ad from Crockery and Glass Journal, *October 4, 1883.*

results of his lucubrations are the factories maintained."

Over the next two months, Hobbs, Brockunier products were mentioned from time to time. The *Journal* discussed both spangled glass (a patented ware developed by William Leighton, Jr.) and craquelle glass as well as cut, engraved and etched ware along with some mysterious "Roman, Grecian and Trojan vases" (November 15, 1883). Also mentioned was a "new set, on the round order with a series of heavy points, especially attractive with the new engraving" (*Crockery and Glass Journal*, December 27, 1883).

A later note about Harry Northwood in a glass trade periodical apparently closes his career at Hobbs, Brockunier. This brief report of a routine meeting at the La Belle Glass Company in Bridgeport, Ohio, just across the Ohio River from Wheeling, is significant for its final sentence:

"The La Belle, at Bridgeport, O., had a meeting of directors last Monday. Capt. Seymour Dunlevy

was elected secretary, and he has assumed charge of the office. There is a good demand for their new design 365 ware, which is very handsome. The new whiskey decanters, water bottles, oil bottles, and fine blown etched ware in Kate Greenaway series is wonderfully beautiful. These consist of a dozen tumblers neatly packed in a case, and are very attractive and handsome. Mr. Harry Northwood, one of the best engravers in the United States, has engaged with the La Belle" (*Crockery and Glass Journal*, February 6, 1884).

Harry Northwood at the La Belle Glass Co.

Just as there is no doubt that Harry Northwood began work at the La Belle in early 1884, there is also good evidence that he resigned in late October, 1887. It is also certain that his employ at the La Belle was not continuous and unbroken. During February, 1884, the La Belle was affected by an Ohio River flood and ceased production for a time. In 1885, like some other Ohio Valley glass plants, the La Belle's productive time was curtailed by a prolonged strike by members of the American Flint Glass Workers Union. In February, 1885, a note in *Crockery and Glass Journal* revealed that the La Belle factory had been shut down for almost a year, so Harry Northwood may have had little time to work before problems arose.

When Harry Northwood decided to cast his fortune with the La Belle Glass Company at Bridgeport, Ohio, he became a member of a well-established firm, one which had competed successfully with both the nearby Hobbs, Brockunier plant and the Pittsburgh-area factories which dominated the tableware industry at this time. As the January, 1884, exhibit at the Monongahela House in Pittsburgh drew to a close, *Pottery and Glassware Reporter* (February 7, 1884) provided this record of the firm's products:

"The La Belle Glass Company, of Bridgeport, Ohio, have out an exceedingly handsome line of tableware, which will be known as No. 365. This set they make plain and engraved, and it is one of the finest lines in the market, the pattern being very neat and tasteful. Among other new goods they have decanters, handled brandies, water and oil bottles, plain, cut and engraved. Also the St. Bernard dish, which is a decided artistic success, and their new tankard pitchers, which they likewise make plain, cut and engraved, are beautiful specimens of the crystal art. S. C. Dunlevy has been appointed secretary of this concern, and the stockholders are to be congratulated on their choice. His reputation is of the highest, and if he

View of the La Belle in Hayes' Atlas *(1877).* **Courtesy of the Fenton Museum, Williamstown, WV.**

fills his present position as acceptably to all concerned as he has filled other places of trust, the results will be thoroughly satisfactory."

In February, 1884, the La Belle Glass Company was forced to cease glassmaking operations because of flooding from the nearby Ohio River. Readily available water transportation in the form of paddle-wheel steamboats was an asset, but a lack of flood control measures made the river's proximity a threat, too. *Pottery and Glassware Reporter* for March 27, 1884, said that the La Belle "have not fired up since the flood. They have a large stock on hand and propose to dispose of it before starting again." Over six weeks later, an

explanatory notice was being run by the firm in this same journal (see next page).

The plants usually began the next "blast," as it was called, just after Labor Day, but this report, in the October 30, 1884, issue of *Pottery and Glassware Reporter*, said that the "La Belle Glass Works ... are making ready to start up, and will probably resume work in December." By that time, however, the Ohio Valley glass tableware plants were embroiled in a bitter labor dispute with their skilled glassworkers, who were represented by the young, but powerful American Flint Glass Workers Union. By mid-December, many tableware factories in the upper Ohio Valley area were shut down. The strike was caused by disagreements between Ohio Valley glass manufacturers and workers over wages and working conditions.

Crockery and Glass Journal for March 1, 1883, had reported that the "Flint glass workers of the region known as Martins Ferry have united on a uniform scale of 'moves' on articles made in the various factories, which will be presented to the manufacturers in a week or two. Slight changes have been made simply to make the rates the same all around, and it is not likely that there will be any disagreement between the men and their employers." The *Journal* could not have been further from the truth. The resulting strike, which began in December, 1884, was long and bitter. Most of the affected companies did not resume operations until the fall of 1885. A few were closed even longer, and the La Belle was among them.

In the midst of the strike, the April 23, 1885, issue of *Pottery and Glassware Reporter* carried this revealing note about the firm: "A meeting of the stockholders of the La Belle Glass Co. ... will be held in May, for the purpose of effecting a complete reorganization of the concern, with a view of starting up upon a stable and solid basis next fall. In times past this firm were noted for the fine wares manufactured by them, to which there were none superior in the market, and it is the intention of the promoters of the reorganization to revivify, improve and permanently maintain the old time prestige of this house." This report suggests that the La Belle was losing ground in the competitive glass tableware industry. Perhaps Harry Northwood, now a young man with a family, was the person to restore the La Belle to its past glory. But they already had Harry Northwood on hand. Or did they?

Harry Northwood at the Phoenix?

Despite the record of his employment at La Belle in February, 1884, there is ample evidence to suggest that Harry Northwood was at the Phoenix Glass Co. in Phillipsburg, Pa., during a large part of the period when the La Belle was beset by the flood and the glassworkers' strike. Northwood was not a union member, and he had a family to support, so the La Belle's management, already in the throes of some organizational problems, may have had little choice in allowing him to leave their employ. It's hard to imagine Harry Northwood sitting idle for over a year, alternately waiting for the river to recede and the strike to be settled!

A retrospective article about Harry Northwood in the *National Glass Budget* (February 22, 1896; see p. 107) alluded to his work at the Phoenix plant, but some interesting contemporary evidence is also available. On October 23, 1885, the *American Glass Worker* reported that a newly-granted United States patent held by John Northwood I of England had been assigned "to Harry Northwood, Bridgewater, Pa." The assignment papers for this patent were dated April 27, 1885, so Harry Northwood was in Bridgewater at that time. The boroughs of Bridgewater and West Bridgewater were just across the Ohio River from Phillipsburg (now Monaca), the site of the Phoenix Glass Company's plant. The patent (#327,406) was granted on September 29, 1885, and Harry Northwood was likely working for the Phoenix at this time, allowing the firm to utilize the patented crimper in making their wares. Later in 1885, Harry Northwood prepared the preliminary paperwork for an improved glass crimper. Listing his residence as "Bridgewater, Beaver Co.," he appeared with two witnesses (Percy J.

Beaumont and Laura M. Hibler) before Thomas M. Taylor, a notary public in nearby Rochester, Pa., on November 19, 1885. For some reason, the patent application was not filed until April, 1887 (see below, p. 17).

The Phoenix plant where Harry Northwood worked was relatively new, having been rebuilt after its destruction by fire on January 29, 1884 (there is a long account in *Pottery and Glassware Reporter* for February 7, 1884). According to a *History of Beaver County, Pennsylvania* published in 1888, the plant was rebuilt "in the autumn of the same year [1884]. " In December, 1884, *Pottery and Glassware Reporter* provided an interesting picture of this enterprise:

"Formerly this firm worked chiefly on chimneys, afterward they commenced on shades, and still later on colored glassware, which is at present their most notable product. They make chimneys yet, however, and the finest lines of decorated shades in the country, but in colored glassware they have achieved a triumph never before consummated in the land. The variety of shapes, shades and colors in this ware they have on exhibition at their factory is perfectly bewildering, and altogether impossible to describe. They have table sets, pitchers of all sizes and descriptions, ice cream sets, finger bowls, water sets, berry sets, and a host of other miscellaneous wares. The diversity of colors in itself is not so remarkable as the fine shading of one color into another and the different shades in one and the same article, which shows a different color as one changes its position in relation to the light. Some of the articles have a body of one color and are plated or cased inside with a different color and the effect is very fine. Also on pieces cased outside the colored part is cut away by machinery in any desired pattern and leaves the crystal to be seen beneath, forming a crystal design on colored ground. Among the colors are carnelian, topazine, amberine, azurine, all shades of opalescent, such as flint, spotted, blue, crystal, canary, pink, etc., rose, blue, green, all shades of red, ruby, amber, blue and gold, and numerous others. They also make kerosene and glass globes and duplex chimneys in all colors and finely engraved, as well as salt and pepper sets, vases and ornamental glass, of every kind. The colors are all brilliant, sparkling and full of life and spirit, if such an expression be permissible, and combinations of shades are here produced that have never before been attempted in this country or Europe" (December 25, 1884).

By April 23, 1885, the Phoenix had regained much of its stature, according to *Pottery and Glassware Reporter*, and had increased the capital stock from $150,000 to $250,000. In May, 1885, the firm received two "medals of first class" at the exposition in New Orleans for opal glass and "best assortment and quality of colored glass" (*Crockery and Glass Journal*, May 28, 1885).

Perhaps the Phoenix's strong interest in colored and decorated wares drew Harry Northwood to the plant at Phillipsburg. A further magnet was the fact that the Phoenix firm had acquired the rights to manufacture "the Celebrated Webb Glass," as it was called in their ads (*Crockery and Glass Journal*, August 20 and November 12, 1885). The firm was very successful throughout 1885, but the editorial notes in *Pottery and Glassware Reporter* and *Crockery and Glass Journal* do not mention Harry Northwood, so one might conclude that his primary efforts were in the area of decorating cold metal, but also that he was observing and learning about glassmaking from Joseph Webb, who was probably the nephew of English glassmaker Thomas Webb.

Other compelling evidence of Northwood's association with the Phoenix is his re-assignment

ANDREW HOWARD, Prest.   W. I. MILLER, Sec'y and Treas.

Phœnix Glass Company,

PITTSBURGH PA.

SOLE MANUFACTURERS OF

THE CELEBRATED WEBB GLASS,

Cut, Etched, Engraved and Decorated, in Crystal, Flint, Colors, Opalescents, Venetian and Art Effects of Every Description.

TABLE WARE VASES, ETC. IN CORALINE, VENETIAN, VERD PEARL, ETC

ALSO KEROSENE GOODS.

FINE GAS GOODS A SPECIALTY.

Section from a Phoenix ad in late 1885; elsewhere, Joseph Webb is identified as "Metal Worker and Designer and Gen. Supt."

of patent rights for the crimper on September 1, 1885. In precise language, the assignment enabled the Phoenix Glass Company to use and profit from the device immediately and allowed Harry Northwood the right to use the invention at any future place of employ: "[Harry Northwood]

Grants exclusive right to make or have made and use and sell said Invention, upon conditions herein recited, but should he sever his connection with said Company and connect himself with any other concern making Glass Articles, he shall have the right to use said Invention at a single Factory, so long as he remains therewith." The Phoenix Glass Company's address was listed in U.S. Patent Office records as Pittsburgh; the office and salesroom were on Water St. in Pittsburgh, although the factory itself was about 27 miles away in Phillipsburg.

In the September 11, 1885 issue of the *American Glass Worker*, Henry Hand wrote a lengthy article about John Northwood's celebrated execution of the Portland vase. Hand concluded with the observation that contemporary American glass production was concerned with "so many dozen pieces for so many cents" and possessed "no taste, no skill, no beauty, no richness of design ...." Two weeks later, Harry Northwood, who was then 25, replied to Hand's remarks. He corrected some misconceptions held by Henry Hand regarding the fashioning of the Portland vase by John Northwood, but the most interesting part of the article is its final paragraph. The young Harry Northwood sketched a remarkably prophetic vision for the American glass industry as well as his own career:

"Mr. Hand's concluding remarks are good, and will be appreciated by all who read them. But the time must come when the taste of the multitude will be cultivated, and the desire for rich, artistic and beautiful goods will predominate. Our glass blowers lack the greatest of all incentives—ambition. They are satisfied to work week after week pulling down a lever or blowing in a mold. Let every young glass blower think that by gaining a knowledge of drawing and cultivating his other talents he may in the future shine as a star in his profession, and so arouse the ambition of others that the United States shall be second to none in her production of rich, artistic and beautiful glassware" (*American Glass Worker*, September 25, 1885).

Harry Northwood's time at the Phoenix was relatively brief, for, as will be seen below, he was once more at the La Belle plant by early 1886. The array of colors made by the Phoenix in the fall of 1885 was probably the work of Joseph Webb.

Northwood Returns to La Belle

On November 20, 1885, the *American Glass Worker* revealed that the La Belle was searching for "a good manager." The firm had evidently regained its financial footing and was preparing to make glass once again. They were still idle in December, 1885, but the firm made news in January, 1886:

"The La Belle Glass Company of Bridgeport has secured the services of Mr. Harry Northwood, formerly of the Phoenix Glass Company, and propose to enter more largely in the manufacture of fine colored glassware than heretofore. Mr. Northwood is the son of Mr. John Northwood, the reproducer of the Portland vase ... and as the son has been trained by this great master the La Belle management is to be complimented on this forward step in the production of fine, artistic glassware" (*American Glass Worker*, January 29, 1886).

Harry Northwood moved from Bridgewater back to Wheeling Island, taking a house at 43 S. Broadway. *Callin's Wheeling Directory* for 1886 lists Harry Northwood as "manager (La Belle Glass Wks)." Among the neighbors on Wheeling Island was the Beaumont family. Percy Beaumont's parents, John and Elizabeth, had immigrated to the United States in 1884, along with his brother, E. G. "George" Beaumont. They lived at 89 Ohio St., and Percy Beaumont was listed as an "etcher." He may have been at the La Belle also or at Hobbs, Brockunier and Co., where he had first found employment in 1882. He had been in the Bridgewater area with Northwood in November, 1885, so perhaps the brothers-in-law returned together.

Crockery and Glass Journal carried a brief note in its January 21, 1886, issue, calling Harry Northwood "an expert in the manufacture of fine colored glass ... thoroughly conversant with its production in fine artistic effects—originality, neatness and beauty in designing." An ad listed no fewer than ten glass colors (see next page).

Three colors were familiar transparent hues — canary, amber, and blue — but the others need some explanation. Topaz (amber), ruby (red glass made with gold in the mixture), citron (yellow), and pomona (green) were probably all transparent. Rose Du Barrie, which may be spelled several different ways, is an opaque pink glass, and Turquoise is probably opaque blue. The term Ivory may refer to an opaque yellowish-white glass, since "opal" [pronounced o-pal] usually designated opaque white (milk glass). The ad also mentioned "all opalescent colors." Presumably, these colors were made by Northwood at the La Belle firm, which also placed a notice in *Pottery and Glassware Reporter*. Many of these colors, or hues similar to them, were made at Northwood's later plants, too.

Within a few weeks, reports began to appear about the La Belle's new glass. *Crockery and Glass Journal* (February 18, 1886) called the sample room "a thing of beauty" and mentioned opalescent lines and "crimped ware made from a patent of Mr. Harry Northwood" [this would be the patent of John Northwood I which had been assigned to Harry Northwood; see above, p. 10]. At this same time, both Hobbs, Brockunier and Company and the Phoenix Glass Company were producing very similar wares, such as opalescent hobnail patterns, which were called "dew drop" by the manufacturers. Colored glass was all the rage, and competition was keen!

A clipping from an unidentified newspaper, dated February 12, 1886, by a member of the Northwood family, was saved in a family scrapbook:

"The La Belle Glass works at Bridgeport is again in successful operation and is turning out a variety of fine colored ware. The sample room contains specimens of ware that are as unique in design as they are variegated in colors. The specimens of opalescent colored ware, such as shades, hall globes, gas globes, duplex globes and other goods of similar pattern, present an array of beauty and is an exhibit that required knowledge and skill to produce. The fine work is executed under the supervision of Mr. Harry Northwood, the metal maker and designer of the works, and all crimped ware is manufactured under a patent which belongs exclusively to him. Another important feature of this factory is that one of the best forces of workmen, in the profession, has been secured — men who thoroughly understand their business.

"In addition to the fancy ware, which this company is becoming famous for, the press shops are rendering like satisfaction in the production of table and bar-room ware, which embraces the latest novelties in this line of business. The works, after a suspension of two years, have resumed operation under the most favorable circumstances, with a bright future; and with such a gentleman as S. C. Dunlevy, president and general manager, likewise his assistants surrounding him, who are thoroughly posted as to their duties, the La Belle is bound to take a front rank in the glass manufacturing business."

A lengthy note in *Pottery and Glassware Reporter* details the firm's products and mentions Harry Northwood:

"The La Belle Glass Co., Bridgeport, Ohio, are now in full and successful operation, and able to meet orders punctually. The lines they are now manufacturing include handsome novelties in table and bar ware, lamps, stationers', gas and kerosene goods. In fancy colored ware they are making canary, amber, Rose du Barrie, ivory, blue, topaz, citron, pomona, turquoise, ruby and opalescent colors. They are making both lime and lead glass, under the superintendence of Mr. H. Northwood, of Stourbridge, England, a place famous for the production of fine fancy glassware. From present indications the La Belle Co. looks for a great run on their new ware, although they are in operation only a short time, it is already attracting the attention of the trade. They have a fine factory here, with excellent facilities in every way, and are assured of a busy and prosperous season " (February 18, 1886).

The La Belle's ad in this same issue of *Pottery and Glassware Reporter* lists S. C. (Seymour) Dunlevy as president of the firm, and this note is revealing: "H. Northwood, Designer and Metal Maker."

Some writers have mistakenly assumed that "metal maker" means "mould maker," i.e., the craftsman who chips out the intricate patterns in the cast iron moulds. In fact, the metal maker is the man who determines the ingredients for the glass batch — the glass color chemist. Glassworkers refer to molten glass as "hot metal," and the appellation "metal maker" in the La Belle ad marks a stage in Harry Northwood's career—progressing from working with "cold metal" in etching and otherwise decorating to the creation of color effects in hot metal. Since the primary hot metal man at his previous employer, the Phoenix Glass Company, was Joseph Webb, Harry Northwood now had both the benefit of his father's instruction and first hand experience with Webb.

An ad similar to the one in *Pottery and Glassware Reporter* began to appear in *Crockery and Glass Journal* (March 18, 1886).

Editorial notes in the trade press from February through June, 1886, allude to success for the La Belle firm, but, unfortunately, no specific glassware lines are described. The *American Glass Worker* mentioned "color combinations" and "fine colored crimped ware" (February 26, 1886) without elaboration. A "Northwood opalescent polka dot shade" and "ribbed combination colored finger bowls" were mentioned in a lengthy article in the *American Glass Worker* (April 9, 1886).

The July 22, 1886, issue of *Crockery and Glass*

This ad appeared weekly in Crockery and Glass Journal *from March 18, 1886 to April 21, 1887.*

LA BELLE GLASS COMPANY,

MANUFACTURERS OF

Fine Crystal and Colored Glassware

BRIDGEPORT, O.

S. C. DUNLEVY, Pres't.
A. THOMPSON, Sec'y.

Hand Lamp

No. 1

No. 2

No. 3

No. 4

DEW DROP CREAM.

DEW DROP SPOON.

DEW DROP SUGAR.

Solid Stem Drip Foot Polka Dot Lamps and Dew Drop Sets made in Amber, Blue, Canary, Crystal, Blue Opalescent, and Crystal Opalescent.

DEW DROP BUTTER.

Ad in Crockery and Glass Journal, *July 29, 1886; note the various colors.*

Journal noted "novelties in peach and a new rare brown color," and the next issue featured a full-page ad showing lamps and an interesting square Dew Drop table set. This pattern, listed as "maker unknown," was called "Hobnail, 4-Footed" in Heacock's *Opalescent Glass from A to Z* (H2, p. 21 and fig. 156). The four-piece table set can be found in all the colors listed in the ad.

In the September 9, 1886, *Crockery and Glass Journal*, the La Belle's new line for the fall of 1886 was mentioned — "Queen Elizabeth." The journal predicted that "it is destined to have even a more popular run than the famous Queen Anne." The Queen Anne pattern, which was designed by Andrew Baggs, had been introduced in 1879-80, and it was, from all reports, quite successful. No illustrations appeared for Queen Elizabeth, so this pattern, which might have been designed by Harry Northwood, remains a mystery.

About the same time as the pattern honoring an English monarch appeared, Harry Northwood sought U.S. citizenship. On September 13, 1886, he appeared at the Circuit Court in Ohio County, West Virginia, declaring his intention to become a citizen. He was given a certificate by the court, and told to return after the statutory three-year waiting period was over.

In the October 14, 1886, issue of *Crockery and Glass Journal*, several interesting La Belle colors are mentioned: "specialties in peach-blow and satin glass and their 883 rose-lined ivory in ruby are great hits." *Crockery and Glass Journal* for October 28, 1886, said that "Mr. Harry Northwood has struck a happy medium in the production of ware that seems to have struck the popular fancy in the right place, and as a consequence the company is doing big business." About this time, the La Belle's officers changed. R. K. Giffin became president and Addison Thompson served as secretary. Seymour Dunlevy went on the road as a travelling salesman, along with C. T. Mustin (*Pottery and Glassware Reporter*, November 25, 1886).

A full-page ad in the November 18, 1886, issue of *Crockery and Glass Journal* listed the firm's "New, Rich and Beautiful Allochroite Ware" as well as a "new line of Pressed Glassware in Rock Crystal" which was termed "the richest Imitation

Cut Pattern ever offered." The *Journal*'s editorial columns mentioned "Rose du Barrie and Autumn Leaf," as well as the new line of rock crystal which "will be ready about the middle of December." On December 2, 1886, their wares were further described as "pitchers in light blue opalescent with satin finish..., a new ruby Dew Drop pattern, and lily vases in ruby with citron edge. They have just put on the market a ruby table set in rich cut nobs of the diamond pattern which is having quite a run." Unfortunately, no illustrations accompanied these descriptions.

Harry Northwood's influence upon the glassware products of the La Belle firm in late 1886 can be seen in two newspaper reports. The first appeared in the Pittsburgh *Commercial Gazette* on December 31, 1886. The reporter described "a beautiful line of gas and kerosene goods, tableware, bar goods and artistic novelties in various colors and effects, such as Nacre de Perle [Mother of Pearl] and Vere de Soir" [Verre de Soie is "glass of silk"]. A similar article in the local Wheeling *Intelligencer* (January 6, 1887) was much more extensive:

"The La Belle glass house, across the river, is open to the mild suspicion that it has been playing 'possum. Since its rehabilitation under favorable auspices, it has been moving ahead quietly, sounding no hewgags. But it has also been turning out a great variety of artistic glass—table ware, colored globes, dome shades, and articles of a purely ornamental character. The sample rooms, large well-appointed apartments, display a range of ware that would be creditable to any American glass house, and which, even now, is not thought of by consumers to be produced on this side of the Atlantic.

"An *Intelligencer* reporter was surprised to see a line of silk glass [verre de soie] in many forms and delicate colors, superb ware justly prized by fanciers of artistic glass. Manager Harry Northwood, who is the good spirit of this fairy land, was kind enough to let the reporter see the process of producing this triumph of the glass maker's art. ...

"Mr. Northwood is not only an accomplished glass manufacturer, but he is the inventor of many labor saving appliances used in the manufacture of glass, and he has the artistic sense in a high degree. He designs forms, produces novel colors, and is able to direct every man's work. Many *Intelligencer* readers will remember an artistic cameo cutting in glass by Mr. Northwood exhibited at the State Fair...."

The *Intelligencer*'s writer also discussed Harry Northwood's father, John Northwood, re-telling the story of the Portland Vase and concluding with this observation: "Having had the forethought to select so promising a father, it is not surprising that our American Northwood is something of a worker in glass himself. He is a young man, competent and in love with his work, and ambitious to establish for the La Belle works a reputation equal to the best." Coincidentally, Verre de Soie was among the products of the Stevens and Williams firm in Stourbridge during 1885-86, where John Northwood I held the post of art director (John Northwood II, pp. 71, 105; Morris, *Victorian Table Glass and Ornaments*, p. 226-229). Mother of Pearl glass was introduced by the Stourbridge firm of Boulton & Mills about 1886, also, so Harry Northwood's creations seem to parallel glassware production in England.

The "rock crystal" line was mentioned several times, without illustrations, by *Crockery and Glass Journal* in early 1887, and the February 17 issue alludes to Harry Northwood's "enviable reputation." In the March 31, 1887, issue of *Crockery and Glass Journal*, another interesting note appeared: "The office force and Harry Northwood keep quiet as mice about the amount of trade they have, but they show the elegant lines of artistically made and finished wares, which are indeed grand." Still another tribute was forthcoming in the April 14 issue: "The inimitable Harry Northwood continues the superb color, and he has proven himself master of the art." The La Belle was on the map, and Harry Northwood was gaining fame.

Did Northwood Work for Buckeye?

In late April, 1887, the trade publications reported that Harry Northwood had left the La Belle for a similar post at the Buckeye Glass Works in nearby Martins Ferry. This account appeared in *Pottery and Glassware Reporter* (April 28, 1887):

"The Buckeye Glass Works, with two men on the road, is doing a good business, though not quite so well as one month ago. This company recently secured the services of Mr. Harry Northwood in the capacity of superintendent. Mr. Northwood has been connected with the La Belle for some time past and is a practical glass man. He has a national reputation and the company is to be congratulated in securing so good a man. Mr. John F. Miller, the secretary, has heretofore looked after everything. ... The Buckeye will get out a number of new lines soon which will take well and will turn out more fancy goods in the

This ad appeared in Crockery and Glass Journal *just once—April 28, 1887; it was replaced the next week by the old ad mentioning Harry Northwood which had run for months.*

future than in the past, which will please the trade. Some new designs of ware are ready for the trade."

The above quote and a similar note (*Pottery and Glassware Reporter*, April 28, 1887) to the effect that Northwood was to be replaced at La Belle by "Mr. Alfred Bournique, formerly of Reading, Pa., and latterly of the Dithridge at Martin's Ferry" have led to the unfortunate and erroneous attribution of many Buckeye creations to Harry Northwood. In fact, Harry Northwood remained at the Buckeye for only a week, hardly sufficient time to lay the groundwork for a host of new color effects in glass. The La Belle may have thought Northwood was lost to them forever, because they did replace his name with that of Stephen McCabe in their customary ad.

There is no doubt that Northwood was gaining stature as a glassmaker, but there may have been another reason for the Buckeye Glass Company's pursuit, albeit unsuccessful, of Harry Northwood. On April 19, 1887, the Buckeye's John F. Miller wrote to the Commissioner of Patents in Washington, DC, about the application process for a glass crimping apparatus developed by Harry Northwood (this application was begun while he was at the Phoenix Glass Co. in November, 1885; see above, p. 10). At the time, all incoming patent applications were assigned serial numbers; the number for Northwood's was 237,004 (these are not the same as patent numbers and serve merely to keep track of correspondence and applications, whether or not they resulted in the granting of a patent). Northwood left the Buckeye within a day or two of Miller's letter, of course. Later in 1887, as will be discussed

below, Harry Northwood, with the help of Connolly Bros., a Washington law firm specializing in patents, was granted a patent for this device.

The full story of Harry Northwood's brief employ at the Buckeye was told in the May 12, 1887, *Pottery and Glassware Reporter*: "The La Belle Glass Works is still running to its fullest capacity and has plenty of orders. Mr. Dunlevy, the traveling salesman, is in and will probably not go out again this season. The manager, Mr. Harry Northwood, recently resigned and got the same position at the Buckeye the next day. Mr. R. A. McCabe, of Meriden, Conn., and Mr. Adolph Bournique, of the Dithridge, were hired to succeed him. Northwood is an excellent glass maker and the company concluded they must get him back. They offered him more money than they formerly paid him and more than he was getting at the Buckeye, and in less than one week the other two gentlemen had been dismissed and he was in charge of the enterprise and had possession of the keys of the batch room. He has always been well liked by the employes, who were so well pleased over his return that they presented him with a gold headed cane and gave him a banquet."

The banquet was held on April 29 at Heinlein's Hall in Bridgeport, and the convivial occasion was noted in some detail by the Wheeling *Express* (April 30, 1887). The cane, purchased from the I. G. Dillon store in Wheeling, was inscribed: "Harry Northwood, from the employes of the La Belle Glass Works." Harry Northwood's granddaughter, Miss Elizabeth Northwood Robb, remembers it among the family's possessions in later years.

17

Workers at La Belle, ca. 1887. Manager Harry Northwood, clad in suit and tie, is seated in the front row. Immediately behind the woman on Northwood's right is a young Carl Northwood, who probably came to the United States for a visit when his brother and sister-in-law returned in August, 1887. The man at the right side of the doorway (standing in the back row with hands in pockets beneath his light-colored apron) may be George Pownall, a glass engraver and cutter, who was a close Northwood friend. **Courtesy of the American Flint Glass Workers Union.**

Success and Tragedy at La Belle

In late June, 1887, just prior to the annual six-week summer stop by the glassworkers, the trade publications summed up the state of affairs at the plant and mentioned the whereabouts of Harry Northwood: " The La Belle Glass Works, with both furnaces on, is doing an immense business. They have a new line of tableware and a new line of dome shades, gas shades, etc., ready for the fall season which will please the trade. This past season has been an excellent one with the La Belle. Mr. Thompson, the secretary, thinks the outlook for next season is very flattering for the reason that the crop prospects are good, there are no prospects of labor troubles and business is generally good. Several buyers have already visited the La Belle from Canada and other parts. Mr. Harry Northwood, the manager, accompanied by his wife, sailed for England to spend a month or so with his parents and get pointers on fine ware" (*Pottery and Glassware Reporter*, June 23, 1887; a similar note appeared in

Crockery and Glass Journal, June 30, 1887).

While the Northwoods were in England, the mid-year glass exhibit was held at the Monongahela House in Pittsburgh. Brief reports in *Crockery and Glass Journal* (July 7 and July 21, 1887) mentioned the 843 ware in "canary, blue, crystal and rose coraline." The La Belle's ad in this publication was changed in August to mention the colors (August 11, 1887); an editorial note in this same issue mentioned the "moderate price" of the 843 set and concluded with this bit of fanfare: "Harry Northwood, the manager, is back from England, burnished up like a new piece of gold, and great things are expected of him this season."

Pottery and Glassware Reporter (August 11, 1887) was even more expansive: "Harry Northwood is back 'in business' again. His seven weeks' trip to England was the first vacation he had in six years. Harry is a graduate of the South Kensington Art School, and the training received there enables him to get up those original and tasty designs, which seem to have 'caught on' the market. The sample room of the La Belle is his pride, and the feeling is pardonable. The whole upper floor above the office is devoted to the display of the products of this factory. All varieties and combinations of colors can be seen there in all imaginable shapes and designs. It is more like an art gallery than a sample room of trade products. While in England he noticed that the English factories are devoting more attention to costly designs and find a ready market for even the most expensive products in our country. Even here the taste of the public is improving, and the demand for the finer grades of glassware is increasing every year. Mr. Northwood thinks the glass business has a big future before it in this country. His whole time is devoted to studying out new and attractive features, and he says that fifteen hours is a regular day's work with him."

On August 30, 1887, Harry Northwood was granted a patent (#369,296) for his glass crimper improvements. The application had been filed during his week of employ at the Buckeye Glass Company in April 1887 (see above, p. 17).

A few weeks after Harry Northwood's return from England, just as the La Belle Glass Company was embarking upon the fall, 1887, season for trade, tragedy struck. The account in *Pottery and Glassware Reporter* (September 27, 1887) is painful to read:

BRIDGEPORT, OHIO.

THE LA BELLE GLASS WORKS, was entirely destroyed by fire on Saturday night. The fire originated in the main factory by the furnace "bucking" and in a few minutes the entire structure was enveloped in flames. On the hill back of the works there is a large reservoir but the works was without hose and soon burned to the ground. Fire engines came over from Wheeling but too late to do any good. The whole place burned like tinder and before any part had fallen in the entire establishment was one brilliantly grand mass of flames from which the sparks shot hundreds of feet into the air. While this was going on fully a hundred men and boys were at work rolling barrels of glass out of the warehouses, nine-tenths of which was rolled promiscuously over the river bank into the water. When the fire was at its height, the mixing room, filled with soda ash and nitrate of soda, arsenic and other materials used in the manufacture of glass, caught fire and made a most beautiful and exceptionally intense blaze. In the upper end of the room was stored a whole car load of nitrate of soda and when the shell of the building burned away the whole mass tumbled into a pond of water and as fast as the sacks in which the material was packed became saturated, they exploded, sending clouds of brick dust, barrel staves, etc., high into the air, shaking the earth for miles and sounding like heavy cannonading that was the subject of much enjoyment to the assembled multitude. The noise was heard twelve miles from the scene. At one time there were fully five acres of solid blazing, seething fire and the conflagration was the grandest and most distinctive which ever occurred in Bridgeport. The La Belle has been unfortunate of late years, but for the past year or so has been doing splendidly under the efficient management of Mr. Addison Thompson and had orders enough to keep it running all winter. One furnace was on and the other one was to have started on Monday. With both furnaces in operation about 275 hands were employed. The total loss is about $100,000, one-third of which is on new ware. The plant was valued at $55,000. The insurance on the buildings, machinery and stock is $54,500, mostly held by foreign companies. The secretary, Mr. Thompson, informed the REPORTER man on Monday that they would lease another factory at once and be ready to fill orders in thirty days.

Before the ashes had cooled, the La Belle's management was besieged with proposals for relocating the glass plant. According to *Crockery and Glass Journal* (September 29, 1887), two towns in natural gas-rich northwestern Ohio—Findlay and Fremont—had offered free fuel plus cash bonuses. By October 13, 1887, the firm decided to rebuild its Bridgeport plant, retaining the management team of Giffin, Dunlevy and Northwood, said *Crockery and Glass Journal*. The other trade publication, *Pottery and Glassware Reporter* (October 13, 1877), had a detailed story:

"The La Belle Glass Co., of Bridgeport, before deciding to rebuild, came near leasing the Union Flint Glass Works here [in Martins Ferry], with one ten-pot furnace, which has been idle since the Dithridge Glass Co. gave it up and went to New Brighton. The La Belle wanted it free of rent for six months and offered to make improvements to the amount of $1,500 or $2,000 and leave everything if they decided to rebuild and left at the expiration of the time or any time in the meantime. This was a liberal offer and as the company had no prospect of selling or leasing the works it was thought that they would accept it. Henry Helling and Henry Floto, the two leading stockholders [in the Union], were willing but the balance were not, so the matter was dropped."

Apparently, some of the stockholders in the La Belle Glass Company did not agree with the financial arrangements contemplated for the plant's reconstruction. Both *Pottery and Glassware Reporter* (October 27, 1887) and *Crockery and Glass Journal* (October 27, 1887) said that Dunlevy and Northwood had resigned, but the latter publication provided some rationale: "So much trouble has been stirred up that the manager, Harry Northwood, has severed his connection, as has also Mr. S. C. Dunlevy, the traveling salesman." Harry Northwood was 27 years old, married, with two young children. He had learned—indeed, he had mastered— the trade. He was an accomplished glassmaker, but now he needed a glass plant in which to ply his trade.

CHAPTER TWO
THE NORTHWOOD GLASS COMPANY AT MARTINS FERRY

For six years (1881-87), Harry Northwood had worked in glass plants owned by relatively large organizations. He had learned his trade well, progressing from an etcher working with cold metal to become the La Belle's glassmaker, a position of considerable repute, rivalling his contemporaries at Hobbs, Brockunier and such companies as the Phoenix, the Buckeye (Martins Ferry) and the Elson (Martins Ferry). Surely the dream, if not the calculated desire, of having his own company must have crossed Harry Northwood's mind. The Northwood family saved this undated clipping, probably from a Martins Ferry-area newspaper in November, 1887:

"It is reported that Mr. S. C. Dunlevy and Mr. Harry Northwood, who recently severed their connection with the La Belle, will arrange for the formation of a company.... Mr. Dunlevy has been connected with the La Belle for years in the capacity of traveling salesman, and has covered their trade entirely, including probably every glass buyer in the United States. Mr. Northwood comes by his ability as a glass maker and mixer through the family by that name in England, where the Northwoods are head and shoulders above all other scientific glass makers. Such a combination as this, backed by a reasonable supply of capital, will make a firm which can hold its own in any market, and under all circumstances. Let them come, and Martins Ferry will welcome them with open arms."

The Northwood plant at Martins Ferry made a wide variety of blown glass tableware items, and many of these were decorated with various techniques, including the use of hydrofluoric acid to create a satin finish. Most of the pattern lines made at Martins Ferry can be found in the four-piece table set, the berry set and the water set as well as an assortment of miscellaneous articles: syrup jugs, salt/pepper shakers, cruets, etc. After a brief look at the investors who were behind the enterprise at Martins Ferry, this chapter will detail the patterns and items made there.

The Investors

In order to establish a glassmaking plant, Harry Northwood needed capital. It came in the form of key investors — Henry Helling and Henry Floto. Both Helling and Floto had been associated with the Union Glass Company in Martins Ferry, a firm which operated from 1882 to 1884. Henry Helling,

a German immigrant who had been a Martins Ferry councilman in 1876-78, was president of the Union Flint concern in June, 1882 (Belmont County Deeds, Vol. 79, p. 612).

Neither Henry Helling nor Henry Floto was a glass man, however. Both were investors, Helling's wealth coming from coal in the Martins Ferry area and Floto's from a well-established bakery. The 1888 *Atlas of Belmont County* describes Floto as follows: "Baker of all kinds of bread, cakes, pies, etc. Dealer in confectioneries, canned goods, teas, spices, fruits, nuts, tobacco, cigars, etc. Also fine saloon attached."

The first manager of the Union Flint Glass Company was Thomas J. Slane (*Pottery and Glassware Reporter*, August 10, 1882). Joseph M. Woods, who left the La Belle, assumed the position of mould room foreman at the outset of the company's activities (*Pottery and Glassware Reporter*, March 23, 1882). Exactly when the Union Flint Glass Company failed is unclear, but the October 2, 1884, issue of *Pottery and Glassware Reporter* noted that the plant was "still idle." Just four weeks later, however, this same journal reported as follows: "The Dithridge Flint Glass Works (formerly the Union), Martin's Ferry, Ohio, are doing first rate under the management of E. D. Dithridge. They are making a full line of blown and stem ware, and will make a specialty of opal shades. F. C. Winship has charge of the office" (October 30, 1884). Positive trade reports appeared from time to time over the next several years, but the March 17, 1887, *Pottery and Glassware Reporter* said that the firm "is moving to New Brighton to go in their new factory." Apparently, the Dithridge's flourishing trade necessitated a larger plant, hence the move to New Brighton, PA. The furnaces were out in Martins Ferry by late June, 1887. Henry Helling and the other investors were without a tenant for their glass factory.

The plant remained idle for some time. The October 13, 1887, issue of *Pottery and Glassware Reporter* indicated that the La Belle Glass Co., which had burned on September 17, 1887, "came near leasing the Union Flint Glass Works here ... which has been idle since the Dithridge Glass Co. gave it up and went to New Brighton. The La Belle wanted it free of rent for six months and offered to make improvements to the amount of $1,500 or $2,000 .... This was a liberal offer and as the company had no prospect of selling or leasing the works it was thought that they would accept it. Henry Helling and Henry Floto, the two leading stockholders, were willing but the balance were not, so the matter was dropped."

C. D. Kaminsky (who had sold land to the Union Flint in 1882) won a judgment of $342.57 against the Union's investors in the fall of 1887 (Belmont County Common Pleas, case #4451). The plant was ordered to be sold at a sheriff's auction on November 29, 1887. To protect their investments, Helling and Floto, along with William C. Handlan and J. O. Payne, re-purchased the plant for $5603.00. Handlan and Payne immediately sold their interests to Henry Floto (Belmont County Deeds, Vol. 91, pp. 338-41).

These transactions were noted in *Pottery and Glassware Reporter*, and the most revealing statements were in an article published December 8, 1887:

"Recently we stated that the UNION FLINT GLASS WORKS had been sold at sheriff's sale.... We are pleased to state that they will [operate] under the partnership of Helling, Floto and Seymour Dunlevy and Harry Northwood. Mr. Northwood will make the glass and be the general manager and Mr. Dunlevy will have charge of the office and will sell goods. These two gentlemen are practical glass men and will make a strong team. Northwood is from the famous district of Stourbridge, England, and Dunlevy has been with the La Belle for seven or eight years. The plant will be fitted with the most modern machinery and equipments and will be put in operation by January 1, if possible. The finest qualities of blown, cut and engraved ware will be made. The works will employ about 150 persons."

Two additional investors, Thomas Mears and William Mann, now entered the picture. Mears was associated with the Martins Ferry Keg and Barrel Works, and he had similar enterprises elsewhere. Barrels for shipping are much needed by any glass factory, and Mears' firm probably became the supplier for the Northwood concern. According to the *History of the Upper Ohio Valley*, Mears was "one of the notable and influential men of Martins Ferry." When his Martins Ferry operation was destroyed by fire in 1891, it was quickly rebuilt, and the *Evening Times* carried frequent reports. Mears also held stock in the Elson Glass Company of Martins Ferry and the Crystal Glass Company of Bridgeport, as well as the Junction Iron Works at Mingo Junction in Jefferson County.

William Mann of Martins Ferry, a Scotsman who had come to the area in 1874, owned several machine shops, and his large foundry was on the corner of First and Locust Streets, opposite the old Union Flint plant. The 1888 *Atlas of Belmont County* described his businesses this way: "Foundry and Machine shops. Practical manufacturer of light and heavy castings of all kinds. Steel plant rolling mill and blast furnace work a specialty." Cast iron is used for glass moulds, of course, and Mann's foundry likely did the rough work before Northwood's own machinists and mouldmakers took over the specialized task of working out patterns and designs in the moulds.

Section of letterhead stationery. **Courtesy of the Martins Ferry Historical Society.**

Establishing the Firm

The Northwood Glass Company was incorporated in West Virginia. According to papers dated December 10, 1887, Henry Helling, Henry Floto, William Mann, Thomas Mears and Harry Northwood held 1 share apiece. The firm was capitalized at $40,000, and the five men appeared before W. M. Lupton, a notary public in Belmont County, Ohio, who prepared their paperwork for submission to the West Virginia Secretary of State. Since the new Northwood Glass Company was to occupy a glass factory building which formerly housed the Union and Dithridge concerns, little time was needed to ready the plant for glassmaking. The January 5, 1888, issue of *Pottery and Glassware Reporter* carried a full account:

"THE NORTHWOOD GLASS WORKS commenced operations in full on Monday and everything started off satisfactorily. Three new lears and a new mold shop have been built, new etch-

This ad first appeared in the January 5, 1888, issue of Crockery and Glass Journal, *and it ran through September 27, 1888. The reference to the La Belle firm was dropped in April, and Northwood was identified as General Manager.*

ing department made, the office and sample room nicely repapered and the entire works thoroughly overhauled, making it a first class glass works. All blown ware is made, of all colors, such as gas goods dome shades, tableware, water sets, berry sets, and all the latest colors and effects. Mr. Harry Northwood, formerly manager at the La Belle, is the general superintendent and Mr. A. W. Kerr, formerly assistant secretary at the Buckeye, is the secretary. ... The Northwood is now ready for the trade and will certainly do well. Their samples are a credit to them. Several good bills have already been sold and the outlook is flattering."

Although there seems little doubt that the fledgling Northwood Glass Company had a successful first year of operation in 1888, reports in the trade publications regarding specific products are almost non-existent. During the first half of 1888, an unidentified "220 line" was mentioned just once (*Crockery and Glass Journal*, February 2, 1888), and *Pottery and Glassware Reporter* (February 9, 1888) carried a general report on the firm's exhibit:

"Capt. S. C. Dunlevy has a beautiful exhibit of the goods manufactured by the NORTHWOOD GLASS CO., of Martin's Ferry, at the Monongahela House. They are chiefly blown lead goods and comprise tableware, water sets, flower holders, molasses cans, shades, gas globes, water bottles, finger bowls, hall globes, tumblers, casters, oil bottles, salt, pepper and oil cruets, and a general line of fancy glassware. The colors are most exquisite and include effects in satin finish, diamond, rib, spot, etc."

Satin finish articles were produced by acid etching, of course, and the diamond and rib motifs were made by first blowing glass into a small, patterned mould and then, in a second mould, blowing once more to expand the item to its desired size and final shape. "Spot" effects

Cruet in spot motif, made in Northwood's Ring Neck mould. **Courtesy of Larry Loxterman.**

were likely opalescent glass creations similar to the "coindot" and "coinspot" products of many different factories which were so popular in the late 1880s. The absence of illustrations in the trade journals makes identification of Northwood products speculative, although the array of items in the trade journals is impressive. The Northwood's stationery made no mention of specific lines or colors.

Crockery and Glass Journal (June 10, 1888) attributed the firm's good fortune to "the careful management of Harry Northwood, and his great success in producing some of the finest effects in colored glassware...." *Pottery and Glassware Reporter* alluded to new lines (June 28, 1888), and its account in the July 19, 1888, issue provided some detail:

"Captain Seymour C. Dunlevy is staying at Room 137 [Monongahela House, Pittsburgh] and represents the NORTHWOOD GLASS CO., of Martin's Ferry, Ohio. This concern has achieved much celebrity in the manufacture of fine blown tableware, fancy goods, globes, shades, fine colors and effects, and their products are without a peer in the market. ... Their specialty, as noted above, is artistic glass ware in fine colors and of a superior quality of metal, and includes a large diversity of articles. They have now ready two complete new lines of blown fancy tableware, Nos. 206 and 244. They have a fine selection of vases, jugs, tankards, casters, fancy straw jars, bitter bottles, water sets, and other things too numerous to specify. The number of shapes is practically without limit and the same may be said of the colors and combinations of color all of which are extremely beautiful, rich and effective. They make both flint and lime glass at this establishment, all of the best kind. No mere written description can give anything like a correct idea of the elegance and attractiveness of these goods; they must be seen and judged for themselves."

Sometime in 1888, a gathering was held at the Northwood residence on Wheeling Island (see photo on next page). Members of the Beaumont and Dugan families were present, so perhaps the Dugans had moved from Pittsburgh to work in the Northwood concern at Martins Ferry (the Dugans were listed in a Martins Ferry city directory published for 1892-93).

During the six weeks' summer stop, the Northwood Glass Company took advantage of the opportunity to make improvements in the factory. Additional lehrs (annealing ovens) were built, and a new glory hole (auxiliary furnace used to "warm-in" glassware) was constructed (*Pottery and Glassware Reporter*, August 2 and 16, 1888).

At the outset of the fall blast, both trade publications had good things to say about the firm:

"The Northwood Glass Co.'s success is something to be wondered at. Harry Northwood seems to have reached his zenith in blending together colors with beautiful effect, and their trade is away beyond the capacity of the works" (*Crockery and Glass Journal*, September 13, 1888).

"Never before in the history of the NORTHWOOD GLASS CO. has business been as good as the past three weeks. The pay on last Saturday was the biggest in the history of the company. Mr. Dunlevy, the traveling salesman, was recently called in on account of increasing business. The line of goods the Northwood is turning out is a credit to the company" (*Pottery and Glassware Reporter*, September 13, 1888).

On November 6, 1888, Harry Northwood was granted another patent (#392,450). Unlike his previous patents, which were mechanical devices for shaping glassware, this invention related to "glassware having an exterior coating of unvitrified sand, acid roughed or etched." Northwood further described the glassware as having a "lusterless" surface which is "very dense and rough." The application for this patent had been prepared

Harry Northwood is at the far right, next to his wife Clara Elizabeth, who is seated. The youngsters are the Northwood children—Harry Clarence (b. 1883) and Mabel Virginia (b. 1884), who is standing next to her maternal grandmother, Elizabeth Beaumont. Standing at the far left is E. G. "George" Beaumont, and his father, John Beaumont, is next, followed by Carl Northwood (b. 1872) and George Pownall, a glass cutter and engraver who was a Northwood family friend. The short gentleman with the dark beard is Samuel Dugan, and his son, Thomas E. A. Dugan, is seated in front of him. Percy J. Beaumont is the tall man standing slightly behind the rest of the group on Clara and Harry Northwood's right. The house, which is no longer standing, was located at 43 S. Broadway, Wheeling Island. **Courtesy of Miss Robb.**

over a year earlier (September 27, 1887), so the Northwood Glass Company may have been producing this glass before the patent was obtained. The patent drawing (see next page) offers a rendition of some of the products envisioned.

The mention of rough surface effects suggests that this technique may explain the "speckled" articles known today in Panelled Sprig and Chrysanthemum Swirl [formerly Chrysanthemum Base Swirl. See H2, pp. 42, 50; H3, p. 18; and H6, p. 22]. The former pattern was made later at both Ellwood City and Indiana, PA. Chrysanthemum

Swirl could be exclusive to Martins Ferry, but other factories made cranberry opalescent articles which are very similar (see H9, pp. 69-70).

Although the Northwood Glass Co. did not have an ad in the thick "Holiday Number" of *Crockery and Glass Journal* (December 6, 1888), the other trade publication provided this brief note: "In a few days the NORTHWOOD GLASS WORKS will have a full line of goods ready for the spring trade which will be entirely different from anything ever attempted in glassmaking. The Northwood has been doing a big business and

Fig.1.

Fig.2.

Fig.3.

Fig.4.

Witnesses:
A.B.A.Blackwood.
G. Smith.

Inventor.
Harry Northwood.
by Connolly Bro.
Attorneys.

UNITED STATES PATENT OFFICE.

HARRY NORTHWOOD, OF WHEELING, WEST VIRGINIA.

MANUFACTURE OF GLASSWARE.

SPECIFICATION forming part of Letters Patent No. 392,450, dated November 6, 1888.

Application filed September 27, 1887. Serial No. 250,431. (No specimens.)

To all whom it may concern:

Be it known that I, HARRY NORTHWOOD, a subject of the Queen of Great Britain, residing at Wheeling, West Virginia, have invented
5   certain new and useful Improvements in Manufacture of Glassware; and I do hereby declare the following to be a full, clear, and exact description of the invention, reference being had to the accompanying drawings, which form
10 part of this specification.

My invention has relation to fancy glassware, and has for its object the provision of a novel and beautiful article of glassware and the provision of means for manufacturing the same.
15 As a new article, my invention consists in a glassware having an exterior coating of unvitrified sand, acid roughed or etched.

My improved method of manufacture con-
20 sists in dipping or rolling a gathering of hot glass, which may be either crystal, colored, flashed, or sensitive glass, in sand until the latter adheres to the surface, then manipulating the coated gathering to form the desired
25 article, and finally acid-roughening or etching the completed article so as to produce a lusterless surface similar to a peach-skin.

Referring to the accompanying drawings, wherein I have illustrated the article in its va-
30 rious stages of manufacture, Figure 1 shows a gathering of glass as it is taken from the pot. Fig. 2 shows the same after having been dipped in or covered with sand; Fig. 3, the shaped article made from the same, and Fig. 4 the
35 complete and finished article.

After the gathering has been dipped, so as to present the appearance shown in Fig. 2, it may be blown, molded, pressed, or in any other

way fashioned to the desired shape; but as the
40 fashioning of the glass forms no part of my invention, and the manner of doing so is well known, it need not be particularly described.

It is essential to the practice of my invention that the glass after being dipped in or covered
45 with the sand should not be subjected to so high a degree of heat as will melt or vitrify the sand, as this would interfere with or entirely prevent the production of the desired effect in the finished article.

50 The article manufactured according to my improved method presents a strikingly beautiful effect, the surface being very dense and rough.

I am aware that it is not new to acid-rough
55 or etch the surface of articles of glassware, and I am also aware that it has been the practice to ornament glassware by sprinkling particles of colored glass, mica, &c., upon the surface of the hot glass; but these processes differ from mine,
60 as I employ simply ordinary sand, not for the purpose of producing an effect of coloring, but to produce a denser and rougher surface than has heretofore been had.

Having described my invention, I claim—

65 As a new article, glassware having a surface of lusterless adherent unvitrified sand substantially as described.

In testimony that I claim the foregoing I have hereunto set my hand this 14th day of September, 1887.

HARRY NORTHWOOD.

Witnesses:
    PERRY J. BEAUMONT,
    R. T. HOWELL.

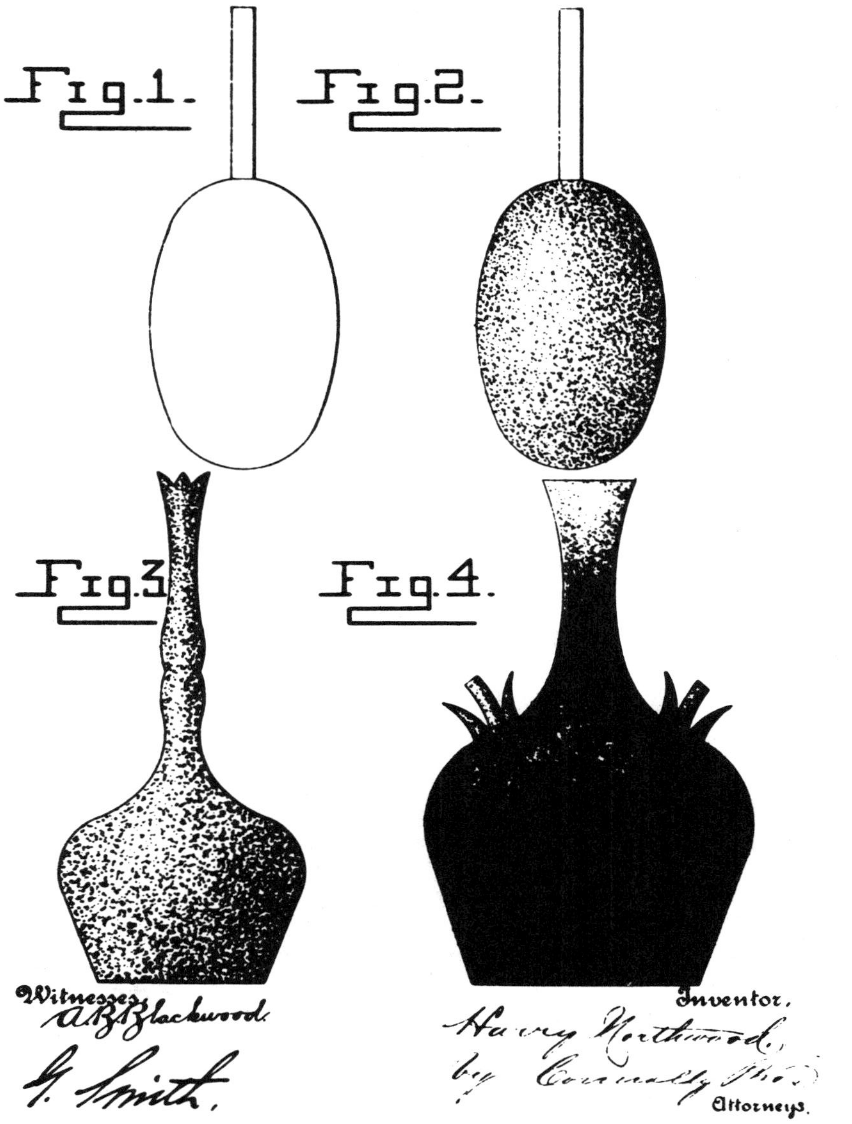

Chrysanthemum Swirl toothpick holder. Note the dense speckled finish. Courtesy of Larry Loxterman.

their new goods will go off with a rush" (*Pottery and Glassware Reporter*, December 13, 1888). In December, both trade journals noted that salesman S. C. Dunlevy and secretary A. W. Kerr had resigned, effective at year's end; Dunlevy joined the recently-reorganized Hobbs firm in Wheeling, and Kerr became a member of the Buckeye Glass Works in Martins Ferry. These changes reflected no difficulties within the Northwood concern; on the contrary, the fledgling firm was soon to enjoy its best years.

No. 245: An Early Pattern Line

Glass factories usually introduced their new patterns and novelties in December (in the Holiday Number of *Crockery and Glass Journal*) or in early January along with the exhibitions at the Monongahela House or the McLure House. Wholesale buyers would view samples of ware and place orders for the "spring trade." Thus, a factory's success depended upon orders placed in mid-winter for later shipment. The volume of purchases often determined the size and nature of the plant's workforce, as workers could be laid off when not needed. If a particular line of goods proved to be a good seller, additional workers, such as decorators or engravers, might be required to meet the demand. Manufacturing glass

tableware was a risky business, for the public taste must be satisfied for a line to be successful.

Pottery and Glassware Reporter (January 3, 1889) carried a fulsome account of the Northwood's pattern line:

"THE NORTHWOOD has an elegant line of new goods ready for the spring trade which will sell at sight. The number is 245 and the goods are of a pillared hexagonal shape made in a new marbled effect which is suggestive of the old Venetian glassware. ... Mr. Harry Northwood, the efficient manager, for some time past has been endeavoring to get out fine goods in a soft mellow color instead of harsh blues, yellows, greens, etc., made by many factories, and in this direction has been quite successful especially in the 245 line, just out. This line, which had not been named when the P&GR man called, is a credit to Mr. Northwood, who is a practical glass man, in fact it is the handsomest thing he ever introduced, which is saying a great deal, and is bound to sell. ... The Northwood Glass Works is constantly getting out novelties in bowls, celeries, etc. Its goods are all of a high character and sell readily."

The trade journal's description makes clear that No. 245 is the pattern known today as Ribbed Pillar. After a lengthy study of the line's origins, Heacock suggested naming it Northwood Pleat, and this appellation will be added parenthetically. The trade journal's comparison with "Venetian glassware" is not precise (see Klein and Lloyd's *History of Glass*), but the phrase "marbled effect" and the reference to "soft mellow color" suggest a spatter or slag effect. *Crockery and Glass Journal* (January 24, 1889) called the line "Marblescent," and this term may have been coined to refer to one or more of the color effects.

Today's collectors can find Ribbed Pillar (Northwood Pleat) articles in these colors: crystal with reddish-pink/white spatter interior; sapphire blue with white spatter interior. In addition, all of these color combinations may be found with an acid-etched, satin finish exterior that greatly reduces the visual impact of the spattered interior. A wide variety of Ribbed Pillar (Northwood Pleat) items is available — four-piece table set; pitcher/tumblers; bowl with sauces; toothpick; sugar shaker; syrup; celery holder; and salt shaker. The spooner doubles as an insert for a pickle caster. Ribbed Pillar (Northwood Pleat) can easily be confused with articles which Heacock called Ribbed Opal Lattice (H9, p. 57). The precise origins of Ribbed Opal Lattice have not yet been ascertained, although Heacock's suggestion that it was produced at Martins Ferry is not unlikely.

Ribbed Pillar (Northwood Pleat) articles from 1889 Butler Brothers catalog.

Business with a Big "B"

The earlier mention of the McLure House, a fine downtown Wheeling hotel, needs some elaboration, since it may have contributed to the Northwood's success. Beginning about 1884, the Monongahela House hotel in Pittsburgh housed semi-annual, month-long (January and July) exhibitions of glass tableware. Most firms rented a suite (sleeping rooms and parlor), and their representatives were present with samples to meet buyers from the major catalogue houses and department stores, as well as wholesale jobbers who bought in large lots and then re-sold the glassware to smaller stores (see Welkers' *Pressed Glass in America*, pp. 215-217). Early in 1889, many Wheeling vicinity plants (the Wheeling area includes the nearby Ohio towns of Martins Ferry, Bridgeport and Bellaire) decided to make the McLure House their exhibition headquarters. A story in *Pottery and Glassware Reporter* (January 3, 1889) provides the background:

"Wheeling — An important change has been made in the management of the glass business in this section which will be of interest to nearly every buyer in the country. At a meeting of the manufacturers of Wheeling and vicinity, held at the McLure House last week, arrangements were perfected to make Wheeling the center of the glass trade as it is of the nail trade. Buyers are to be induced to come to Wheeling instead of going to Pittsburgh. Representatives of the Central and Hobbs, of Wheeling; Elson, Buckeye and Northwood, of Martin's Ferry; Riverside, of Wellsburg; Belmont and Aetna, of Bellaire and oth-

ers were heartily in favor of doing this. Other factories in Wellsburg, Steubenville, Fostoria and probably other towns can, it is thought, be induced to come to Wheeling. One well known glass man told the representative of this paper that this movement would make Wheeling the centre for glass buyers. Heretofore nearly every factory in this section has displayed their samples at the Monongahela House, at Pittsburgh, for the inspection of buyers. Since the Wheeling district has become the great producer as well in point of variety as quantity, the manufacturers decided that by concert of action, Wheeling could as easily be made the headquarters. This district produces pressed table ware, fancy white and colored ware in great variety, lantern globes, bottles and a wide range of specialties. The Martin's Ferry, Bridgeport, Bellaire, Wellsburg and at least one of the Fostoria factories will be on hand at the McLure House with a full line of samples. The Wheeling factories, which are conveniently located, will display samples in their own sample rooms, and the Aetna, of Bellaire, at its Wheeling office on Main street. This arrangement will save buyers the trouble of visiting the Bellaire, Bridgeport and Martin's Ferry factories. A glass

Ruby opalescent Ribbed Opal Lattice salt/pepper shaker. **Courtesy of Larry Loxterman.**

27

works has from 200 to 800 customers and large numbers of them will commence coming next week."

About a month later, *Pottery and Glassware Reporter* summarized the impact of the exhibit at the McLure House and preserved some of the social atmosphere which prevailed:

"Large numbers of glass buyers have already visited Wheeling, and still they come. Some big orders have been left, but for some reason many are holding off. None has left without buying something. They go from Wheeling to Pittsburgh, or vice versa. Many have expressed themselves being pleased with the idea of having samples displayed here semi-annually instead of having them all at Pittsburgh, as it affords them a better chance to inspect goods and in consequence they can purchase more satisfactorily. ... The gentlemanly representatives of the different factories who are at the McLure House have rented a first class piano and had it placed in the parlor. There is considerable talent in the party and in this way many pleasant hours have been spent. Occasionally a party of ladies and gentlemen, Wheeling's best talent, drop in and have impromptu concerts, which are enjoyed by the salesmen, buyers and all present. One New York buyer present at one of these concerts on Saturday night said he didn't think Wheeling had so much good talent. Nearly all the buyers appear to enjoy their stay and few appear to be in a hurry about leaving, which is an evidence that they are not tortured to death by the salesmen" (January 31, 1889).

Perhaps the most optimistic report of the Northwood Glass Company's fortunes appeared in the February 21, 1889, issue of *Pottery and Glassware Reporter*: "Business is booming with a big "B" at the NORTHWOOD GLASS WORKS, which is running to its fullest capacity. Immense quantities of the spring pattern are being made and still the demand is in excess of the supply. The Northwood will have a great run on these goods, which are as pretty as they can be." A week later the same journal noted "the demand for the new spring pattern ... is increasing and it is bound to be a great seller. The factory is running almost entirely on this line. The company has no salesman and if business continues as it has been they will not have use for one."

On April 23, 1889, the directors of the Northwood Glass Company passed the following motion: "Resolved that the Northwood Glass Co. does this day voluntarily dissolve and cease to be a corporation, and its affairs be at once settled up." This ominous-sounding resolution did not

foretell the closure of the glass plant. President Henry Helling, who was seriously ill and did not attend the meeting, may have been seeking to liquidate his financial interest. Helling died about a month later, and a local newspaper carried a moving tribute to him from the glass company.

Courtesy of Jane Thiel Boddorf, great-granddaughter of Henry Helling.

The Northwood company was soon reconstituted as an Ohio corporation. Henry Helling's son Charles Helling, who had been the firm's secretary for about three months (*Crockery and Glass Journal*, February 7, 1889), became a stockholder, along with these familiar names: Henry Floto, Thomas Mears, William Mann and, of course, Harry Northwood. One new stockholder was listed — Percy J. Beaumont. Apparently, Beaumont had left the Hobbs, Brockunier firm in 1887 or 1888 when the company was being re-

These ads appeared in Pottery and Glassware Reporter *(top) and* Crockery and Glass Journal. *The latter ran from February 28, 1889, until mid-June, 1890.*

organized due to the departure of Charles Brockunier.

Percy Beaumont married Laura Dillon in Springfield, Ohio, on April 23, 1889, and *Crockery and Glass Journal* (April 25, 1889) reported that he was then employed at the Northwood plant. A later trade journal note (*Pottery and Glassware Reporter*, March 13, 1890) says he was "head shipping clerk," but this seems incompatible with his talents, for Beaumont was surely an accomplished glassmaker by that time. Notebooks of glass formulas kept by Percy Beaumont in the 1880s are preserved at the Rakow Library in the Corning Museum of Glass.

The May-June, 1889, trade reports of the Northwood firm are mixed. In early May, one publication said "Orders are very plentiful" (*Pottery and Glassware Reporter*, May 5, 1889), but the May 9, 1889 *Crockery and Glass Journal* said "Trade ... is fair at this time." By late May, *Pottery and Glassware Reporter* characterized the trade as "moderately good" and said the firm "is making six days a week" (May 30, 1889). The next few months were even more positive for the company, as a second successful line was introduced.

No. 263: Another Northwood Winner

In June, 1889, at the McLure house in Wheeling, the Northwood Glass Company had samples of its new fall line, No. 263 (generally known as Leaf Umbrella today; see Peterson's *Glass Salt Shakers*, p. 32s). After some initial confusion regarding the name of the line, a correspondent for *Pottery and Glassware Reporter* (June 20, 1889) penned an enthusiastic account: "MARTIN'S FERRY — Rose Du Barry is the name of the new fall line [incorrect! see below] of the NORTHWOOD GLASS WORKS and it ought to be a great seller. It is made in ruby and crystal and the shapes are classical. The goods are being made in berry sets, tea sets, toilet sets, sugars, molasses cruets, etc. A number of good orders have been booked for this line and it promises to be a great seller. It is believed to be the nicest and best ever made at the Northwood. Cracker jars, nut bowls and water sets are made in various styles, also odd berry bowls and artistic novelties."

The correspondent erred on the name of the line, which was simply No. 263. The mistake was corrected in the July 4, 1889, issue of *Pottery and Glassware Reporter.* "A slight error crept into our last letter where mention was made of the new fall goods made at Northwood. [The new line] is made in rose Du Barry, ruby and crystal and is not called rose Du Barry as stated. The error was laughable and we cheerfully make the correction." Rose Du Barry is an interesting opaque color, often called mauve (H3, p. 31) or simply pink. It was sometimes made as a cased glass and may be found with an opal (milk glass) inner lining. According to the July 18, 1889, issue of *Pottery and Glassware Reporter*, "a full line of samples of the artistic glassware manufactured by the NORTHWOOD GLASS CO., of Martin's Ferry, Ohio, [are] on exhibition at Room 138, Astor House, New York City, where [J. M. Usher] will remain until the latter part of the month."

The display at Wheeling's McLure House also attracted considerable attention from the glass tableware periodicals, and this lengthy account in *Pottery and Glassware Reporter* (July 25, 1889) contains considerable information about the firm's products in addition to the new No. 263 line:

"THE NORTHWOOD GLASS CO., of Martin's Ferry, has a large line of samples at Room No. 121 [McLure House], in charge of Mr. B. Long, who has already booked some good orders. Mr. Long has a full line of everything made by the Northwood, consisting of tableware, dome shades and novelties. No. 263, the new fall line of tableware made in rose du Barry, ruby, and crystal is the finest ever made by the Northwood, which is saying a great deal. Tooth picks are also made in this line. All the dealers who have seen the new line express themselves as highly pleased with it. A new line of lemonade sets [pitcher and six tumblers] in P.O. [pink opalescent], F.O. [flint opalescent] and B.O. [blue opalescent] have been brought out. The number is 260. A nut bowl in ruby, with marble edges, is ready for the fall trade, also other novelties. The straw jars, P.O., F.O. and B.O. and in No. 245, are the finest in the market. They have fifteen different water sets. In 14 inch dome shades, they exhibit the largest variety of colors in the market and new ones are constantly added. The latest is No. 248 in ruby and crystal crackled. They have a large assortment of casters with 2, 3 and 4 bottles, and hand made bowls for fruit, nuts, roses and oranges. The rose bowl in royal ruby is great. Their royal ruby line, the finest they make, and others all introduced within a year, are going off very well."

Several conclusions are clear from this report. First, the No. 263 line seems to have been limited, at least initially, to just two colors — Rose Du Barry and ruby, both of which were covered with an outer layer of crystal. The other hues known to collectors today (ruby with white spatter; sapphire blue with white cased interior; light yellow; and light yellow with white cased interior) were probably produced about the same time,

although they attracted no notice in the trade press, which always tends to concentrate on the introduction of new pattern lines. The blue and yellow examples are known with satin finish, too.

The No. 263 line also contains some interesting variations. Two sizes of creamers are known (4 1/2" and 4" tall), but the corresponding sugar bowls are fitted with identical lids. Furthermore, some cruets and water pitchers have colored handles, while others are clear; a similar situation is found with the finials on sugar bowls. A crystal, satin-finish cruet occurs with a curious smoky effect, too.

Albert Christian Revi's article, "Northwood's 263 Ware" (*Spinning Wheel*, December, 1964, p. 18), described the pattern as "stylized acorns and oak leaves arranged below a representation of twisted rope or chain." *Crockery and Glass Journal* (October 31, 1889) mentioned a "new line of jugs or pitchers in turquoise, topaz, and rose agate [ruby with white spatter] — the 263 ware — that cannot help but be popular." A full-page ad in the Holiday Number of *Crockery and Glass Journal* (December 5, 1889) may be the source for the sketches used by Revi which are reproduced here (see next page).

Leaf Umbrella cruet, satin finish with "smoky" effect.

263 – 8ⁱⁿ Bowl

263 Sugar & Cover

263 Tumbler

263 Finger Bowl

263 Ware made in Ruby, Rose Du Barry, Rose Agate, Turquoise and Topaz

263 ½ gal Jug

263 Salt

The quote from *Pottery and Glassware Reporter* also reveals that the Northwood firm was making opalescent glass, for "P.O., F.O. and B.O." refer to pink opalescent, flint opalescent and blue opalescent, respectively. The references to many different water sets and shades indicates the variety of production at the Northwood in 1889, and the remarks about "royal ruby," although not capitalized, may reveal an original name for the No. 245 line — Ribbed Pillar (Northwood Pleat).

The "straw jars" could be the Chrysanthemum Swirl motif which poses many problems in attribution (see H9, pp. 69-70). The occurrence of items in satin finish and Northwood's patented "speckled" finish are strong reasons to attribute the pattern to Northwood, as are the known colors — cranberry ["pink"] opalescent, flint opalescent, and blue opalescent — which parallel the hues mentioned in *Pottery and Glassware Reporter*.

On the Personal Side

As the Northwood Glass Company became better and better known in the glass tableware trade, the activities of its namesake, Harry Northwood, became newsworthy. The Martins Ferry *Evening Times* and the glass trade periodicals included frequent notes regarding Harry

Two different salt shakers and a sugar shaker in Chrysanthemum Swirl. **Courtesy of Larry Loxterman.**

Northwood personally. Some of these relate to Northwood's career as a glassmaker, of course, but many simply preserve details of his life. For example, *Crockery and Glass Journal* (February 7, 1889) reported on a number of glassmen, including Harry Northwood, who were members of the loosely-organized Wheeling Wit Club, a group which met in the barroom of the McLure House! A humorous expose' of hotels and travelling salesmen, Sam. B. Harrison's *Front!* (1889), credits "Harry N — — , of Martins Ferry" with founding a "society for prevention of cruelty among glass buyers," and whiskey glasses figure prominently here, too.

On a more serious note, various notes in the *Evening Times* during 1891-92 record Harry Northwood's activities as a charter member of the local Republican Club as well as a partnership, Northwood & Connelly, which leased the Opera House in Martins Ferry (*Evening Times*, August 4, 10, 11, and 14; September 9, 1891). When Clara Northwood's brother, Percy J. Beaumont, was married in April, 1889, *Pottery and Glassware Reporter* duly mentioned that "Mr. Harry Northwood and wife attended the wedding of Mr. Beaumont...." (April 25, 1889).

Both *Pottery and Glassware Reporter* (March 14, 1889) and *Crockery and Glass Journal* (March 14, 1889) wrote that the Northwood family planned to "visit England next summer, having already secured one of the best rooms on the splendid steamer Alaska, which leaves New York June 18." About a week prior to the Northwoods' departure, the June 13, 1889, issue of *Crockery and Glass Journal* said "it will be a combined business and pleasure trip with him, as Harry expects to

spend much of his time freighting his mind with new ideas for the American glass trade."

Among the sources of inspiration for Harry Northwood was the Paris Exposition. The August 29, 1889, issue of *Pottery and Glassware Reporter* mentioned that Northwood "picked up many valuable pointers" and *Crockery and Glass Journal* said that "Harry Northwood ... brought with him several large trunks of samples and trinkets that will be utilized in time in adding to the already brilliant variety of goods already made at these works" (September 19, 1889). *Pottery and Glassware Reporter* carried a full report of the Northwoods' trip:

"Mr. Harry Northwood, manager of the NORTH-WOOD GLASS WORKS, returned last week from a three months' sojourn in England and France, where he picked up many valuable pointers regarding glass making, by which the Northwood will be benefitted. Mrs. Northwood and children, and Mr. George Pownall, foreman in the cutting department, were along with him. Mr. Northwood reports the glass and iron business better in England than it has been for fifteen years. He spent four days viewing the Paris Exposition, and didn't see one fourth of it. On the ten cent stands considerable cheap common glassware was seen. While of English birth, he was proud of the American made machinery and agricultural implements. The latter beats the world and are seen in the fields all over England and France. The railway exhibit of the United States is poor. He says

Note the difference in the widths of the stripes on these Chrysanthemum Swirl cruets. **Courtesy of Larry Loxterman.**

that every person who can afford it should see the Paris Exposition. He went on the Alaska and returned on the Arizona, having secured excellent rooms last February. He knew that the glass business was dull in the United States but found it better at the Northwood than he expected" (September 19, 1889).

On October 8, 1889, Harry Northwood appeared in Probate Court in Belmont County, Ohio. He presented a certificate issued on September 13, 1886, in Ohio County, West Virginia, in which his intention to become a U.S. citizen was first declared. Two witnesses, both associated with Northwood in the glass business, George Pownall and Charles Helling, affirmed that Harry Northwood had resided in the United States for five years and that he had been in Ohio for at least a year. By order of Probate Judge Isaac H. Gaston, Harry Northwood became a citizen of the United States of America, vowing "to renounce forever all allegiance and fidelity to any Foreign Prince, Potentate, State or Sovereignty, and particularly to Victoria, Queen of England...."

In mid-March, 1890, the residents of Martins Ferry witnessed a spirited debate regarding proposals to change the name of the city. Some argued that the name suggested merely a small town consisting of a ferry landing and a few houses, not a thriving center of manufacturing. Their opponents asserted that Martins Ferry's industrial products and, hence, the name of the city itself, were known worldwide. Strident letters appeared in local newspapers, and the controversy was fueled by the posting of handbills under cover of night, usually near the business places of those involved in the exchange of views. At least one advocate, perhaps Harry Northwood, suggested re-naming the town "Stourbridge," perhaps with tongue in cheek, and the opposition howled with displeasure (four published letters are preserved in a scrapbook owned by Miss Robb). In its August 7, 1897, issue, *Crockery and Glass Journal* mentioned that Martins Ferry was first named after the father of Lucian B. Martin, a prominent glassman associated with Hobbs, Brockunier of Wheeling and, later, with the Fostoria Glass Company.

On April 3, 1890, Harry Northwood purchased a lot on the northeast corner of Broadway and Monroe streets in Martins Ferry (Belmont County Deeds, vol. 95, p. 361). A mortgage was obtained from the Enterprise Building Association (Belmont County Mortgage Record, vol. 42, pp. 517-518), and the Northwoods arranged to have a large wood frame home erected. The June 5, 1890,

issue of *Crockery and Glass Journal* termed it "an elegant residence," and a columnist in *Pottery and Glassware Reporter* (December 4, 1890) said Northwood "built the house after a palace in England, his native country."

Apparently, construction took some time, but when the Northwoods finally took possession, *Crockery and Glass Journal* recorded the event and added an observation: "[Harry Northwood] moved into a handsome $10,000 home he built for himself at Martins Ferry. But his genius deserves the good things in life" (December 4, 1890). For some reason (possibly to divest himself of assets in his name), Harry Northwood sold his interest in the home to his wife Clara for $5000 on March 31, 1891 (Belmont County Deeds, vol. 100, p. 431). Several years later, when the Northwoods were in Ellwood City, Pa., the home was sold to Thomas Mears (see p. 102).

Also in April, 1890, Harry Northwood was threatened by a disgruntled employee. *Pottery and Glassware Reporter* had the details: "Recently Charley Martin ... was discharged for getting drunk while on duty. That evening he appeared in the factory accompanied by a friend and assaulted Mr. Harry Northwood, the manager, drawing a revolver on him, threatening to kill him and using the foulest language, all because Mr. Northwood had discharged him. A warrant was sworn out for Martin's arrest but he skipped. If arrested Martin would have probably gone to the penitentiary. Mr. Northwood was unarmed at the time and thought his end had come" (April 10, 1890). Some months later, the correspondent for *Pottery and Glassware Reporter* (December 4, 1890) saw a warning sign at the Northwood factory and wrote this: "A notice printed on a good-sized board in black letters attracted my attention. It is on the side of the main entrance to the factory, and reads as follows: 'Notice. Visitors and persons seeking employment must go to the office. Intruders will be fired out.' This should be the rule at all factories."

By late 1890, the Northwood name was such a fixture in the glass trade press that even the most ordinary event was recorded. For example, when Eva Northwood, one of Harry Northwood's six sisters, visited the United States, *Pottery and Glassware Reporter* (September 25, 1890) mentioned that he went to New York to accompany her to Martins Ferry. Fred Northwood, who had arrived in the United States on the *S. S. Wisconsin* with Carl Northwood in June, 1891, was mentioned in the *Evening Times* (August 5, 1891), but it is not clear when he returned to England. Carl

Northwood stayed in the United States to work in the glass business after arriving in June, 1891, although he had been in the country for visits prior to this time.

In December, 1890, a glass trade publication carried this note in one of its reporter's columns: "A fine setter dog, with a pedigree as long as your arm, belonging to Mr. Henry [sic] Northwood, of the Northwood Glass Co., died last week. Mr. N. is not only one of the best glass men in this country and a clever gentleman, but is quite fond of hunting and owns four other blooded dogs. A friend tells me that "Arry" doesn't know how many dogs he has." Miss Elizabeth Robb recalls family stories that Northwood was an avid sportsman, quite interested in hunting, and that he once kept several dozen dogs. Both the Martins Ferry *Evening Times* and records from the American Kennel Club confirm this bit of family history. Northwood had several prizewinning English setters (Benzine and Amy Robsart) and a fox terrier called Painter. One of Painter's pups was named "Frank Northwood."

The Best Years, 1890-91

By late 1889, the successes of pattern lines No. 245 (Ribbed Pillar or Northwood Pleat) and No. 263 (Leaf Umbrella) had established the reputation of the Northwood Glass Company. Harry Northwood had been recognized as a talented glassmaker, of course, but now the firm which bore his name had made its niche in the highly-competitive glass tableware market. The next two years would be marked by even greater vitality as Northwood created new patterns and utilized a wide variety of glass colors (particularly ruby) and decorating effects. About this time, Harry Northwood posed for a portrait, looking very much the successful young businessman.

The October 10, 1889, issue of *Pottery and Glassware Reporter* briefly mentioned the new lines being prepared by Northwood for the January, 1890, glass exhibitions: "The Northwood Glass Works is making two new lines of useful tableware in crystal, called the 'Rustic' and 'Parisian.' The goods are made in fruit baskets, bowls, celeries, etc., and are both entirely new and of such figure as to make them as brilliant as cut glass. They are the first crystal ever made at the Northwood."

Although these two patterns in crystal glass were short-lived and neither has been identified, the last sentence in this trade report may be significant. It reveals that the Northwood firm had not made clear glass (crystal) pattern lines until

Courtesy of Miss Robb.

this time, although crystal was used to overlay the colors used in patterns such as Leaf Umbrella. The January 9, 1890, issue of *Crockery and Glass Journal* mentioned that the Northwood's "Parisian and Rustic crystal goods are ... quite popular," but the journal seemed more interested in reporting that "Mr. Harry Northwood went to Paris to gather ideas to strike Americans with and now there is no combination of colors under the sun that cannot be found in the Northwood's exhibit ...."

Crockery and Glass Journal (February 6, 1890) contains another clue about the Parisian and Rustic lines: "Mr. Harry Northwood with pardonable pride listens to the encomiums passed upon one of his elegant new crystal lines. Everybody guesses at how it is made, but none can tell." A note in the March 27, 1890, issue of *Crockery and Glass Journal* adds to the mystery: "Harry Northwood has just completed some beautiful effects in bright crystal ware, one of which has a sort of wavy, silken effect that is very rich and striking." A later issue of *Pottery and Glassware Reporter* (July 17, 1890) also described these Northwood lines: "In crystal they have three fine effects, "Sea-shell", "Parisian" and "Rustic". The former is embellished by the introduction of air

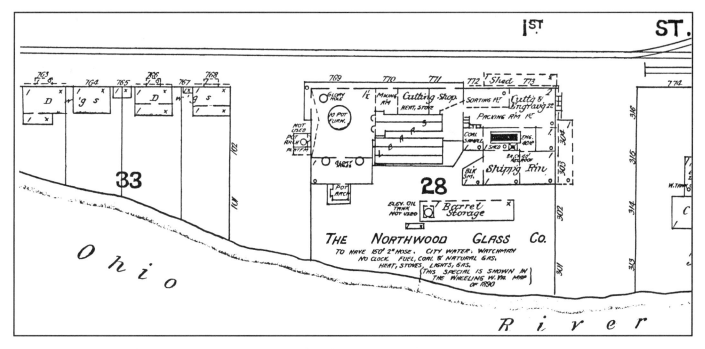

This drawing of the Northwood plant at Martins Ferry is from a Sanborn fire insurance map dated June, 1890.

bubbles in the glass, a unique novelty. We have no room for further details, and if we had it would be of no use to give them, as no words can satisfactorily describe the extent and beauty of this display."

Eventually, the Northwood's new spring lines for 1890 were well-described in a lengthy article in *Pottery and Glassware Reporter* (February 13, 1890):

"Martin's Ferry — THE NORTHWOOD GLASS WORKS is running every day and doing well. This enterprise has a very large line of novelties for the spring trade, which are selling like hot cakes. No. 273, made in crystal sea shell ware and consisting of epergnes, flower vases, water bottles, plates and round and heart shaped bonbons is very artistic [This has not yet been identified. It may be blown cranberry with crystal applied rigaree similar to rows of sea shells, previously thought to be English only]. Pretty casters and bottles are made in crystal engraved and ruby, the number of which is 274. Opalescent salads, oils and vinegars, salts and peppers, the number of which is 272, are goods that are bound to become popular. Brownies, Greenaways and tumblers in etched are very pretty, also their crystal engraved pitchers and tumblers, and decanters in both lines of crystal and ruby, with tumblers to match. The No. 264 bowls and nappies in crackled, crystal and ruby; No. 267 twist salts and peppers, in blue, canary, and ruby; No. 275 plain ruby jugs and tumblers; No. 280 crystal engraved decanters, and No. 281 crystal jugs and tumblers,

engraved and cut, are also among the new spring ware. These goods are all new and a credit to the Northwood. Some of them have already become popular. Mr. Harry Northwood, the efficient manager, is to be complimented for bringing out such a fine line of spring goods."

The prosperity of the early months of 1890 enabled the Northwood firm to enlarge its facilities. In June, 1890, a two story addition, intended for an expanded cutting and engraving department, was erected on the north side of the plant (*Crockery and Glass Journal*, May 8, 1890; *Pottery and Glassware Reporter*, June 5, 1890).

As the time for the July glass exhibitions neared, the glass trade periodicals kept watch on the Northwood concern. *Pottery and Glassware Reporter* (June 19, 1890) offered the bland observation that the Northwood's "line of goods for the fall trade ... will sell on sight," but *Crockery and Glass Journal* (June 19, 1890) was effusive: "The irrepressible 'Arry Northwood is never satisfied unless he has something new to hit the trade with, and the harder he can hit them the better he likes it."

The next patterns introduced were to prove "heavy hitters," indeed. Ads began to appear during July, 1890 (in both *Crockery and Glass Journal* and *Pottery and Glassware Reporter*) for the two new patterns — No. 287 Royal Ivy and No. 285 Aurora. The latter was called Hobb's Optic and, finally, Prima Donna by Heacock, who credited the pattern to Hobbs, Brockunier and Company in several of his publications before pinpointing its

Northwood's Aurora toothpick, Ring Neck mould, in rubina. **Courtesy of Larry Loxterman.**

this and their new Aurora ware. The Northwood is widely known for the excellence of its colored wares, but this last production far surpasses anything they have yet brought out. The Royal Ivy consists of a spiral pillared or columned base, commencing at the top with a rich ruby (for which the Northwood is famous) gradually diminishing or dying away into a beautiful crystal. Ivy leaves are raised in heavy relief and twine around the whole. This makes a new and pretty effect but when the body is etched, leaving the ivy leaves bright, the effect is beautiful and artistic."

The article goes on to describe the Aurora line as "another pretty effect ... a ruby dying away into a bright crystal" before concluding with these statements: "The Northwood not only produces the newest and prettiest effects in colored goods but also has a line of flint novelties in fine cut and machine etched, water sets, celeries, spoons, water bottles, bowls, etc. Taking it altogether, the Northwood has made such progress of late that we predict for them a great future. Mr. Northwood, the superintendent and manager, certainly did not take the Paris Exposition with his eyes closed and we learn that since his return he

Northwood origins (see H3, p. 34 and CG2, p. 12). Since other factories made Aurora patterns, this should be known as Northwood's Aurora.

The similarity, in both design and colors made, of other glassware items (see H3, pp. 39, 45) — Ring Neck with Inverted Thumbprint, Ring Neck Optic, Ring Neck Stripe and Venetian Diamond — suggests that all are Northwood products, but their relationships to the Aurora line are not altogether clear. Northwood's Aurora — a rather plain blown line — is usually seen in rubina, but it is also to be found in spatter effects, including pink with minute silver flecks over opal (the Royal Silver line which was introduced later, see p. 43). The Aurora pitcher ball-shape mould was also used for Northwood's crystal, machine etched ware (see p. 39). Some articles in the various Ring Neck moulds and Venetian Diamond moulds are also known in rubina and spatter effects as well as in cranberry opalescent treatments.

The July 10, 1890, issue of *Pottery and Glassware Reporter* provides a detailed account of the Royal Ivy line:

"'The Northwood Glass Co. have two very attractive engravings of their new Royal Ivy line in this issue, and it is safe to predict a good run for

Northwood's Aurora syrup jug, Ring Neck mould, in cranberry opalescent stripe. **Courtesy of Larry Loxterman.**

has devoted the whole of his time to these new goods. They will have a complete line of samples at the Monongahela House, Pittsburgh, from July 7 to August 30, in charge of Mr. J. G. Anderson and occasionally "Arry" will put in a few days himself for he cannot miss this opportunity to shake hands with his many friends."

The July 17, 1890, issue of *Pottery and Glassware Reporter* reiterated its description of Royal Ivy with a bit of elaboration: "The Royal Ivy is finished in three different ways, each perfect in itself. The coloring is exquisitely shaded, so that it is almost impossible to define where the ruby ends and the crystal begins as they seem to melt into one another. There are water bottles, tankards, sugar sifters, tumblers, finger bowls, water sets, molasses pitchers, caster bottles and a variety of other articles in these lines." Collectors today have located the four-piece table set, the water and berry sets, the toothpick holder and a wide variety of condiment pieces: syrup jug, sugar shaker, salt shaker, cruet, and pickle caster (made by inserting the spooner in a silver-plated frame). A small oil lamp is also known (Smith 1, fig. 431). Heacock recorded a salt shaker with amber stain on the ivy leaves (H3, p. 52).

Many Royal Ivy pieces follow the shape of Parian Swirl, a separate line whose original name and number remain elusive. In addition to the typical rubina color, Royal Ivy pieces are known in other colors and effects. Red/yellow spatter over

Northwood's Aurora sugar shaker in rubina (this was formerly called Ring Neck Optic). **Courtesy of Larry Loxterman.**

opal casing (sometimes called "rainbow") is especially attractive, and, on some articles, the red is decidedly pink and the yellow is a yellowish-green or chartreuse hue. Both red/yellow spatter and

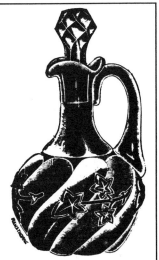
This ad ran for about five months (July-December, 1890).

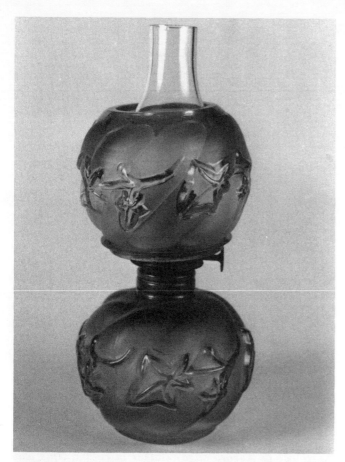

Royal Ivy miniature oil lamp (frosted rubina). **Courtesy of Larry Loxterman.**

to John Northwood's geometrical glass etching machine in the 1860s. In brief, clear glass items were covered with a thin coating of wax before being placed on the machine, which utilized a complex series of wheels, cams and levers to bring a needle close enough to the object to take the wax away from the surface of the glass in sharply-defined lines. Once removed from the machine, the glass item was subjected to hydrofluoric acid, which attacked the unwaxed areas, emphasizing the geometric pattern

Parian Glassware "Ruby."

55133 The Parian Glass Assortment contains nothing but useful pieces of glassware, such as come constantly into use, as will be seen by the following articles They are all hand-made, of the very best quality lead-blown glass, and warranted perfect: Table set. consisting of butter dish, sugar bowl, spoon holder and cream pitcher: one large berry dish, six small sauce dishes, one half-gallon pitcher, six tumblers, one oil bottle, one syrup can. one small night lamp, three salt bottles, three pepper bottles and one toothpick holder. They are packed securely in a strong wooden box and weigh about 40 lbs. Per set...$5.40

Northwood's Parian Swirl from Montgomery Ward catalog. **Courtesy of the University of Wyoming's American Heritage Center.**

rubina items may exhibit a "cracquelle" effect produced by subjecting hot pieces to immersion in water before final finishing and annealing. Royal Ivy items may also have a satin finish, and some are known in the Royal Silver line (pink spatter and minute silver flecks on opal). Collectors should realize that not all of the pieces occur in all of the colors.

The Parian Swirl line was shown in a Montgomery Ward catalog for 1895 (see Kamm 5, p. 89). The table set, water set, and berry set were illustrated, along with such other pieces as the syrup jug, salt/pepper shakers and toothpick holder. A miniature oil lamp completed the set. Parian Swirl articles are well-known in ruby opalescent, but both ruby with satin finish and blue with satin finish may be found as well as light opaque green. All of these may be decorated with delicate flowers.

Also mentioned by *Pottery and Glassware Reporter* (July 17, 1890) was "a selection of machine etched and cut lead glass," and a later ad (*China, Glass and Lamps*, December 17 1890) shows some of these articles, which usually had "circle" or "Greek key" motifs. The method used to produce this interesting crystal ware goes back

Jug from Northwood ad in China, Glass and Lamps, *December 17, 1890.*

imparted through the wax by the machine. The result was etched glassware which rivaled engraved ware but cost much less, since the machine could be operated by an unskilled worker (for an excellent description of the invention, see *John Northwood* by John Northwood II, pp. 20 - 22).

Brief, but enthusiastic, reports appeared in the trade press throughout the summer and fall of 1890, and this note from *Pottery and Glassware Reporter* (October 9, 1890) is typical: "The Northwood Glass Co. is still running the works to its fullest capacity and continues to make large shipments. Never in their history have they been so busy and their new lines have verified all that has been said of them in this paper from time to time. Dealers wishing shipments in time for the holiday trade should place their orders at once. Mr. J. G. Anderson, the western salesman, is home and it is thought that he will not have to travel any more this fall. Mr. Northwood is to be congratulated on the success of the new lines."

By late November, 1890, the Northwood concern was readying several more new lines for the January, 1891, exhibition and the subsequent spring trade. The "two new lines for next season" mentioned by *Crockery and Glass Journal*

(November 20, 1890) were dubbed No. 315 Royal Oak and No. 317 Jewel.

A splendid advertisement for the Northwood Glass Company appeared in the Holiday Number of *Crockery and Glass Journal* (see next page). In addition to alluding to the "two new lines for Spring trade," the ad mentions the color "ruby" prominently and shows three articles in Royal Ivy. Also of significance is the mention of "opalescent" glassware. Elsewhere in the Holiday Number, the journal's editorial columns summarized the Northwood firm's fortunes:

"It [the new pattern] is the product of that rare genius, Mr. Harry Northwood, whose new pattern this year brought to this company the largest and best business they have ever had; yet each new design seems to be better than the last one. That they are popular is evinced by the fact that with the factory running constantly they have accumulated no stock, and during all of the season until this month were from two to four weeks behind in their orders. Now they are catching up some, and are ready to do business on the new line [Royal Oak] presented in this number, which will be a holiday treat to the dealers who get in first. Mr. John G. Anderson represents the Northwood on the road, and Mr. Charles Helling is the efficient secretary."

In its first issue, the new trade publication *China, Glass and Lamps* (December 17, 1890) said that 1890 had been "a very prosperous run" for the Northwood concern, and the publication called the firm "the leading house in colored blown ware in this country." *Crockery and Glass Journal* (January 1, 1891) was equally enthusiastic: "...they make no common ware, and the rich glass, beautiful designs and elegant novelties count up rapidly. The demand during all of the past season was fully up to their capacity, and the two rich lines they will display this month promise even greater returns. They will exhibit at the Monongahela House in Pittsburgh."

When the semi-annual gathering of glass manufacturers and buyers was in full swing, the writer for *China, Glass and Lamps* (January 14, 1891) had a full account of Northwood's new lines:

"The Northwood Glass Co., of Martin's Ferry, Ohio, have a beautiful assortment of ware in Room 119, with Mr. J. G. Anderson in charge. No. 317, Jewel, in crystal and crystal ruby flashed, twist rib with delicate thread going around, is one of the newest products and they have a complete line of it. The Royal Oak, No. 315, is a square shape, in bright ruby, flashed and etched [satin finished], and crystal etched, with oak leaf in

Ad from Crockery and Glass Journal, *December 11, 1890; note similarities to the firm's letterhead (see p. 23).*

Ad from China, Glass and Lamps, *January 14, 1891.*

heavy relief and acorn knob. It is impossible to describe verbally the elegance of these goods and they must be seen. The firm are doing a big business in machine etched goods. They have a line of ruby flashed ware in sea shell pattern, consisting of seven pieces which are very attractive [possibly cranberry blown ware with applied rigaree]. They show three new opalescent jugs with tumblers, and lemonade sets which are hummers. The company have another new departure in a line of bar bottles which they expect big things from."

The No. 317 Jewel line was first called Threaded Rubina by Heacock (Hl, p. 48), who later amended the name to Threaded Rubina Swirl (H3, p. 44) and finally to Threaded Swirl (H6, cover and p. 3 and PGP1, p. 1). Henceforth, the name Jewel should be restored, since original manufacturer's names are preferred by most pattern glass collectors. Most of the articles made in the Jewel line are reminiscent of Northwood's earlier pattern No. 263 (Leaf Umbrella), and the finial on the butter dish matches Royal Ivy (PGP2, p. 14). In addition to the crystal and rubina items, collectors should know that Jewel salt shakers have been seen in blue opalescent (H6, p. 3) and in cranberry with white opal stripes.

The No. 315 Royal Oak line has been well-documented for many years in pattern glass literature (Kamm 5, plate 20, is erroneously dated April 22, 1889; the ad first appeared January 14, 1891). Three major color effects are known — crystal with satin finish, rubina, and rubina with satin fin-

ish — but the array of items is extensive: four-piece table set, pitcher and tumblers (water set), individual berry or sauce and large bowl (berry set), cruet, salt shaker, toothpick holder, syrup, sugar shaker and pickle caster. One item has been recorded in cranberry opalescent, a creamer. Articles in crystal with satin finish in which the oak leaves have an amber stain have been reported, too, although a note of caution must be sounded here, for it is possible that the amber color was added later.

The January 22, 1891, issue of *Crockery and Glass Journal* captured the excitement generated by the Northwood's two new lines for 1891:

"Gorgeous is the word to apply to the new lines of the Northwood Glass Co., Martins Ferry, now being shown at the Monongahela house by John G. Anderson. Their fame has gone abroad and lots of people who have no direct interest in the trade have been in to see them." About this time, Harry Northwood went on the road for two weeks, seeking to reach buyers in the Midwest who did not attend the exhibit. Upon his return after "a two weeks' trip to Cincinnati, Indianapolis, and Louisville," *China, Glass and Lamps* (February 4, 1891) spoke with Northwood and summarized trade conditions: "He reports a bright and cheerful outlook for business — every mail brings a large number of orders from customers — and Mr. Anderson is sending in large business, secured from the most discriminating buyers, who visit him at his sample rooms in Pittsburgh. Their new styles Royal Oak and Jewel are going off rapidly

Royal Oak creamer in cranberry opalescent. **Courtesy of Larry Loxterman.**

— while the demand for their regular last season's goods is quite large."

Just when the Northwood firm was at the height of its prosperity, the nearby Ohio River reached flood stage in late February, 1891. A first report, in *Crockery and Glass Journal* (February 26, 1891), mentioned "heavy losses by the flood" and said the "fire in [the] furnace [was] almost put out." A week later, *China, Glass and Lamps* (March 4, 1891) reported on the flood damage to a number of Ohio Valley glass plants, including the Northwood operation at Martins Ferry. The account begins with a rueful quotation: "'Slightly disfigured, but still in the ring.' Such was our greeting from Harry Northwood, when we called at the Northwood Glass Co. The flood came upon them, the natural gas was shut off and eight pots were lost. Six of these, however, were old, having been in use since last July. They lost no material. Some few of their out buildings were moved by the water, but not damaged to any extent. The principal loss will be in the time taken for cleaning up and getting ready for the start." On March 18, 1891, *China, Glass and Lamps* noted that the firm had "recovered from their wetting" and

"commenced making glass on the 12th," so the effects of the flood seem to have been quickly overcome. By March 26, *Crockery and Glass Journal* reported business "fairly booming" and said that the firm was "shipping all their goods as fast as possible, much to the gratification of the invincible Harry Northwood."

The May 13, 1891, issue of *China, Glass and Lamps*, in this general report, alludes to some forthcoming Northwood products: "The Northwood Glass Co. have been idle for the past two weeks, but will start up full on Monday. Business with them is looking up considerably. Mr. Anderson is sending in some nice orders from the West and direct orders are coming in better. Two new and beautiful lines will be offered this fall. They will show in a marked degree the skill and taste which has made the goods of this factory so popular. They have not yet been christened or brought into the sample room, so we will have to postpone a formal introduction. The Northwood will add to their business this fall the manufacture of oil lamps and we may look for something very attractive and novel." The new line, called Royal Silver, was not illustrated in a small ad in this same installment of the trade magazine. The ad, like the editorial report, calls attention to the "new and beautiful effect."

Royal Oak butterdish with amber stain decoration.

Mixed reports about the Northwood's business success appeared. The May 28, 1891, issue of *Crockery and Glass Journal* noted "two new magnificent lines in floral shapes," but the June 4 issue of this same publication commented that "the Northwood's excellent lines of tableware were not sold in as large quantities as they would have been at lower figures." *China, Glass and Lamps* (June 10, 1891) was more optimistic: "Everything is on full at the Northwood Glass Co's. The season's business has been entirely satisfactory, and during the early part of the fire they were rushed with orders. The styles and shapes introduced have all sold well and will only give place to still more attractive goods that will be offered to the fall trade."

Finally, in the July 15, 1891, issue of *China, Glass and Lamps*, a reasonably full account of the Northwood's new pattern line, No. 333 (now called Leaf Mold), can be found: "The Northwood Glass Co., Martin's Ferry, Ohio, have their interests looked after by John G. Anderson in room 54. They have a great many new things, No. 333 in three effects, two onyx and one spangled, a full line and brilliant in color and finish. They have water sets, berry sets, rose bowls, and a number of other articles in these. The triple flower holders in the same three effects are very handsome too."

The account in *China, Glass and Lamps* also mentions a number of other products and colors, many of which remain unidentified: "They have a large line of 335 and 337 bowls in different shapes, tulip, three-cornered, crimped, fluted, etc., also fruit baskets and a number of other novelties. The

selection of new lamps is very fine: crystal etched [satin], onyx light, onyx satin and spangled. There is a line of night lamps in the same effects. All these lamps have glass founts so that the amount of oil in them can be seen. They are showing also Nos. 287 [Royal Ivy], 315 [Royal Oak] and 285 [Aurora] as formerly noted by us. The line of crystal etched goods made here is larger and finer than ever."

About a month earlier, *Crockery and Glass Journal* (June 11, 1891) reported that Harry Northwood "struck an idea" while on a business trip to the East, and, consequently, "the two new lines of the Northwood this season will be of more brilliant effect than was contemplated prior to his visit...." The June 25, 1891, issue of *Crockery and Glass Journal* had previously reported "added lustre to the brilliant lines they were preparing for the fall season .... The latest is sprinkled with gold or silver, which at once gives a brilliant effect to an elegant line of goods." On July 3, 1891, *Crockery and Glass Journal* described Royal Silver as "a blending of modest colors spangled with silver...." These may be the Leaf Mold opal items with red spatter and minute flecks of silver. A few articles in Northwood's No. 285 Aurora pattern was also produced in this same color effect.

The reference above to a growing line of "crystal etched goods" needs some elaboration, for the arrival in the United States of one of Harry Northwood's cousins had some part in this. *China, Glass and Lamps*, June 24, 1891, said that "Harry Northwood has recently returned from New York accompanied by a brother and cousin ... lately arrived from England." The brother, of

Northwood's Aurora toothpick holder, Ring Neck mould, in Royal Silver effect. **Courtesy of Larry Loxterman.**

course, was Carl Northwood, now 18, who had visited this country before. The cousin was, in all likelihood, Charles O. Northwood, a son of William Northwood or Joseph Northwood, who were John Northwood I's brothers. Both *Crockery and Glass Journal* (July 9, 1891) and *China, Glass and Lamps* (July 8, 1891) mentioned Charles Northwood, and the latter said he "has assumed charge of the etching department."

Records from the *S. S. Wisconsin*, which docked in New York on June 3, 1891, list both Carl Northwood and Fred. Wm. Northwood (another of Harry's brothers). The latter probably returned to England in 1891, accompanying Eva Northwood, who had spent nearly a year with Clara and Harry Northwood in Martins Ferry. Carl Northwood was mentioned from time to time in the Martins Ferry newspaper, sometimes in connection with social events (*Evening Times*, January 2, 1892) or with trips to dog shows (*Evening Times*, April 1 and 14, 1892).

The July 3, 1891, issue of *Crockery and Glass Journal* called Royal Silver "just what its name denotes," and also mentioned "a very rich effect called Yellowine," but, unfortunately, without any description or elaboration. The curious name Yellowine might refer to the red/white spatter on

canary yellow glass that is so striking in the Leaf Mold pattern (see p. 67). This color combination is also known with a satin finish produced by acid.

A quote from *China, Glass and Lamps* (July 8, 1891) reveals that Leaf Mold, Northwood's No. 333, was known by at least two different names, each of which described a color effect: "Some very rich and elegant designs have been produced by the Northwood Glass Co. in tableware, vase lamps and novelties. Their Royal Silver, No. 333, and Royal Onyx, No. 333, are beauties. A full line of samples will be seen at their rooms at the Monongahela House, Pittsburgh, where Mr. John G. Anderson will be glad to welcome all visitors" (a similar report was carried in the July 9, 1891, issue of *Crockery and Glass Journal*).

The Leaf Mold pattern line is extensive, embracing the table set, the water set, condiment pieces (cruet, salt/pepper, and sugar shakers), and items such as the celery, toothpick holder and bowls of various sizes. Among the more unusual articles are the two-piece fairy lamp and the cologne bottle, both of which are known in white/red spatter on canary yellow glass. Another miniature lamp in what appears to be Royal Silver is pictured by Smith (fig. 555).

Sharp-eyed Northwood glass collectors will find some interesting characteristics as well as some idiosyncrasies in the Leaf Mold line. The Leaf Mold finial is identical to the finial found on Parian Swirl items. The water pitcher may have a crystal or a colored handle. Some lime-colored items with satin finish have crystal handles which are reeded and twisted slightly.

Over the next few months of 1891, the trade periodicals carried only brief reports of glassware made at the Northwood plant. The July 30, 1891 issue of *Crockery and Glass Journal* called the firm's trade "only moderate" but predicted "lots of orders." During the summer stop, *China, Glass and Lamps* August 5, 1891) mentioned "nice orders" for Royal Silver and Royal Onyx, and, two weeks later, this same publication said the Northwood was "anxious to fire up and begin producing more of these desirable and popular goods" (*China, Glass and Lamps*, August 19, 1891). *Crockery and Glass Journal* (August 27, 1891) reported the Northwood was making "large shipments" and, a week later, had this comment about the firm's namesake: "'Arry Northwood is a hustler, and likes to see things hum about the works."

By mid-September, the *Journal* (September 17, 1891) reported "an immense business this season" for the Northwood, and the *Evening Times*

Leaf Mold fairy lamp (compare with Smith 1, fig. 555).
Courtesy of Larry Loxterman.

water sets and odds and ends, berry bowls and other novelties; two new etched tankards, four new lemonade sets, six new fancy bowls; new set in ruby; several new designs in machine etchings and a number of new baskets are what the firm show."

The quotation above seems to be the lone mention of Northwood's Royal Art line. Like Royal Silver, it seems to be a color effect rather than a pattern motif, although this is not known for certain. Heacock associated the Rainbow Twister toothpick (*1000 Toothpick Holders*, p. 44) with this line, and he discussed several articles similar to the creamer shown on the front cover of this book in his *Collecting Glass* (vol. 3, pp. 42 and 52).

Additional Northwood Products

Many articles made by the Northwood Glass Co. in Martins Ferry do not show up in the firm's advertising, simply because some colors and/or pattern lines were more widely advertised and publicized than others. Furthermore, the company's diverse offering of "novelties" changed frequently. Many of the novelty wares, like the limited or short-lived pattern lines, received little mention in the trade press and are not pictured in company advertising. Illustrated sheets and cata-

had this note: "The Northwood glass works are running to the full capacity and can't get their goods out as fast as wanted, and have large numbers of orders ahead. The outlook for goods in their line is very encouraging for a prosperous run." About a month later, *Crockery and Glass Journal* reported "no falling off in sales of Royal Onyx and Royal Silver" (October 15, 1891). No special Northwood ad appeared in *Crockery and Glass Journal*'s Holiday Number, but a large Usher & Osborne display mentioned the Northwood concern (see next page).

Early in 1892, *Crockery and Glass Journal* (January 7, 1892) mentioned three Northwood lines — 339, Spangled; 341, Royal Art; and 343 Marbelized. An article in *China, Glass and Lamps* (January 13, 1892) provided some details: "John G. Anderson is at No. 54 with the exhibits of the Northwood Glass Co., of Martin's Ferry, Ohio. The company always shows something new in artistic and fancy glass and they do not belie their reputation on this occasion. Their Royal Art line, No. 341, in two effects, bright and satin, are things that the trade ought to see. No. 343, of which they have a full line, is a thing the trade should make a note of. No. 339 in spangled ware they have in

Leaf Mold cologne bottle (stopper probably not original).
Courtesy of Larry Loxterman.

We are always rolling out goods and rolling in orders to manufacturers represented by us.

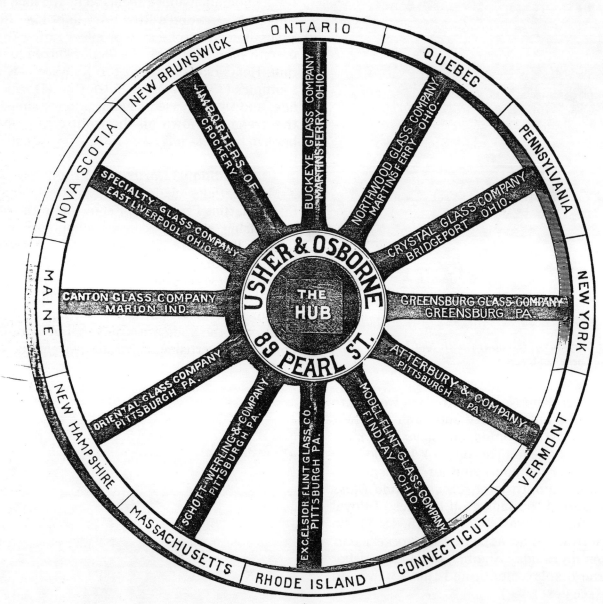

Buyers are respectfully invited to inspect the above lines before placing spring orders. We are in the front rank and we know it.

Our new importations of crockery will interest the most conservative. If unable to visit us, correspond with us. We have some goods you want.

NEW YORK OFFICE, 96 CHURCH ST., Cor. BARCLAY.

A. G. MENZIES Manager.

Ad from Crockery & Glass Journal's *Holiday Number*, December 3, 1891.

logs would be invaluable, but, unfortunately, none from this era has yet come to light.

Another approach to identifying probable Northwood products depends upon similarities in patterns, colors and decorating techniques, especially when "unknowns" bear strong resemblance to documented Northwood products. This method also involves careful study of the advertised products of Northwood's competitors during the Martins Ferry period — Hobbs, Brockunier and Co.; the Union Glass Co.; the Buckeye Glass Co; the West Virginia Glass Co.; and the short-lived American Glass Co. — all of whom advertised in the trade publications and received coverage in the editorial columns as did Northwood.

Using a combination of the above methods, William Heacock isolated a number of probable Northwood novelty items and patterns. These were reported in his own periodical publications — *Pattern Glass Preview*; *The Glass Collector*; and *Collecting Glass* — as well as in contributions to the *Toothpick Bulletin*, *Glass Review*, *The Antique Trader*, etc. (*Old Pattern Glass According to Heacock* contains many of these individual articles). The remainder of this section lists and discusses such probable Northwood products from the Martins Ferry era. Some of these were likely made at Ellwood City, Pa., also, since the company transported its moulds to the new location.

Several ruby (now called cranberry) opalescent lines can be attributed to Northwood through careful study of characteristic Northwood shapes (see p. 82 for an opalescent "Stripe" jug in Northwood's Aurora pattern and the Ring Neck shape mould) and other colors, as in the discussion of Chrysanthemum Swirl above). In Heacock and Gamble's *Cranberry Opalescent from A to Z* (pp. 72-73), Northwood's "Opal Swirl," as they call it, is identified in both the Royal Oak and the Jewel shape moulds. A "Twist" shaker has been found in blue opalescent, and items called Ribbed Opal Rings have been tentatively linked to Northwood because of their similarity to Ribbed Coinspot.

The Christmas Snowflake items (pitcher, tumblers and cruet) may be from the Martins Ferry era. The water set is known in blue opalescent, flint opalescent and ruby opalescent, and the pitcher comes in several mould shapes — ribbed (H9, fig. 178) and twist handle (H9, fig. 183). The cruet, known only in flint opalescent, was made in the Parian Swirl shape mould, and this is the strongest evidence that Christmas Snowflake may date prior to 1895.

Christmas Snowflake cruet from Parian Swirl mould, in flint opalescent. **Courtesy of Larry Loxterman.**

Some Northwood products from the Martins Ferry era which remain unidentified, despite trade journal accounts. The short-lived Parisian and Rustic lines in crystal (see p. 34), for example, remain mysteries, as do those lines which were known simply by number. Many Northwood novelties are equally elusive. *Pottery and Glassware Reporter* (March 27, 1890) carried this brief quote: "One of the best selling novelties ever brought out by any glass works in the Ohio valley is the flower vase or holder made of glass in the shape of a horn, with silk cord and tassel. This company has been having an enormous run on it."

The Decision to Relocate

In February, 1892, the Northwood Glass Company, like many other independent glassmaking concerns in the tableware field, began to ponder its future. The recently-formed United States Glass Company — which controlled 18 plants in Ohio, Pennsylvania and West Virginia — was certain to present formidable competition in an already difficult environment.

Natural gas supplies in the Ohio Valley were

47

generally dependable, but the almost absurdly low prices of the past, once used as an inducement to attract or retain businesses, were giving way to higher rates set by city gas boards which felt the increasing political pressure of citizens who demanded lower rates and insisted that industries pay their fair shares. In October, 1891, the Martins Ferry Council (of which investor Charles Helling was a member) pondered the adoption of a controversial gas ordinance which would have increased charges to the manufacturing firms. The Martins Ferry *Evening Times* (October 15, 1891) warned against price increases which "would result in shutting down every factory in the place." The gas company threatened to cut off residential customers, but Harry Northwood was quoted in the *Evening Times* (October 21, 1891) as "satisfied" with the promises of the company to serve citizens and businesses alike. Less than a month later, the *Evening Times* (November 19, 1891) reported gas shortages at nearby Bridgeport and Wheeling, although Martins Ferry-area customers seem to have been spared any inconvenience.

Some glassmaking enterprises drilled gas wells or maintained relationships with independent natural gas companies. Harry Northwood had a financial interest in the Glens (or Glenn's) Run Oil and Gas Co. while he was at Martins Ferry, and he signed a number of leases for natural gas rights (Belmont County Leases, vol. 7, p. 493; vol. 8, pp. 3, 5, 7, 83 and 87). This firm was formed in January, 1891, by Charles Helling and four other investors, but an open letter in the *Evening Times* (March 3, 1892) was signed by Harry Northwood, who was then president of the corporation's Board of Directors. The letter sought citizen subscriptions to raise an estimated $550.00 to continue drilling a gas well on the Thorburn farm near Martins Ferry. Northwood wrote that a successful gas well would assure both "the welfare of the city ... and handsome returns ... to those who have invested in the project." About two months later, however, the firm had foundered, and some of its property was sold by Constable W. H. Moore to satisfy claims (*Evening Times*, April 20 and May 3, 1892).

Both *Crockery and Glass Journal* (February 18, 1892) and *China, Glass and Lamps* (February 17, 1892) reported the rumors of a possible Wheeling-area combination among the tableware plants. The supposed advantages were clear: a lessening of competition through control of production plus the leverage of combined effort when dealing with city gas boards and the labor unions. Ultimately, however, the factories valued more highly their individuality and autonomy, perhaps as reflections of the strong personalities of their owners or managers. Discussions among manufacturers continued through April, 1892, but the May 4, 1892, issue of *China, Glass, and Lamps* laid the proposition to rest under the headline "No New Combination of Tableware Manufacturers Probable" and said that "the individual companies can operate their plants more economically than they could be operated by one company." *Crockery and Glass Journal* (May 19, 1892) attributed the decision to a committee composed of Edward Muhleman, Chas. J. Gill and David W. Baird.

In January, 1892, the Northwood firm considered moving its glassmaking operation to another locale. An *Evening Times* (January 5, 1892) story, under the headline, "Have No Intention Of Removing," revealed the possibilities: "For several days it has been reported on the streets that the Northwood glass house had determined to remove their plant from this city — some said to Steubenville, others to New Brighton, Pa. One of the stockholders was seen today by a *Times* reporter and asked in regard to the report, and was informed that while several good offers had been received as an inducement to locate elsewhere, they were not such as would justify them in making any changes, and unless a great deal better offer than any they have received was made them, which was very improbable, they would continue to do business in the old stand." A few days later, in noting the revival of a glass plant in Steubenville, the *Evening Times* (January 9, 1892) made this comment: "If Martins Ferry were to lose some of its industrial establishments, it would awaken to a realization of the fact that such things are the life of the town and worth looking after."

Unlike most of the other Wheeling-area plants, which had entertained offers from northwestern Ohio and/or east central Indiana, the Northwood Glass Company looked toward Lawrence County, Pennsylvania. The *Evening Times* (February 27, 1892) noted that the investors went to Elwood, Pa., to pursue the offers being made for their possible relocation. Two days later, the *Evening Times* (February 29, 1892) reported that "while the offer looks favorable, nothing definite has been determined." Both *China, Glass and Lamps* (March 2, 1892) and *Crockery and Glass Journal* (March 3, 1892) carried similar reports, the latter saying that "The Northwood Glass Co. have been considering a proposition from Elwood, Pa., for the removal of their business to that place for some time, and at the last meeting of the company the board of directors were authorized to make an examination of the matter and take such actions as they may deem wise."

Two weeks later, the question was still unresolved: "The Northwood Glass Co. have not yet come to a conclusion as to the removal of their plant, but have the question still under consideration. Meantime they are doing a right good business where they are and the outlook is most cheering" (*China, Glass and Lamps*, March 16, 1892). The April 13, 1891, issue of *China, Glass and Lamps* reported the Northwood firm was "operating their works to full capacity."

In mid-April, 1892, the decision was made to leave Martins Ferry and to build a new factory at Ellwood City, PA. The *Evening Times* (April 15, 1892) had a report on page one: "It is stated on reliable authority that contracts between the Northwood Glass Company and the Elwood, Pa., people, whereby the factory of the former is to be removed to that place, have been signed and the present fire will wind up the operations of the company in this city." Shortly thereafter, *Crockery and Glass Journal* (April 28, 1892) carried the news, mixed with other particulars: "Elwood, on the Pittsburgh and Western railroad, about twelve miles from Beaver Falls, is another prospective glass making town not far from here [Pittsburgh]. The Northwood Glass Co., now of Martins Ferry, O., have decided to remove there, the Peerless Lead Glass Works [a lamp chimney manufacturer] have chosen it for their location, and your correspondent has it on good authority that the largest flint bottle works in this city will be removed there and installed in a four-furnace plant." Elsewhere in the same issue, it was reported that the Northwood firm had "received part of their bonus" for putting down a gas well in Ellwood City. Bonus arrangements were commonplace in the 1880s and 90s, as the relocated companies received monies raised by citizen subscriptions and/or large investors.

The decision of the Northwood Glass Company to leave Martins Ferry raises this question: Why did the firm decide to leave Martins Ferry and move to Ellwood City? The answer really has two parts: (1) the difficulties encountered in Martins Ferry, discussed below, and (2) the perceived advantages of Ellwood City (see p. 54).

There is no indication of consternation among the investors. On the contrary, the Northwood operation must have been successful financially, for the entire Martins Ferry group, which had been in both the West Virginia and the Ohio organizations, became part of a new Pennsylvania corporation, and, in fact, held an overwhelming controlling interest. On June 2, 1892, the Northwood Glass Company applied for a corporate charter in Pennsylvania. Four investors were from the Martins Ferry operation — Henry Floto, Thomas Mears, William Mann, and Charles Helling. Each held 75 shares of stock, as did Harry Northwood. Three gentlemen from Beaver, Pennsylvania — William C. French, James J. Davidson and James H. Cunningham — joined the group, although each held but one share. The charter was granted on July 6, 1892.

The plant at Martins Ferry, despite improvements made during several summer stop periods, was relatively small, and the ten-pot furnace simply may have lacked the capacity to meet demand. Even when noting that the Northwood firm "have just closed one of the greatest seasons in their history," *Crockery and Glass Journal* (January 1, 1891) observed that "the wonder is that one furnace should yield so much." Furthermore, the factory had been inundated by flood waters at least once (February-March, 1890), and Harry Northwood surely remembered the calamity at the La Belle Glass Company, when the fickle Ohio River, swollen by heavy rains, came over its banks and closed the plant. Although the *Evening Times* seemed confident that the Northwood plant would remain in Martins Ferry, this newspaper quoted the Bellaire *Independent* to the effect that the company was "hampered for room" and had "suffered some from floods" (March 8, 1892).

Another factor in the decision to leave Martins Ferry may have been the relationship between the firm and its unionized employees, the skilled glassworkers who belonged to the American Flint Glass Workers Union. The AFGWU, which was founded in 1878, gained in strength throughout the 1880s, and the Local Unions in Martins Ferry were very strong. The glass tableware concerns formed a confederation in 1888. Called The Associated Manufacturers, its sole purpose was to represent the manufacturers in their yearly negotiations with the workers. By 1891, The Associated Manufacturers had fewer than a dozen firms listed as active members, although other companies tended to accept the terms of agreements reached by the association in their dealings with the workers.

The United States Glass Company, a combine of 18 individual companies, was formed in 1891, and it soon decided to run its operations with non-union workers. A lengthy strike ensued, and, although the United States Glass Company closed some of its plants, the AFGWU was weakened by the contest. Other manufacturers were tempted to run nonunion, and this note about Northwood may be significant: "The workmen at the Northwood factory got a notion in their heads last week that the new factory being built by the company at Elwood, Pa., was to be a non-union factory, and they concluded not to make any samples to secure trade for it, and all quit work, leaving eight pots filled with glass. The matter was adjusted, however, and the men returned to work after a conference with President Smith of their union, and things were run along as usual" (*Crockery and Glass Journal*, June 30, 1892).

The nature of glassmaking in the Northwood's Martins Ferry plant was complex, and workers of considerable skill were needed in both the hot metal (blowing and finishing) and cold metal (decorating) areas. This interesting note about some workers appeared in the July 28, 1892, issue of *Crockery and Glass Journal*: "Four of the glass workers formerly employed by the Northwood Glass Co. have engaged to work in the World's Fair factory of the Libbey Glass Co. They are Nicholas Walters, who is said to be one of the finest workmen in the United States; his brother Walter, who is a finisher; Adolph Littleson, a blower; and John Hoar, a gatherer. That all are experts is evidenced in their engagement." The Martins Ferry *Evening Times* mentioned Northwood workers by name from time to time in stories occasioned by weddings (Robert Baggs; October 13, 1891), Christmas parties (Jennie Volhardt; December 26, 1891) and injuries (Fred Harrick, October 30, 1891; Harry Craig, November 13, 1891). Sometimes the news was colorful: "Two of the girls at the Northwood glass house got into a hair pulling during the noon hour yesterday and made things lively until separated by friends. No damage was done except the loss of a few bangs from the head of each of the girls" (*Evening Times*, April 13, 1892).

Although the Northwood Glass Company had determined to leave Martins Ferry in April 1892, the firm remained active there until the time of its closure. The May 4, 1892, issue of *China, Glass and Lamps* called its readers' attention to "a handsome new tea set of four pieces in lead blown ware, ornamented with needle etching, which has a fine effect and will doubtless meet with high favor from the trade." The Northwood concern joined with other manufacturers in the Wheeling area in opening a center to display the firms'

wares. The plan was similar to the exhibitions at the McLure House, but the new facility rented space and was open all year. The formation of the Wheeling Glass, Crockery and Lamp Exchange was announced on the front page of *China, Glass and Lamps* (May 11, 1892).

Just prior to the July, 1892, exhibition at the Monongahela House, the Northwood firm introduced a new line of lamps in *Crockery and Glass Journal*, which had this to say about the venture: "The Northwood Glass Co. are in the lamp business, and with the same skill and ingenuity they have displayed in the artistic designs in tableware and novelties. They continue all of their former business, but with their enlarged capacity they have made a line of lamps in opalescents, coraline, onyx, ruby and crystal, and they have added a new line of novelties. These lamps are works of art in the glass line, and bear the stamp of ingenuity displayed by the inimitable Harry Northwood in all his creations, and dealers will do well to see them when buying this season. Their other lines are all in great shape, too, and it will be well for the shrewd dealer to see or hear from this company" (June 9, 1892). Later notes alluded to "a flood of inquiries" (*Crockery and Glass Journal*,

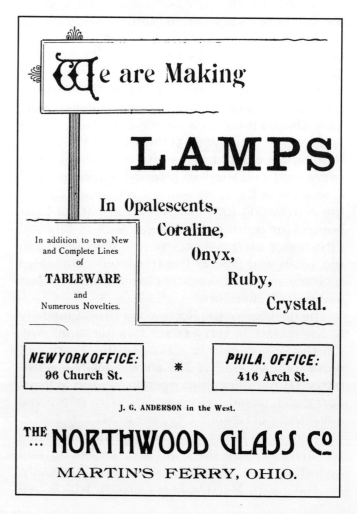

June 23, 1892), although the ad ran only a few weeks (it appeared in both *Crockery and Glass Journal* and *China, Glass and Lamps*).

Monies were raised by the sale of lots in Ellwood City in May (*Evening Times* May 26, 1892). *China, Glass and Lamps* (May 25, 1892) said the Northwood firm was "preparing to wind up affairs here [Martins Ferry]." Ground was broken for the new plant in mid-June (*Evening Times*, June 14, 1892). George Pownall, foreman of the Northwood's cutting department and longtime family friend, listed his Pearl Street home for sale (*Evening Times*, June 6-24, 1892) and moved to Ellwood City, where he purchased a lot in the developing town.

Glassmaking at Martins Ferry probably ceased in early July, 1892, with the beginning of the annual summer stop. By mid-July, *Crockery and Glass Journal* reported that Harry Northwood "moved with his family to their new location" (July 14, 1892). The company had an exhibit at the Monongahela house in July, 1892, and it featured a distinctive line (see p. 90) which was named for the plant's new location, although most of the ware was surely made in Martins Ferry.

By August 4, 1892, *Crockery and Glass Journal* referred to Northwood's Martins Ferry plant as "the old factory" and reported that "Charles Helling is getting off the stock ... in great shape." Helling and the rest of the office workers left for Ellwood City just after mid-September (*Crockery and Glass Journal*, September 29, 1892). The Martins Ferry era was, for all practical purposes, over.

The Legacy of "the old Northwood plant"

Although Harry Northwood and his fellow investors had left Martins Ferry, the glass plant was not razed. The Northwood firm would have taken its moulds and any portable fixtures, of course, but the ten-pot furnace, the lehrs and many other functional appurtenances likely remained. The March 15, 1893, issue of *China, Glass and Lamps* reported this bit of speculation: "It is rumored that the plant ... lately operated by the Northwood Glass Co., now of Ellwood City, Pa., will be started up by two brothers of Harry Northwood, president of the above named company." One object of this speculation might be Carl Northwood, but the other "brother" could be Percy Beaumont, Harry Northwood's brother-in-law, or Charles O. Northwood, a cousin. Harry Northwood's brother Fred could have been involved, since he came to the United States in

June, 1891, but he was not a glassman and was probably in the United States on a visit.

Attempts to re-open the plant went on for quite some time. The November 8, 1893, issue of *China, Glass and Lamps* carried a story in which some unidentified "Wheeling and Martin's Ferry capitalists" sought a bonus of $10,000 from the citizens of Martins Ferry. A later account (*China, Glass and Lamps*, December 20, 1893) lowered the bonus to three or four thousand dollars, and the January 17, 1894, issue of *China, Glass and Lamps* identified the prospective firm as the Columbus Glass Co. Apparently, some member of the company held a patent on a device which made a bottle and a lamp chimney simultaneously, and *Crockery and Glass Journal* (December 28, 1893) said the plant would be "revived early in the year." The patented device aroused controversy with the American Flint Glass Workers Union, but the January 18, 1894 issue of *Crockery and Glass Journal* revealed the company's determination to settle the matter with the union or to run the plant with non-union workers.

Repairs were begun in February, and *Crockery and Glass Journal* (January 25, 1894) predicted "the plant will be operated this spring." Then, a snag developed, as reported in *Crockery and Glass Journal*:

"The Columbus Glass Co. have not yet closed their deal for the old Northwood glass factory. The company is organized and the bonus of the town has been fully subscribed, but the five owners of the plant want to get $2,000 each out of it, and the new company regard the price as too stiff. This is all that has prevented operations being commenced there" (February 1, 1894). The five owners, of course, were Henry Floto, Charles Helling, William Mann, Thomas Mears and Harry Northwood. In March, 1895, during a tumultuous strike at the Union Glass Company in Martins Ferry, *China, Glass and Lamps* carried this rumor: "The union glass workers say they would buy or lease the old Northwood plant and start it up if they had the money" (March 27, 1895). Neither the Columbus Glass Company nor the union workers ever operated the glassworks in Martins Ferry, and *China, Glass and Lamps* (June 6, 1894) reported "no prospect" of the plant's resumption, although it was said to be "in good repair."

In late 1895, the vacant Northwood plant was rented to a new concern, the Beaumont Glass Company. Its prime mover, of course, was Percy Beaumont, Harry Northwood's brother-in-law. A lengthy article in *China, Glass and Lamps* (November 13, 1895) gave the full particulars and provided an account of Beaumont's glassmaking career:

"The Beaumont Glass Co. leased the old plant of the Northwood Glass Co. ... last week and will do all kinds of decorating, staining, etching and gold banding. Preliminary arrangements were made at a meeting held on Wednesday night and a charter will be taken out at once. Percy Beaumont, formerly of the Hobbs Glass Co., Wheeling, and Northwood at Martin's Ferry, and latterly of the West Virginia [a firm in Martins Ferry which was "closed indefinitely" according to *Crockery and Glass Journal*, July 4, 1895], will be manager, and Samuel Taylor, who has been in the employ of the West Virginia Glass Co. for years, will have charge of the office. Among the stockholders are James Higgins, Wm. Higgins, Fergus Whaley, Frank Swift, Capt. John Smith and Percy Beaumont. The newly organized company expects to have a full line of samples ready by the first of the year. The work of making changes and building kilns was commenced last week and they expect to be ready to begin operations by the middle of December. The plant leased is large and roomy and well adapted for the purposes ... the business should grow. The company will not [manufacture its] own glass, but do as above stated."

The firm began with a small work force of decorators. When the State of Ohio's factory inspector visited the Beaumont concern in 1898, he reported a total of 8 employees, three of whom were women. Eventually, the Beaumont firm began to manufacture glass, and, from all reports, the company operated in Martins Ferry with some success (in 1900, there were over 100 employees). The lease arrangement apparently continued for a few years, and Thomas Mears, the Northwood investor and cooperage owner, became a stockholder and member of the board of directors. The Beaumont Glass Company purchased the Northwood plant on April 20, 1899 (Belmont County Deeds, vol. 121, p. 270).

After the Beaumont concern moved to Grafton, West Virginia, in 1902, the plant was sold to the Haskins Glass Company, which made lighting goods and other glassware there for a number of years. A fire in 1909 destroyed most of the plant. In May, 1909, the journal *Pottery and Glass* reported that the plant "was owned by the Haskins Glass Co., who have not used it since moving to their larger factory."

The financial affairs of the Northwood's Martins Ferry organization remained unsettled for quite some time. On February 24, 1896, two suits

Ruins of "the old Northwood plant" after its destruction by fire in 1909. Courtesy of the Wrixon Studio Collection, Martins Ferry, OH.

were brought against the Northwood Glass Company in Belmont County Common Pleas Court. In the first action (case #8623), four plaintiffs (Charles Helling, Henry Helling, William Helling and Louis Helling) asked for $2500.00 plus interest from July 2, 1894. In the second matter (case #8624), Charles Helling sought $1500.00 as well as interest from October 10, 1895. In both cases, the legal papers were delivered by the sheriff of Belmont County to Thomas Mears at the old Northwood plant, which was then occupied by the Beaumont Glass Company. Case #8623 was not settled until March 17, 1897, when a trustee, E. G. Kranter, was ordered "to carry out an agreement between plaintiffs and William Mears," who may have been Thomas Mears' son and heir. Case #8624 ended with a judgment against the Northwood Glass Company on May 11, 1896, and the property was ordered to be sold. If such a sale took place, there is no record of it, for the Northwood Glass Company had a clear title when it sold the premises to the Beaumont Glass Company on April 20, 1899 .

A third lawsuit in Belmont County (case #8796)

was filed on August 11, 1896, on behalf of the creditors of Thomas Mears, Henry Floto and William Mann. This action was brought against Harrie [sic] Northwood, Sophia Helling (executrix of Henry Helling's estate), the Northwood Glass Company and the First National Bank of Bridgeport. A series of legal maneuvers followed (including a deposition from Thomas Dugan on April 27, 1897), all of which culminated in this terse entry in the Appearance Docket for the Summer Term, 1899: "settled and dismissed."

Members of the Helling family were investors at both Martins Ferry and Ellwood City, and several of them were employees of the glass company as well. Both Charles Helling and Charles J. Helling appear in the city directory for Ellwood City borough (New Castle-Lawrence County) in 1895-96. Perhaps as the Ellwood City operation was winding down, they and the others felt compelled to take these legal actions. Despite the financial problems which developed later among Harry Northwood and the other investors, the Martins Ferry plant was probably both productive and profitable. Even when other glassmaking firms occupied the premises years later, the factory was remembered for its association with Northwood. Indeed, the last line in an article cited earlier about the Haskins firm (*Pottery and Glass*, May, 1909) is an appropriate one with which to close this chapter on the Martins Ferry enterprise: "Harry Northwood ... made colored and plain glass there years ago."

CHAPTER THREE
THE NORTHWOOD PLANT AT ELLWOOD CITY

Like its predecessor at Martins Ferry, the Northwood factory at Ellwood City made mould-blown glassware. Some distinctive colors were developed, but the articles made were generally the members of "seasoning sets" (salt/pepper shakers, cruets, and syrup jugs) rather than the extensive tableware lines produced earlier. Some of the lines, such as Parian Swirl, were in production at both locations, and this pattern also served as the basis for the manufacture of opalescent motifs, particularly Daisy and Fern.

In regard to the move of the Northwood Glass Company from Martins Ferry to Ellwood City, PA, two questions emerged. The first, addressing the various difficulties encountered in Martins Ferry, was considered in the previous chapter. The second question remains: What were the perceived advantages of Ellwood City? Clearly, several factors attracted the Northwood Glass Company and its investors to Ellwood City, and an understanding of them necessarily begins with a brief history of Ellwood City itself. Fortunately, an excellent source is available; the Ellwood City Historical Association prepared *A History of Ellwood City, Pennsylvania*, for a celebration of the city's 50th year in 1942.

From Hazel Dell to Ellwood City
Ellwood City was the creation of Henry Waters Hartman, an iron and steel magnate who, in association with Andrew Carnegie, founded a steel company in nearby Beaver Falls. Hartman soon established several subsidiary concerns, including a rod mill, a wire mill, a nail mill and other plants which made steel mats and wire fences. After Hartman and Carnegie separated their interests about 1888, Hartman decided to acquire a large parcel of land in Wayne Township near the Beaver and Lawrence county lines, not far from the Connoquenessing Creek. Within the area was then a small hamlet called Hazel Dell.

Over the next five years, Hartman proceeded to develop the town, both by locating his own plant and by working with The Pittsburgh Company, an entrepreneurial group of real estate men, investors, contractors, etc. Once the land had been acquired, The Pittsburgh Company sought to attract industries, arranged for houses to be built, and otherwise developed the town, which was first called Ellwood (the name was changed to Ellwood City to avoid confusion with

another town of the same name). The Pittsburgh Company sold lots to many persons connected with the Northwood enterprise, such as George Pownall (foreman of the cutting room at Martins Ferry), Charles Helling and George Beaumont, as well as to Harry Northwood and two of his cousins, Samuel Dugan and Thomas E. A. Dugan.

The August 24, 1892, issue of *China, Glass and Lamps* provides an interesting overview of Ellwood City in which the enthusiasm of the times is captured:

ELLWOOD, PA.
The new town of Ellwood in Lawrence county, this state, outside of its present status and future promise as a manufacturing center, is one of the most salubrious, prettiest and most picturesque spots within a radius of 500 miles of Pittsburgh; and that its merits as such have remained practically unnoticed until within a comparatively recent date is certainly a matter of surprise, considering its proximity to so many populous towns and cities, and the readiness of access to it from all directions. It is only about 40 miles from Pittsburgh and is reached from there in about an hour by either the lines of the Pittsburgh & Western, the Pittsburgh & Lake Erie or the Pennsylvania Co.'s railroads. It is located on the Connoquenessing Creek, above the beautiful gorge on that stream, surrounded by the most magnificent natural scenery, including great trees, rocks and waterfalls, and is connected with Beaver Falls by the slack-water system of navigation, affording unlimited opportunities for water communication with that thriving town. The water power is unfailing, the supply of natural gas large and hitherto unlimited and there is an abundance of fine coal underlying the adjacent hills. As a manufacturing town, Ellwood therefore possesses all the elements of prosperity, and far-seeing and prudent investors have already availed themselves of the prospects. Among the prominent enterprises already at the point of completion here are the extensive plants of the Peerless Lead Glass Works and the Northwood Glass Co. Both of these will be ready for operation next month, and will the unexampled facilities they will possess for both the manufacture and distribution of their wares, it may be readily supposed that their future record of success will greatly eclipse the high prestige gained by them when established in other localities. Besides these concerns, there is a foundry and machine works at Ellwood, brick works, planing mill, shafting and tube works and enamel works and several manufacturers of other goods are now negotiating for sites. There is already one first class hotel, the "Hotel Oliver," located here, and for ample accommodations, furnishings, modern conveniences, good management and cuisine it has no superior at the sea shore, or in the large cities, or outside of them elsewhere.

The article went on to detail the dimensions of the Northwood factory, which was then under construction: "The new plant of this company will be as complete and thoroughly equipped as any in the country and no trouble or expense has been spared in making it so. Following are the dimensions of the principal buildings: Factory proper, 90 x 90 feet, with one 14-pot furnace; lear room, 85 x 90; selecting and packing room, 96 x 80; cutting room, 40 x 96; etching and engraving room, 40 x 96; and pot room, storage and warehouse occupy 175 x 80 feet of space."

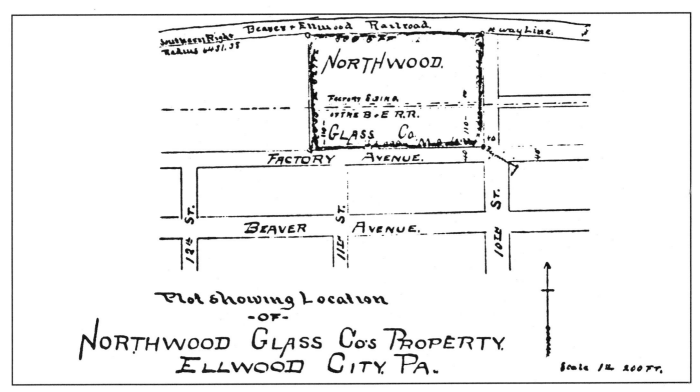

Plant location as shown on the original deed, dated November 20, 1893.

Before the Ellwood City plant was completed, this ad in China, Glass and Lamps *(July 27, 1892) reiterated the lines of lamps made at Martins Ferry and announced the firm's presence at the Monongahela House exhibit. Similar ads appeared in July and August, 1892.*

(Chapter 3 continued on page 89.)

NOTES ON COLOR ILLUSTRATIONS

The color photography for William Heacock's Northwood projects encompassed nearly a decade of effort by at least three professional photographers. The colored backgrounds used and the "style" of these photos will vary considerably, even from one page to the next. All the photos, however, share these traits — sharp detail and accurate color.

Some plates will include a few pieces that are *not Northwood* glass, as the captions will indicate. Bill may have placed these articles in the photo because he thought they might be Northwood-made (proved otherwise by his research) or because he wanted to compare Northwood's colors or shapes with the production of other glass factories. Glass made by Northwood after 1900 will be discussed in a forthcoming book — *Harry Northwood: The Wheeling Years, 1901-1927* — and Northwood's competitors will be covered in a yet to be titled work on Indiana, Pa., glass factories, including the Dugan and Diamond firms.

The items shown are numbered consecutively, following the practice of earlier Heacock books. Each page is also numbered to facilitate the cross-references provided in the various chapters and the index at the end of this book.

A

B

C

D

E

1

Several English pieces reflect Harry Northwood's heritage and training as a glassmaker. The carved cameo vases (A and B) probably represent the work of his father, John Northwood. The other vases (C and D) are typical of the commercial cameo pieces made at Stevens and Williams during the 1880s. The wall plaque (E) bears two separate signatures and dates: "E. G. Thomson 1876" and "W. Northwood 1880."

The opal/blue cameo is inscribed "Hy. Northwood 1882" on the reverse. It was exhibited at the West Virginia State Fair in September, 1882.

The canary Hobnail, 4-Footed creamer (Fig.1) was made at the La Belle Glass Company in 1886 while Harry Northwood was "designer and metal maker" at this important firm, so he may be responsible for both the design and the glass color.

Harry Northwood's genius as a glassmaker is readily evident in this stunning assortment of pitchers and tumblers from his various factories.

2. Royal Ivy pitcher in light yellow/pink spatter with satin finish (Martins Ferry). Note the slight cracquelle effect. 3-4. Northwood Parian Swirl tumbler and pitcher, decorated blue satin (Martins Ferry or Ellwood City). 5-6. Daisy and Fern tumbler and pitcher in cranberry opalescent, Parian Swirl mould (Ellwood City or Indiana). 7-8. Apple Blossom decorated tumbler and pitcher in opal (Indiana).

9-10. Leaf Umbrella tumbler in Rose Du Barry and pitcher in opal-cased blue glass (Martins Ferry). 11. Jewel (Threaded Swirl) pitcher, rubina (Martins Ferry). 12. Ribbed Pillar pitcher in white/pink spatter (Martins Ferry). 13-14. Panelled Sprig tumbler and decorated pitcher in a light rubina effect (Martins Ferry).

15. Panelled Sprig opal decorated pitcher (probably Indiana, but possibly Ellwood City). 16. Royal Oak rubina pitcher (Martins Ferry). 17-19. Netted Oak opal decorated pitchers and tumbler; note the different decorations (Indiana).

20   21   22   23

24   25   26   27

28   29   30   31

Ruby glass was among Harry Northwood's favorites, and several different effects and surface treatments are shown here. Unless otherwise indicated, these are Martins Ferry products.

20-23. Parian Swirl covered sugar bowl, covered butterdish, tumbler and pitcher, satin finish with enameled floral decorations. Note the crystal applied handle on the pitcher and the crystal base to the butterdish; both have been acid-etched to produce a fine satin finish (Martins Ferry or Ellwood City).

24. Parian Swirl cruet, ruby. 25. Daisy and Fern cruet in Parian Swirl mould, cranberry opalescent (Ellwood City or Indiana). 26. Leaf Umbrella cruet, ruby. 27. Jewel (Threaded Swirl) cruet, rubina.

28-31. Leaf Mold covered butterdish, spooner, creamer and sugar shaker in various shades of ruby with satin finish. Compare the finial of 28 with 20 and 21.

Northwood's No. 263

32   33   34   33

35   36   37   38   39

40   41   41   42   43   44   45

Except for the rose agate pitcher (32), all of these Leaf Umbrella items are in Northwood's famous ruby color, which was developed at his Martins Ferry location. The covered cracker jar (39) and the celery holder (45) are very scarce. Note the slightly different colors present in the salt and pepper shakers (41). Compare the butterdish (36) and sugar bowl (38) finials with Ribbed Pillar (Northwood Pleat) and Panelled Sprig pieces (figs. 114, 117, and 120-121).

32. Leaf Umbrella pitcher in rose agate (note the crystal handle).

33-34. Leaf Umbrella tumblers and pitcher.

35-39. Leaf Umbrella four-piece table set and covered cracker jar (note the clear finials on 36, 38, and 39).

40-45. Leaf Umbrella toothpick, salt/pepper shakers, cruet, sugar shaker, syrup jug and celery holder (note the clear stopper in the cruet and the clear handles on 42 and 44).

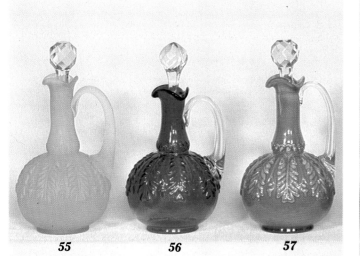

This gathering of No. 263 (Leaf Umbrella) articles shows the wide variety of colors in which this pattern was made at Northwood's Martins Ferry plant. The clear glass outer layer is easily visible on the toothpick holders. Pieces in the ruby with white spatter effect may vary considerably in the amount of white present.

46-49. Leaf Umbrella toothpicks in ruby, ruby with white spatter, Rose Du Barry, and blue cased with opal.

50-51. Leaf Umbrella syrups in ruby and Rose Du Barry.

52-54. Leaf Umbrella sugar shakers in lemon yellow cased with opal, blue satin finish (cased inside with opal), and ruby with white spatter.

55-60. Leaf Umbrella cruets in crystal satin finish, ruby, Rose Du Barry, blue cased with opal, lemon yellow cased with opal, and ruby with white spatter. Note the colored handles on 58 and 59.

61   62   63   64   65

66   67   68   69

70   71   72   73

The Jewel (Threaded Swirl) line was made at Martins Ferry, and most table service items can be found. The water bottle (63) is unusual, as is the small tumbler (62). There are two different syrups (70-71). Notice that the rubina effect varies from covering a small area near the top of the item (61, 62 and 72) to almost completely enveloping the article (68, 70 and 73)

61-65. Jewel celery holder, tumblers, water bottle and pitcher.

66-69. Jewel four-piece table set.

70-73. Two different Jewel syrups, toothpick holder and sugar shaker.

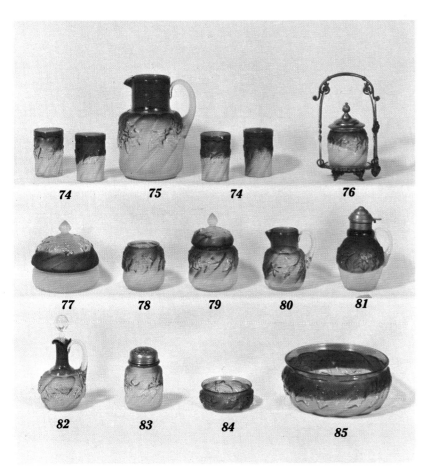

74   75   74   76

77   78   79   80   81

82   83   84   85

Another Martins Ferry product, Northwood's Royal Ivy is well known in both rubina and the acid-treated, satin finished rubina (often called frosted rubina) which is shown here.

74-76. Royal Ivy tumblers, pitcher and pickle caster in silver plate frame.

77-81. Royal Ivy four-piece table set and syrup jug.

82-85. Royal Ivy cruet, sugar shaker, individual berry or sauce and round bowl.

These Royal Ivy pieces were described by Heacock as "cased rainbow spatter," and his phrase captures the beauty of this Martins Ferry product. All are opal inside, and the red/yellow spatter is beneath a layer of clear glass. The spatter effect varies in intensity, and the yellow may be yellow-green.

86-89. Royal Ivy cased rainbow spatter pickle caster, cruet, sugar shaker and pitcher.

90-93. Royal Ivy cased rainbow spatter four-piece table set.

94-96. Royal Ivy cased rainbow spatter individual sauce or berry, round bowl and toothpick holder.

86   87   88   89

90   91   92   93

94   95   94   96

97   98   99   99A

100   101   102   103

106

105

104

The Royal Oak pattern, another Martins Ferry product, was available in both rubina and frosted rubina (the acid-treated, satin finish often used on Jewel and Royal Ivy). The Leaf Mold items, among the last lines produced in Martins Ferry, may be the color effect advertised as "Royal Silver."

97-99. Royal Oak frosted rubina pitcher, tumbler and cruet (compare 99 with the other cruet, 99A, which has not been frosted).

100-103. Royal Oak frosted rubina four-piece table set.

104. Royal Oak frosted rubina toothpick.

105-106. Leaf Mold individual berry or sauce and round bowl in Royal Silver, an opal-cased, red spatter effect with minute silver flakes (these can be easily seen in the round bowl). For more items in Leaf Mold, see figs. 139-184.

107   108   109   110   111

112   113   112   114   115   116   117

118   119   120   121   122   123

Panelled Sprig was a late pattern at Martins Ferry which was also made in other colors at both Ellwood City and Indiana. The Panelled Sprig rubina items shown here have a less intense red to them than characterizes other Northwood products in this hue (see figs. 61-73 and 97-104). Ribbed Pillar (Northwood Pleat) was probably pattern No. 245, one of the earliest lines introduced at Martins Ferry. These Ribbed Pillar (Northwood Pleat) articles have an opal inner lining, and the red spatter is beneath a crystal outer layer.

107. Panelled Sprig rubina pickle caster with painted floral decoration. 108-111. Ribbed Pillar (Northwood Pleat) sugar shaker, syrup, cruet (note the satin finish) and pitcher in red spatter effect.

112-113. Panelled Sprig rubina shakers and cruet. 114-117. Ribbed Pillar (Northwood Pleat) four-piece table set in red spatter effect (compare the finial on items 114 and 117 to their counterparts in Panelled Sprig, 121 and 120).

118-123. Panelled Sprig rubina sugar shaker, toothpick holder and four-piece table set (note the considerable variations in the rubina effect).

Chrysanthemum Swirl was probably introduced at Martins Ferry, but the blue speckled pieces in the bottom row suggest that it was also associated with Ellwood City. The two un-numbered items at the upper left are a pattern called Reverse Swirl, made at the Martins Ferry-based Buckeye Glass Company.

124-126. Chrysanthemum Swirl ruby opalescent shakers, pitcher and tumbler (a taller version of the shakers is also known, see p. 32). 127. Heacock called this Chrysanthemum Swirl variant in his Book 9, which was devoted to cranberry opalescent glass.

128-134. Chrysanthemum Swirl ruby opalescent cruet, toothpick holder, spooner, covered butterdish, creamer, sugar shaker and syrup.

135-136. Chrysanthemum Swirl blue syrup and satin-finished blue sugar shaker. 137-138. Chrysanthemum Swirl ruby and blue syrups with speckled finish; note the different handles, both acid-treated to obtain a satin finish.

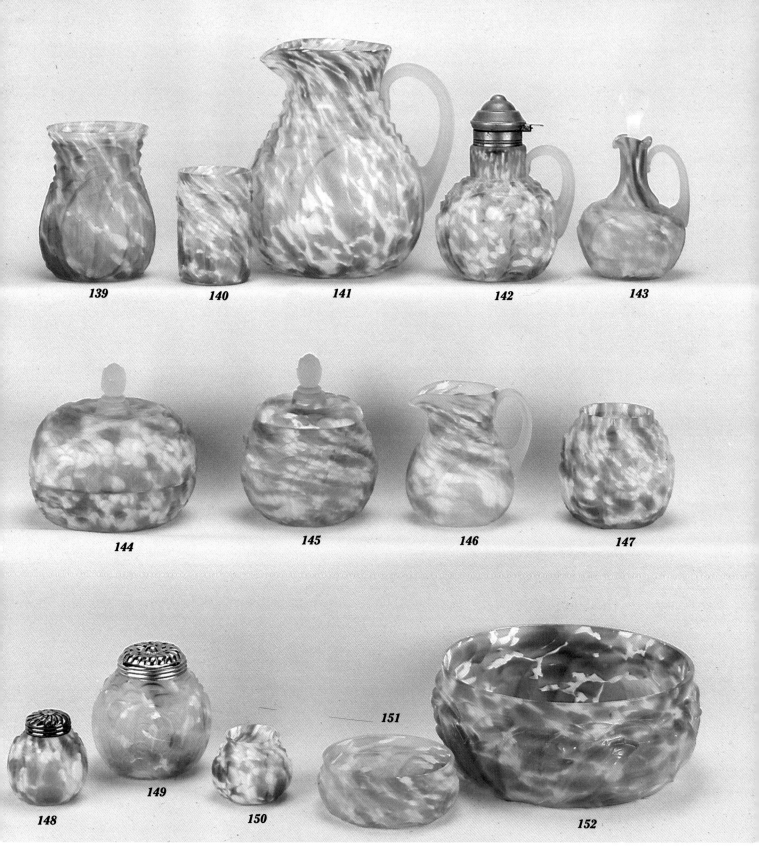

These Leaf Mold items may be the color effect called "yellowine" by one of the trade journals. The red spatter effect in light canary glass is greatly subdued by the acid-etched satin finish.

139-143. Leaf Mold celery holder, tumbler, pitcher, syrup, and cruet (note the crystal satin stopper).

144-147. Leaf Mold four-piece table set.

148-152. Leaf Mold salt shaker, sugar shaker, toothpick holder, individual sauce or berry and round bowl.

67

153 *154* *155* *156* *157*

158 *159* *160* *161* *162* *163* *164*

165 *166* *167* *168* *169*

This selection of Leaf Mold articles shows some of the many color effects in which this pattern occurs.

153-157. Leaf Mold pitchers and tumblers in red spatter canary, lime green with satin finish and opal-cased red spatter with minute silver flecks (Royal Silver). Note the twisted handle on the lime green pitcher.

158-161. Leaf Mold toothpick holder, sugar shaker, salt shaker and syrup in red spatter canary.
162-163. Leaf Mold cruet (note twisted handle) and spooner in lime green with satin finish.

164. Leaf Mold celery holder in the extraordinary color Heacock called "tortoise shell spatter."

165. Leaf Mold opal-cased sugar shaker with red spatter. 166-169. Leaf Mold salt shaker, toothpick, cruet and syrup in opal-cased red spatter with minute silver flakes (Royal Silver).

170   171   172   173

174   175   176

177   178   179   180

181   182   183   184

These sugar shakers and toothpick holders in Leaf Mold show still more of the many colors in which this pattern can be found. The rubina (177) is quite scarce, and satin-finished crystal (179) is hard to find, although collector demand for it is not nearly as strong as for the other colors.

170-176. Leaf Mold toothpick holders in canary with red spatter (satin finish), canary with red spatter, opal-cased with red spatter and minute silver flakes (Royal Silver), light blue (satin finish), ruby (satin finish) and opaque turquoise. Note the difference in the amount of red in Figs. 172 and 173.

177-180. Leaf Mold sugar shakers in rubina, dark blue (satin finish), crystal (satin finish) and lime green (satin finish).

181-184. Leaf Mold syrup and sugar shaker in opal-cased with red spatter and minute silver flakes (Royal Silver), syrup in canary with red spatter (satin finish), and canary with red spatter. Compare 183 with 161 to see different metal tops.

185   186   187   188   189

190   191   192   193

194   195   196

The long-lived Daisy and Fern in ruby opalescent was made by Northwood at both Ellwood City and Indiana, and his successors at Indiana kept it in the line until at least 1903. Daisy and Fern was made in a wide variety of shape moulds, some of which are shown here. Most of these pieces can also be found in crystal opalescent, and a few are known in blue opalescent. The un-numbered item is the Beaumont Glass Company's Daisy in Criss Cross pattern.

185-186, 190-193. Northwood's Parian Swirl pitcher, tumbler, individual sauce or berry, round bowl. sugar shaker and cruet.

187-189. Ball-shape pitcher, tumbler and shoulder mould pitcher. Compare the tumblers (186 and 188).

194-196. Wide Waist mould sugar shaker, rose bowl and spooner or pickle caster insert (made in Apple Blossom shape mould at Indiana).

197   198   199   200

201   202   203   204

205   206   207   208

Ruby opalescent Coinspot motifs were very popular during the 1890s, and this page shows the products of various factories, including Northwood.

197. Star crimp pitcher. 198-200. Cruet and three-tier tankard pitcher with unusual handle (called "question mark" by Heacock) and tumbler. The other pitcher is a Beaumont product.

201. Ball-shaped pitcher. 202. Coinspot and Swirl cruet from Northwood's Parian Swirl mould. The bar bottle was attributed to Hobbs by Heacock. 203-204. Ribbed Coinspot syrup jug and pitcher. This ribbed motif is similar to Northwood's Christmas Snowflake pieces.

205-206. Aurora cruet and sugar shaker made in Ring Neck mould. 207-208. Sugar shakers in Nine Panel and Wide Waist moulds. Heacock attributed the two cruets to Buckeye and Phoenix, respectively.

209   210   211

213   215

212   214   216

Unless otherwise indicated, these items were made at Northwood's Martins Ferry plant.

209-211. These Northwood cruets are distinctive: Royal Ivy in yellow-green/pink spatter; Parian Swirl ruby; and Daisy and Fern ruby opalescent (Ellwood City or Indiana). Note the shape of the pouring lips.

212, 214, 216. Cruets in ruby Leaf Umbrella, rubina Jewel (Threaded Swirl), and opaque green Quilted Phlox (possibly Ellwood City, but probably Indiana). Note the similarly shaped pouring lips.

213, 215. Rubina toothpick from Ring Neck mould and Royal Art toothpick (this was called Rainbow Twister in Heacock's 1000 Toothpick Holders, p. 44); compare with the creamer shown on the cover.

217   218   219

220   221   222   223

224   225   226

This array of pattern glass salt/pepper shakers from Northwood's Ellwood City and/or Indiana plants shows the variety of opaque green and blue/green hues in which many of them can be found.

217-219. Cactus shakers in a very pale green, a very light blue green with crystal outer layer, and the opaque green which is most often found.

220-223. Opaque green Quilted Phlox, Crocodile Tears in different shades of opaque green, and Grape and Leaf in opaque green (the glass is quite thin).

224-226. Opaque blue/green Beaded Crosstie shaker, Flat Flower shaker and Swirl and Leaf shaker.

Courtesy of Bob and Carole Bruce.

73

227   228   229   230

231   232   233   234

235   236   237

These salt/pepper shakers are also from the Ellwood City and/or Indiana plants, and they reflect the wide variety of glass colors and decorating treatments developed by Northwood. Compare the colors with those shown on the previous page.

227-230. Four opal decorated shakers: Grape and Leaf with pink and green decor; tall Quilted Phlox with light blue flowers; Cactus with pink and blue decor; and Quilted Phlox with light blue flowers.

231-234. Grape and Leaf in blue opalescent (note white stripes); Cactus in opaque blue, opaque pink and ruby with opalescent stripes.

235-237. Tall Quilted Phlox in opaque blue/green; Bow and Tassel in opaque blue; and Quilted Phlox in opaque pink.

Courtesy of Bob and Carole Bruce.

238   *239*   *238*

240   *241*   *242*   *243*

244   *245*   *246*   *245*

248   *247*   *247*

Along with Klondyke, Northwood's Alaska pattern was key to the firm's success in 1897-98. Alaska was first advertised in pearl blue, pearl yellow, and flint opalescent. Emerald green was made shortly thereafter.

238-239. *Pearl blue Alaska tumblers and pitcher.*

240-243. *Pearl blue Alaska four-piece table set.*

244-246. *Pearl blue Alaska celery tray, salt/pepper shakers and cruet.*

247-248. *Pearl blue Alaska individual berry dishes and master berry bowl with fluted edge.*

Northwood's Louis XV

249   250   249

251   252   253   254

255   256   257   257   258

Louis XV was the first pattern for Northwood's new Ivory color. An immediate success, it paved the way for other lines in Ivory. Louis XV bears similarities to Klondyke as well as to Geneva and Inverted Fan and Feather. Louis XV was also produced in dark emerald green with gold decor.

249-250. Ivory Louis XV tumblers and pitcher.

251-254. Ivory Louis XV four-piece table set.

255-258. Ivory Louis XV individual berry dish, master berry bowl, salt/pepper shakers and cruet.

259 260 261 260 262

263 264 265 266

267 268 269 268 270

A beautifully-decorated line in Ivory glass, Wild Bouquet was later produced in opalescent colors by Northwood's successors at Indiana.

259-262. Ivory Wild Bouquet cruet, tumblers, pitcher and covered sugar bowl.

263-266. Ivory Wild Bouquet four-piece table set (compare the sugar lid with the one in the row above).

267-270. Ivory salt shaker, individual berry dishes, master berry bowl and toothpick holder.

271 272 273 274 275

276 277 276 278 279 280 279 281

282 283 282 284 285

Klondyke was introduced in 1897, and Ivory articles (sometimes called Jackson today) were probably produced a year or so later. Although fragments have been found at Indiana, Beaded Circle cannot be dated precisely; the scalloped edges and fluting resemble Pagoda (Chrysanthemum Sprig), which was introduced in 1900.

271-275. Ivory Beaded Circle four-piece table set and pitcher.

276-278. Ivory Beaded Circle salt/pepper, cruet, and master berry bowl.

279-281. Ivory Klondyke salt/pepper, cruet and master berry bowl.

282-285. Ivory Klondyke tumblers, pitcher, covered sugar bowl, and creamer.

286   287   288   289   288

290   291   292   293   294

295   296   295   297   297

Although only a few Ivory fragments in Northwood's Maple Leaf have been found at Indiana, Pa., this is yet another pattern designed by Northwood which was continued by his successors. The Ivory ware is certainly Northwood-made, probably ca. 1899.

286-289. Ivory Northwood's Maple Leaf cruet, jelly compote (compare with the individual berry dish below), tumblers and pitcher.

290-294. Ivory Northwood's Maple Leaf four-piece table set and toothpick holder.

295-297. Ivory Northwood's Maple Leaf individual berry dish, master berry bowl, and salt/pepper shakers.

298 299 300 299 301

302 303 304 305

306 307 308 309 310

Northwood's Intaglio pattern in Ivory glass was introduced in early 1899. Ivory items may be decorated with light blue/gold or green/gold. The Intaglio line was also produced in dark emerald green with heavy gold decor as well as opalescent colors (flint, blue and green).

298-301. Ivory Intaglio cruet, tumblers, pitcher and butter dish.

302-305. Ivory Intaglio four-piece table set.

306-310. Ivory Intaglio salt/pepper (note the green and blue decorations), berry bowl (7 1/2") and individual berry, and jelly compote (a larger berry bowl, 9 1/2" d., is also known).

311   312   313   314   315

316   317   318   319   320

321   321   322   323   324

Opaline Brocade, introduced by Northwood in early 1899, is generally known today as Spanish Lace. It was advertised in four colors, but only the "pink" (ruby opalescent) was mentioned at first.

311-315. Three Opaline Brocade pitchers—Ribbon Tie mould, Squat mould and Nine Panel mould—and tumblers.

316-320. Opaline Brocade four-piece table set and cracker jar with silver plated lid.

321-324. Opaline Brocade salt/pepper shakers, sugar shaker in the Wide Waist mould, syrup jug from the Ball Shape mould, and cruet.

81

325 326 327 328 329 330 331

332 333 334

335 336 337 338 339 340 341

325-331. *Ruby opalescent Stripe pitcher and Coinspot cruet in Ring Neck moulds; Opal Lattice cruet in Indiana mould; Coinspot Three Tier tankard pitcher and cruet in Indiana mould; Opal Lattice Ball Base cruet and Opal Lattice pitcher with twisted handle.*

332-334. *Daisy and Fern pitchers in the Parian Swirl and Northwood Ball Shape moulds; Opal Lattice pitcher with its top crimped in the shape of a star. The Seaweed (note square top) pitcher was made by Hobbs and, later, Beaumont.*

335-341. *Coinspot sugar shaker in Nine Panel mould; Opal Lattice salt shaker in Quilted Phlox mould; Daisy and Fern sugar shaker in Wide Waist mould; Daisy and Fern rose bowl; Daisy and Fern sugar shaker in Parian Swirl mould; Daisy and Fern caster insert in Apple Blossom mould; and Opal Lattice spooner in Pillar (Northwood Pleat) mould.*

342   343   344   345   346

347   348   349   350

351   352   353   354

For many years, this pattern was called Chrysanthemum Sprig and no reliable dates of production were established. The original name was Pagoda, and it was first marketed in Ivory and turquoise in 1900. Most pieces are signed with the Northwood script signature on the underside of the base (tumblers, cruets and salt/pepper shakers are not signed).

342-346. Ivory Pagoda celery vase, tumbler, pitcher, condiment set (cruet, salt/pepper shakers on round tray) and toothpick holder.

347-350. Ivory Pagoda four-piece table set.

351-354. Turquoise Pagoda cruet; Ivory Pagoda jelly compote, oval master bowl and individual berry or sauce.

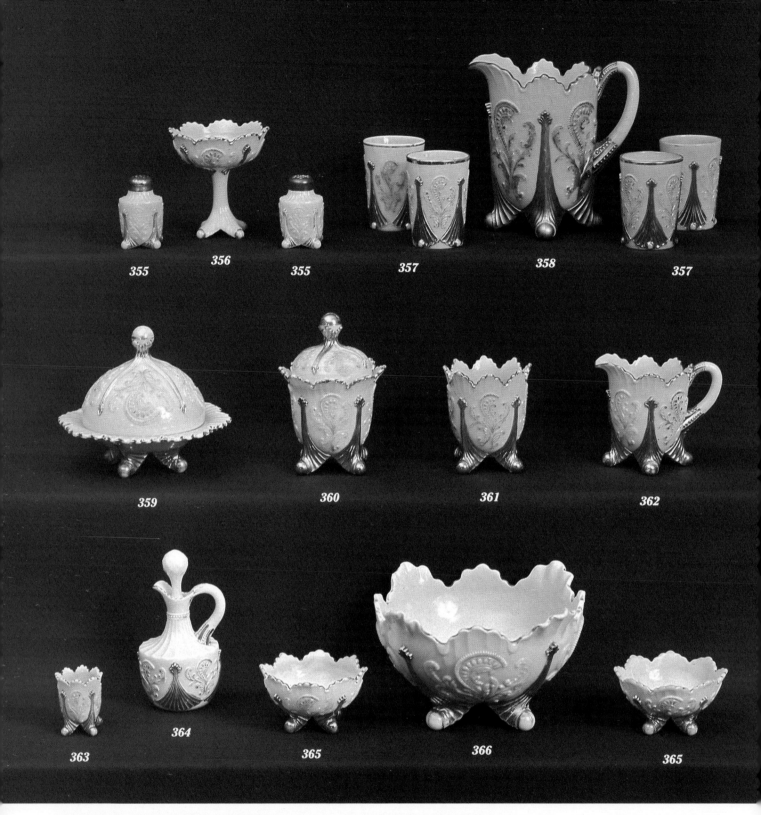

355 356 355 357 358 357

359 360 361 362

363 364 365 366 365

Although the Inverted Fan and Feather pattern cannot be dated with absolute precision, it was likely developed by Harry Northwood in the late 1890s, just before he left Indiana, Pa., for London.

355-358. Ivory Inverted Fan and Feather salt/pepper shakers, jelly compote, tumblers and pitcher.

359-362. Ivory Inverted Fan and Feather four-piece table set.

363-366. Ivory Inverted Fan and Feather toothpick holder, cruet, individual berry dishes and master berry bowl.

367

368

367-368. *Ivory Inverted Fan and Feather punch bowl and eleven individual cups.*

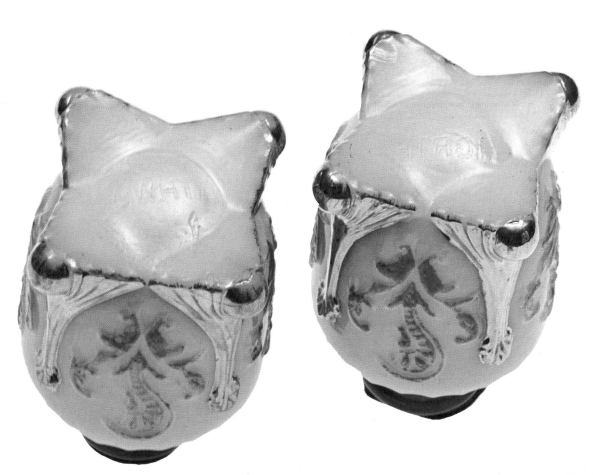

This close-up shows the "backwards" block letters which spell Northwood on some Inverted Fan and Feather salt/pepper shakers. Similar letters have been seen on the bottom of a blue opalescent Coinspot sugar shaker made in Northwood's Nine Panel mould (CG3, pp. 41, 52).

369   370   371   372   373

374   375   376   377

378   378   379   380   381

The Nautilus line, called Argonaut Shell today, was introduced under the aegis of the National Glass Company's Northwood Glass Works in early 1900. Most articles have the Northwood script signature.

369-373. Ivory Nautilus jelly compotes (369 has a bit of seaweed lacking on the other one), pitcher, tumbler and cruet (note the interesting shell-shaped stopper).

374-377. Ivory Nautilus four-piece table set.

378-381. Ivory Nautilus salt/pepper shakers, toothpick holder, berry bowl and individual sauce dish.

382   383   384   385   386   387

388   389   390   391   392

393   394   395   396   397

These Geneva pieces were probably Northwood designs which were made at both Northwood's Indiana plant and, later, the McKee and Brothers Glass Works of the National Glass Company.

382-387. Ivory Geneva jelly compote, tumblers, pitcher, cruet, and syrup jug. Compare the two tumblers; the green/gold decor (378) is likely Northwood, while the red/green decor is probably McKee-made.

388-392. Ivory Geneva four-piece table set and toothpick holder.

393-397. Ivory Geneva oval berry bowl, oval sauce dish, salt shaker, round berry dish and master berry bowl.

398   *399*   *400*   *401*

402   *403*   *404*   *405*

406   *407*   *408*   *409*

This assortment of pitchers reflects both Harry Northwood and his influence.

398-401. Wild Bouquet in Ivory and green Alaska (note the gold decor and the delicate white leaves and tiny, light blue flowers made with six dots); the two tall tankards are likely Northwood designs.

402-405. Blue opalescent Nautilus (made by National and/or Dugan after Northwood left, but bears Northwood script signature); pearl blue Klondyke with low-relief moulded flowers decorated with gilt; pearl yellow Klondyke with painted decoration; and turquoise Pagoda (Chrysanthemum Sprig) with Northwood script signature.

406-409. Flint opalescent Intaglio (gilt almost completely worn off); dark green Louis XV with gold; dark green Inverted Fan and Feather with heavy gold; and Jewelled Heart, a Dugan pattern often attributed to Northwood.

Continued from page 55.

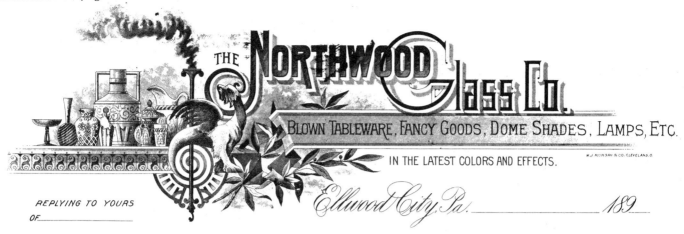

The factory's letterhead stationery was almost identical to that used in Martins Ferry. Courtesy of the Fenton Museum, Williamstown, WV.

There is some evidence that the Northwood Glass Company received a monetary bonus for the relocation of its plant, and the firm probably secured assistance in drilling for natural gas, too (*China, Glass and Lamps*, May 4, 1892). When a successful well was struck, the Martins Ferry *Evening Times* (April 18, 1892) carried the news. Incidentally, Harry Northwood had a financial interest in the Manufacturers Gas Company of Ellwood City, as did Charles Helling and Henry Floto, but it is not known whether this firm supplied natural gas to the plant.

Most interesting, however, is the likely influence of Harry Northwood's uncle, Thomas Dugan, who had come to the United States in the 1850s and who was among the investors in Ellwood City during the early 1890s. Dugan had been associated with several hotels in Pittsburgh in the 1870s-80s, and he was attracted to Ellwood City about 1890 when Hartman and others were publicizing their development of the town. Although Dugan was then about 55 and considering retirement, he built the Dugan Hotel at Ellwood City and made substantial investments in real estate (Lawrence County Deeds, Grantor Index, vol. D). He was also a stockholder in the Manufacturers Gas Company, but he did not have stock in the

Northwood Glass Company, at least not at the time of its incorporation in Pennsylvania.

By constructing its own plant in Ellwood City, the Northwood Glass Company could plan carefully for the needs of its operation. The plant was located on Factory Avenue between 10th and 11th Streets, just east of another new industrial enterprise, the Ellwood Tin Plate Company. The Northwood's new factory, with its 14-pot furnace, was probably 50% larger in capacity than the Martins Ferry operation, and special attention was given to the etching department and other facets of glass decorating, such as engraving and cutting. The company's gas well (*China, Glass and Lamps*, May 4, 1892), made it less dependent upon public utilities for fuel.

The glass trade press lost little time in covering the activities of the Northwood concern at its new location. *China, Glass and Lamps* (May 4, 1892) carried a brief report, and, about a month later (June 8, 1892), the same journal said "The Northwood Glass Co. have broken ground for their new factory at Ellwood, Pa., which they will occupy next fire."

Glassmaking did not begin until early October, 1892, about a month after the usual start of the fall blast. The October 10, 1892, issue of *China,*

This ad ran from April, 1893 through January, 1894.

Glass and Lamps reported the firm "in pretty good shape with their new plant, having begun to make glass on Monday last, October 3. They are feeling bright over their opening, everything having come off so well." A month later, they were "very busy on orders ... running their new factory to the full limit" (*China, Glass and Lamps*, November 2, 1892).

Unfortunately for today's glass collectors, Northwood's Ellwood City operation did very little advertising. In her notes on Northwood glass, Minnie Watson Kamm remarked that the Northwood was "sparing" in this area (Kamm 5, p. 88). *Crockery and Glass Journal* mentioned the Northwood's "opal and fancy glass" in its November 24, 1892, issue, but the firm did not have an ad in the December 8, 1892, Holiday Number. There was no advertising until April 20, 1893, when a small strip ad appeared in *Crockery and Glass Journal* (see previous page). Perhaps there were some financial constraints at the firm's outset, and these had an impact on the advertising budget. In any event, the effect of reduced advertising can be seen in scant editorial coverage, as the Northwood firm received fewer mentions in the trade journal columns.

"Granite Ware"

Although their plant at Ellwood City was not yet in operation, The Northwood Glass Company had a display at the Monongahela House during July, 1892. The glassware shown there was made at Martins Ferry, of course, but a report in the July 27, 1892, issue of *China, Glass and Lamps* indicates how the firm was already adapting to its new home:

"The Northwood Glass Co., of Ellwood, Pa., have their samples in room 100 in charge of John G. Anderson. They have a big selection of fine crystal and rich colored ware, comprising some novelties not shown before. Among the latter is the Ellwood "Granite" ware, a new departure, entirely novel and very attractive. As its name implies it resembles granite in appearance, but is more varied in color and richer in effect. There is a large line of these goods in divers [sic] table articles. They have also a pretty assortment of lamps in fancy colors — another new departure for them. In these are the bell-shaped foot and one in imitation cut, both in a large variety of colors. There are also night lamps in ivory and blue, very pretty things, and stand lamps besides. Among specialties are new lines of baskets, two and four bottle casters, new condiment set in crystal and colors, a large line of etched crystal

goods, comprising jugs, decanters, whiskey bottles, champagnes, trays, &c., all of the most elegant finish. The assortment altogether is very extensive and we can only mention a few articles. Dealers will find it replete with attractions and cannot afford to miss examining them."

The "Granite ware" mentioned above was really an innovative color effect on a modified Northwood pattern. The basic shape of No. 245, Ribbed Pillar (Northwood Pleat), was followed in the new line, which is now known as Panelled Sprig. The granite-like color effect is made by a relatively dense covering of white "speckles" (as described in Northwood's patent a few years earlier) on blue glass. Some of these articles were further decorated with gold paint, and a few of these also have opalescent top rims. The report quoted above seems to be the only mention of "Granite ware," so this color effect may not have proven popular with the buyers.

The Panelled Sprig pattern itself, however can be found in other colors (see CG2, p. 69, for a salt shaker in light blue). A crystal and ruby line was introduced later at Ellwood City as pattern No. 183. A cruet in flint opalescent with a lattice motif

Panelled Sprig cruet in flint opalescent (note the lattice effect). **Courtesy of Larry Loxterman.**

is known. Panelled Sprig in opal with blue decorations is also known, and this dates from later production at Indiana, Pa. (see pp. 111-112), although there is one published reference to "delft" decorated ware at Ellwood City early in 1896 (see p. 102).

The lengthy quote from *China, Glass and Lamps* also mentions "large lines of etched crystal," but no specifics are provided beyond a recitation of the kinds of articles — jugs, champagnes, etc. The trade paper also mentions night lamps (small kerosene-fueled lamps referred to as "miniature" lamps today), and two colors are given, ivory and blue. The latter is probably a shade of transparent blue, but ivory likely means an opaque yellowish-white glass that collectors chose to call "custard" many years later. Ivory glass later became very important in Northwood's success at Indiana, Pa., and it is unfortunate that its role at Ellwood city is so difficult to discern.

Trade Reports, 1893-1894

For about the first two years of its life in Ellwood City, Pa., the Northwood Glass Company received relatively limited coverage in the editorial columns of the various glass trade publications. As noted earlier, this reduced volume of reporting was probably due to the relatively small amount of paid advertising done by the Northwood firm in these same journals. Nonetheless, the quotes from the glass trade periodicals provide some insights into the wares being made at Ellwood City.

The firm had its products on display at the Monongahela House in January, 1893, and the January 11, 1893, issue of *China, Glass and Lamps* carried this report:

"John G. Anderson has the very elegant exhibit ... in Room 54. All their samples have not arrived yet, but the display will be complete in a day or two. There are new tea sets in green and ruby and hyacinth [refers to shape] glasses in ruby 7, 8 and 9 inch. The line of novelties in diverse shapes, colors and combinations of colors is very large, comprising baskets, jugs, tankards, vases, oils, sugar sifters, syrups and a lot of other things, too numerous to describe in short space. The company are strong in lamps too and have a beautiful assortment. They have the finest blown footed line we have yet seen. There is a big line of crystal sets, tumblers, whiskeys, champagnes, ales and beers, etched and engraved, which compose no insignificant part of the display. To carefully inspect these samples and note their merits is a liberal education in fancy glassware."

Although much of the above report is quite general, some conclusions are possible. Etched and engraved glass, especially bar wares, apparently were an important part of production, and the line of lamps announced from Martins Ferry seem to have been continued at Ellwood City. As was the case at Martins Ferry, novelties were made in considerable variety and quantity, but no specifics are available.

The new green and ruby pattern line for 1893 remains unidentified. Incidentally, the phrase "tea set" simply refers to the four-piece table set — creamer, covered sugar bowl, spooner and covered butterdish. The ruby color is typically Northwood, of course, and the green-to-clear color effect may be comparable to the ruby-to-clear effect (now called rubina), which was pioneered by Northwood at Martins Ferry. A similar color effect was also made at the West Virginia Glass Company in Martins Ferry, which advertised "blue tint, emerald tint, violet tint and ruby tint" in 1894, sometime after the Northwood would have been making the new pattern. The glass chemist at the West Virginia firm was Percy J. Beaumont, Harry Northwood's brother-in-law (*China, Glass and Lamps*, December 13, 1893, contains a report on this firm, and Beaumont is mentioned).

This unidentified pattern line may have been designated by No. 403, for a subsequent note (*China, Glass and Lamps*, March 29, 1893) mentions "a pretty assortment of No. 403 in green and ruby sets" as well as an "etched caster frame with green and ruby salts and peppers."

The March 15, 1893, issue of *China, Glass and Lamps* said the Northwood concern was in "fine shape" and noted "an abundance of orders" before making this revelation: "The company have now a Venetian glassworker in their employ, who is fully versed in the crystal art as practiced in Venice, and he is turning out for them some beautiful fancy ware in original shapes and variegated colors." There was no follow up to this story, so whomever the workman was and whatever products resulted from his expertise must remain, at least for now, a mystery.

The Northwood factory representative in New York City was the firm of Usher and Osborne, whose showroom also held the goods of at least two competitors, the Crystal Glass Company of Bridgeport, Ohio, and the Model Flint Glass Company of Findlay, Ohio. In a brief note about salesman Aleck Menzies and the wares on display there, the March 29, 1893 issue of *China, Glass and Lamps* had this to say: "The Northwood show a pretty assortment of No. 403 in green and ruby sets, vases, flower bowls and casters. A neat novelty is etched caster frame with green and ruby salts and peppers. No. 404 is ruby, canary and blue lamps and a pretty variety of baskets and bowls in mixed and mottled colors is also included." The reference to "mixed and mottled" colors probably reflects the continued production of Granite ware and/or some of the spatter effects made earlier at Martins Ferry which were continued at Ellwood City.

In late June, 1893, a full-page advertisement appeared in *China, Glass and Lamps* (June 28, 1893). The ad, which ran only a few weeks, contained no illustrations of glassware, but the verbiage reveals something of the Northwood's then current lines. No colors or designs are mentioned for the decorated lemonade sets or lamps, but the intriguing reference to "neutral tints" may explain many of the colors in which Ellwood City-made salt shakers are found. As mentioned below when the Cactus pattern is discussed, some of the colors are subdued pinks, greens and blues. Some have a clear glass outer layer (similar to the Leaf Umbrella line, No. 263, produced in Martins Ferry). The overall effects are soft and "neutral," that of a pale pastel color, unlike the vividness and color differentiations of rubina or various opalescent shades.

The July, 1893, exhibit at the Monongahela House in Pittsburgh was much smaller than in previous years, and the Northwood concern did not have their wares on display. The July 6, 1893, issue of *Crockery and Glass Journal* reported that the Northwood "intend[s] to run their factory through the summer months and will have a full assortment of their new designs in colored and fancy glassware ready for the earliest buyers that come along. They have out many new things in lamps, berry and ice cream sets, lemonade sets, jugs and various odds and ends, and their stock is full of novelties."

The August 24, 1893, issue of *Crockery and Glass Journal*, in describing the Northwood's wares, made an interesting observation, which may bear on the "neutral tints" mentioned earlier: "they make a line which is particularly adaptable to times like the present, for the appearance and finish of their wares are such as to attract buyers when many other kinds will be passed by. 'Arry Northwood thinks they are unmistakably "in it" yet, and there is no panic around Ellwood City."

The Northwood Glass Company did not have an ad in the Holiday Number of *Crockery and Glass Journal*, and the firm received little cover-

Notice in China, Glass and Lamps *(June 28, 1893).*

age in the trade press during the January glass exhibition. *Crockery and Glass Journal* (January 18, 1894) noted only a "fine line of samples" and "colored and fancy tableware and novelties in a number of new designs...." A note on Usher and Osborne salesman Alex Menzies mentions "colored berry and lemonade sets." Incidentally, according to *Crockery and Glass Journal* (December 20, 1894), Menzies later came to work for Northwood as a salesman.

On February 6, 1894, Carl Northwood applied for American citizenship at the Prothonotary's office in the Lawrence County courthouse at New Castle, Pa. He had emigrated less than three years earlier, arriving in the United States on June 3, 1891, although he visited this country once or twice before coming over to join his brother Harry in the glass business. The Prothonotary gave him a certificate, and the five-year statutory waiting period began. In 1894, Carl Northwood, then just 22 years old, was a travelling salesman for the Northwood firm. Later, while Carl Northwood was at Indiana, he completed the citizenship process (see p. 135).

Sometime in May, 1894, the crown of the Northwood's 14-pot furnace fell in, and the factory's glassmaking operation had to be shut down, although the etching and decorating departments were able to continue until the stock on hand was exhausted. The company "contracted with M. L. Murphy for one of his new furnaces" (*Crockery and Glass Journal*, May 31, 1894). *China, Glass and Lamps* (June 20, 1894) revealed that "the Northwood Glass Co. have had a great deal of trouble with their furnace during the past twelve months and decided some time ago to change it and put in the Murphy producer...." The Murphy furnace did not use natural gas, and it was much preferred in areas where natural gas supplies were undependable. The patented Murphy process used coal to "produce" a gas which was then burned to provide heat. *China, Glass and Lamps* said the firm "would be making glass by July 10." The estimate was probably in error, for the July 12, 1894, issue of *Crockery and Glass Journal* said the new furnace "will start ... in a few days."

As noted earlier, Harry Northwood was an enthusiastic sportsman. He enjoyed outdoor activities in general and was particularly interested in cycling. There is a bicycle visible in an 1888 photo of the Northwoods' Wheeling Island home, and at least one ambitious bicycling trip was mentioned in the trade press (*Crockery and Glass Journal*, August 6, 1896). This report, from the July 11, 1894, issue of *China, Glass and Lamps*, associates Harry Northwood with cycling, albeit in a less active role:

"The Northwood Glass Co. manufactured a remarkable piece of cut glassware to be presented by them to the winner of a five-mile bicycle road race on Friday, July 6. It was a monster punch bowl, 22 inches in diameter, and weighing 50 pounds when finished, 10-1/2 pounds of metal having been cut away in working it. The decorations were in twist prism and diamond, and are both elaborate and beautiful. The article is in two pieces, the bowl being removable, and when the foot is inverted it forms a handsome orange bowl. The piece cost $200, but the company say they would not like to duplicate it for that money. It was on view in this city for several days, and attracted a great deal of attention and won much praise for its artistic tastefulness and beauty as well as for its gigantic size." Northwood's donation of this article would have given him some local publicity, of course, but the Northwood name was already well-known, for he was serving as Burgess [mayor] of Ellwood City. His election was reported to the glass trade in the February 15, 1894, issue of *Crockery and Glass Journal*.

Northwood's Lines for 1895

As 1894 drew to a close, the Northwood Glass Company, like others in the glass tableware business, was readying its lines for the January, 1895, Monongahela House exhibit and the subsequent spring trade. A full page advertisement depicting eight Northwood articles appeared in the Holiday Number of *Crockery and Glass Journal* (see next page). This ad offers proof of the items made by Northwood at Ellwood City. Several of the items are previously unknown to Northwood glass collectors, although Daisy and Fern has been linked to Northwood in previous Heacock works (H2, p. 43; H3, p. 22, H6, p. 25; H9, p. 47-48).

Daisy and Fern flint opalescent cruet (stopper probably not original). **Courtesy of Larry Loxterman.**

Daisy and Fern articles can be found in flint (crystal) opalescent, blue opalescent and cranberry (originally called ruby or pink) opalescent. Many of the Daisy and Fern pieces were made with Northwood's Parian Swirl moulds used to provide basic shapes (see H3, p. 22). Heacock sometimes designated Parian Swirl with the term "Northwood Swirl" (see H9, p. 47), but the phrase

Are We In It?—
Well, I Guess Yes!!

AND WE WILL CONVINCE YOU OF IT.   HOW?

1st.—Because we kicked over the traces, and will do business with legitimate trade only.

2d.--We have the largest and newest lines of colored and crystal novelties in plain, etched and decorated wares ever offered by one house.

Don't buy until you see our line. Write for prices or ask for agents to call.

THE NORTHWOOD GLASS Co

General Offices, ELLWOOD CITY, PA.

NEW YORK OFFICE:	GENERAL SALESMAN:	ST AND SOUTH:
ALEX. G. MENZIES, 96 Church St.	JOHN G. ANDERSON.	CARL NORTHWOOD.

From Crockery and Glass Journal *(December 6, 1894).*

Parian Swirl is retained in this book since the design is exclusively Northwood-made.

The opalescent effect is obtained by reheating (warming in) after the article has been blown to shape and any necessary finishing completed. Cranberry articles have two layers of glass — a ruby inner layer and a crystal outer layer. The crystal layer contains bone ash, and the raised portions of a design will turn white upon warming in. Cranberry items must be blown, as the ruby glass mixture is very sensitive to changes in temperature and does not work well in pressing.

The Daisy and Fern line was also made later in Indiana, Pa. Shape molds range from the Ball Shape, a Martins Ferry motif, to Apple Blossom, an early Indiana pattern made primarily in opal glass. The Daisy and Fern pitcher is illustrated in Pitkin and Brooks catalogs from 1897-1900, in a Falker and Stern catalog (spring, 1898), and in Butler Brothers catalogs from 1903, so collectors must realize that this popular design was used by Northwood and his successors at Indiana, Pa. Photos taken in Northwood's Indiana plant ca. 1897-98 clearly show tumblers in Daisy and Fern (see p. 121). Collectors should also differentiate Northwood's Daisy and Fern pieces from some what similar patterns, such as the opalescent fern motifs made at the West Virginia Glass Company and the Beaumont Glass Company (see H9 for illustrations and discussion).

The basket has a distinctly English look. The feet resemble applied "rigaree," and the fine crimped edge and handle are reminiscent of English wares. Likewise, the "pump" is a most interesting piece. It is not like some of the later pressed Northwood pumps (see H2, p. 38) which have feet and come with an accompanying trough. If the ad is an accurate depiction, this Ellwood City creation of Northwood's was mould-blown, as one can see from the bulbous base. The pump's handle, which resembles the handle on the basket discussed above, was applied in a separate operation, as was the small spout. The bucket hanging from the spout is, of course, another piece with an applied handle (it looks smooth in the ad). The top rim of the pump is irregular, unlike the later, unfooted specimens which are so well known in carnival glass (Edwards' *Standard Encyclopedia of Carnival Glass*, pp. 206-207). Northwood's Ellwood City pump may have been inspired by a similar English creation linked to the area of Northwood's home in England, Stourbridge (Manley, *Decorative Victorian Glass*, fig. 228).

The small vase is strikingly similar to "art glass" products of this era (Revi, *American Art Nouveau Glass*, p 124). It is unfortunate that no size or colors are mentioned in this ad, for the vase is so similar to many American-made and imported wares of the 1890s that little hope exists of isolating distinctive Northwood characteristics.

The Flat Flower syrup jug (previously attributed to Dithridge in H3, p. 24) has been seen in opal, opaque blue, opaque green, and transparent emerald green. The pattern's name comes from Peterson (*Glass Salt Shakers*, p. 29a). The salt shaker and sugar shaker are also known. The opaque blue articles are usually a bright, vivid hue, and this color was probably called turquoise in its own time.

Two interesting salt shakers are shown — Bow and Tassel and Cactus. In his *Glass Salt Shakers* (p. 122), Peterson says Bow and Tassel is "common in white [but] very rare in pink," and his photo (p. 155o) shows the shaker in an opaque color, presumably pink! The shaker is known in opaque blue, too, and Cactus ones have been seen in the identical shade. A similar Bow and Tassel shaker (Heacock, *Old Pattern Glass*, p. 185), which is a bit taller and has a bulging ring just below the lid, was made by the Eagle Glass and Mfg. Co. several years later.

Peterson also pictures the Cactus shaker (p. 24e), which is known in a surprisingly large number of hues, including six opaques (opal; two different shades of green as well as green cased with opal; blue, usually called turquoise; light pink, cased inside with opal), three opalescent stripe (ruby, canary and blue) and two transparent (amethyst and blue). The opal shakers may be decorated with pink and blue paint.

Neither Cactus nor Bow and Tassel is part of any pattern line, insofar as present research indicates, but the distinctive colors invite comparison with other pattern salt shakers which could also be Northwood products. In an article in the June, 1988, issue of *The Pioneer*, researchers Carole and Bob Bruce have noted the similarities in design between Northwood's Cactus and two other patterns: Jewel and Flower (see H2) and Crocodile Tears (see H1 and H4); the latter pattern was definitely made at Indiana (see p. 126), but production could have begun at Ellwood City. Several other Northwood patterns known to have been made later at Indiana (Quilted Phlox, Swirl and Leaf, and Grape and Leaf) also occur in colors similar to Northwood's Cactus. Fragments of Grape and Leaf (called Vineyard in carnival glass) have been found at Indiana.

Yet another possible Northwood pattern at Ellwood City is Swirl and Leaf (H3, p. 43), which has been confirmed in Indiana (see p. 127). The Swirl and Leaf salt shaker and toothpick holder are known in several shades of opaque green and in opaque pink and opaque blue. The syrup jug is pictured in opal (H3, p. 43), and Heacock reported items in "yellow" (probably custard) and opaque gray. Swirl and Leaf fragments have been found at Indiana, where it was made as pattern No. 101, but production could have begun at Ellwood City.

Swirl and Leaf toothpick holder. **Courtesy of Larry Loxterman.**

The Monongahela House displays opened early in January, 1895, and a reporter for *Crockery and Glass Journal* (January 17, 1895) visited the Northwood exhibit:

"The Northwood Glass Co., of Ellwood City, Pa., have a big display in Room 79, and John Anderson does what talking seems necessary, which is not much, as the goods are shouters. No. 183 is a new line in crystal and ruby, enameled and gilt — four effects. This line comprises tea-set, bowls, nappies, jugs, oils, peppers, sugar dusters, and some other articles. No. 191 is in three effects — flint opalescent, [blue] opalescent and ruby opalescent. No. 178 ruby edge bowls and the new berry sets are very striking. Nos. 149 and 165 are more particularly for the jewelers' and silver platers' trade, and they have them in several different effects. Other things shown are five new lines of opalescent lemonade sets, bud vases and vases of larger size, night lamps, cast-

ers, and a great many fresh novelties. A new article is the Anarchist beer mug, specially designed for the Chicago trade. It holds as much as the average nickel growler, and the man who uses it gets the worth of his money. The company have cuts of their ware ready, representing all the colors with exactness."

China, Glass and Lamps also visited the Northwood exhibit, but their reporter's account differed considerably with respect to pattern numbers:

"The Northwood Glass Co., of Ellwood City, Pa., represented by John G. Anderson, have their exhibit in room 73. No. 91 is a full line in opalescent in three colors flint, blue and pink, very showy as well as neat in shapes. No. 182 comes in two colors, crystal and ruby flash, also in gilt and gilt with enamel decorations, being entirely new and the largest line the company ever made. The gilt ornamentation harmonizes well with the flowers in enamel. This line is made in two patterns, flint and ruby. There are half a dozen new lemonade sets, the decorations on which, it is worth remarking, are a great improvement on all that have preceded them in this line. There is a new molasses can, of unique shape, and half a dozen new salts and peppers. These with new crimped bowls, a large assortment of night lamps, both new and old, fancy baskets, sugar sifters and the usual line of novelties complete a very attractive display" (January 9, 1895).

The No. 191 (not 91) line was Daisy and Fern, for there is a cruet so numbered in a Pitkin and Brooks catalog issued in 1899, when the pattern was being made at Indiana (see H9, p. 23). The No. 182 or 183 pattern, as the case may be, probably designated the line now known as Panelled Sprig, for the crystal/ruby and the mention of gilt and enamel decorations is in accord with articles known today.

The mention of decorated lemonade sets reveals another important aspect of Northwood production. Pitchers were made in several basic shapes and/or colors, and these, along with corresponding tumblers, could be decorated with a wide variety of handpainted floral motifs. The full-page ad from mid-1893 (see p. 92) mentioned "decorated lemonade sets," but without any elaboration as to design or color.

From time to time, the glass trade periodicals carried personal notes regarding Harry Northwood. The February 28, 1895, issue of *Crockery and Glass Journal*, noting that Northwood had been visiting friends in Pittsburgh, said this: "Mr. 'Arry Northwood, the

Ad from China, Glass and Lamps, *April 17, 1895; this ad ran through January, 1896.*

versatile glassman whose company bears his name, was mingling with old friends hereabouts last week. He is the same wide-awake energetic hustler as when he was located in the Valley."

In March, 1894, the Northwood Glass Company sought membership in the National Association of Manufacturers of Pressed and Blown Glassware. This organization's chief purpose was the representation of the manufacturers' interests in yearly negotiations with the unionized skilled workmen. These annual conferences, as they were called, determined wages and moves (the number of pieces to be made per turn). At this time, the Northwood's workers were not union members, but it was common practice for the non-union plants to follow the lead of the National Association in dealing with their workforces.

The American Flint Glass Workers Union had tried to organize the plant in the summer of 1893. At the AFGWU annual convention in July, 1893, the union noted a protest filed by the management of the West Virginia Glass Company of Martins Ferry. This firm complained that the Northwood company had recently cut prices about 15%, in addition "to a previous difference of $2.00 per dozen in some goods" (*Convention Proceedings*, July, 1893, p. 57). Price-cutting by non-union firms was common in the competitive tableware market, but the unionized firms tended to hold to price agreements made necessary by the higher wages paid to union workers and the agreements regarding the number of pieces to be made during a turn.

A four-man AFGWU organizing committee — William J. Clarke, William McLaughlin, A. Aulbaugh, and George E. Poth — held a gathering of the Northwood's workers, at which several of the employees spoke out against AFGWU president William Smith. An AFGWU *Circular Letter*, issued August 8, 1893, listed the Northwood employees who attended the meeting: [blowers] Joseph Burt, Joseph Moore, John Elwell, John Lawley, Sam Dugan, Fred Cartwright, James Baker, Eugene Camp, William McKinney and John Sudgrue; [handlers] Sam Dugan and A. Eislen, Jr.; [presser] Ralston; [gatherers] William Jones, William White, Augustus Ruckert, E. Johnson, Howard Hoskins, Thomas Mercer, William Bitter, Charles Fransizen, Sam Melvay, and Charles McCloirs. The organizing effort was not successful.

By August, 1895, however, the Northwood's stockholders decided to run the plant with union labor when the fires were lit after the summer stop. A new plant manager, Henry Findt, was hired. He had been employed at the Martins Ferry plant, and his association with Harry Northwood goes back to their days at the La Belle (*China, Glass and Lamps*, August 28, 1895). The decision to run with union labor may reflect a need to obtain workers whose skills were superior to the nonunion force. The September 25, 1895, issue of *China, Glass and Lamps* reported that "several Martin's Ferry glassworkers went to Ellwood City, Pa. last week to work for the Northwood Glass Co.," but their names were not revealed. The Ellwood City Borough section of the *New Castle Official City Directory* for 1895-96 lists the following glassworkers: Charles Allquire, Charles Andy, E. G. Beaumont, Felix Bullock, Andy Carbon, Harry Craig, Randolph Craig, William Craig, Andy Cubin, Harry Debois, Alfred Dugan, Samuel Dugan, Sam Dugan, Jr., Thomas E. Dugan, Oscar Ednesgad, Joseph Everick, John Fay, Victor Force, Charles Frangins, Charles Gladder, James Haden, Evan Halley, Charles Handle, John Hoffman,

Ad from **Crockery and Glass Journal,** *April 25, 1895.*

Samuel Kinney, Andy Krizen, Charles McClain, James Moore, George Powell [should be Pownall], and Michael Reilley. Some may have been employees of the Peerless firm, which made lamp chimneys, but many of these men were likely at the Northwood concern.

A brief note in the April 17, 1895, issue of *China, Glass and Lamps* comments on general trade conditions and mentions a few specific Northwood products: "Trade has improved in a very satisfactory manner with the Northwood Glass Co., and they are running all the shops they can make room for in the factory. They are adding many new and attractive things to their offerings, among the latest devised being two lines of stand lamps in crystal and colors; a line of fancy crystal vases ranging from 6 to 30 inches in height, and combining great beauty with utility. All these new goods are sure to prove prime sellers."

In this same issue of *China, Glass and Lamps*, a small ad appeared for the Northwood firm; this ad continued unchanged through January, 1896. Also in April, 1895, an ad appeared in *Crockery and Glass Journal* (April 25, 1895); shortly thereafter, the ad was modified slightly to include an illustration of a basket.

The April 25, 1895, issue of *Crockery and Glass Journal* carried a short report on the Northwood concern, bidding their readers to see the new advertising: "The Northwood Glass Co., of Ellwood City, have something to say for themselves in another place in this issue of the JOURNAL, and the trade might well read their statements with advantage to themselves, as their representations as well as the goods they make are always to be depended upon. They produce wares unique and original in design, and hard to match elsewhere, and those who handle them never have any trouble with their customers. John G. Anderson was here part of the week, and will start on another trip in a few days."

A similar note appeared in the May 30, 1895, issue of *Crockery and Glass Journal*: "This is the time of year when the Northwood Glass Co., of Ellwood City, shine pre-eminent in seasonable specialties. Their goods are well in evidence at all times, but they come out strong in summer and give dealers a chance to make things lively during the usually dull period of the year. Ice cream sets, berry sets, lemonade sets, fruit and cake baskets and lots of other needful things in a variety of neat shapes and fancy colors are now out. They

Ad from **Crockery and Glass Journal** *which ran from May 2, 1895 through January 16, 1896.*

Ad from China, Glass and Lamps *(June 12, 1895). Note the salesmen's names.*

are of good glass, and the prices cannot fail to interest buyers. The company have illustrations ready, and will send them to those who write. John Anderson, Bert Graeser and Carl Northwood are on the road and doing themselves proud."

The August 14, 1895, issue of *China, Glass and Lamps* had an account of the Northwood's products, although the firm was mistakenly located in its old Martins Ferry location:

"MARTIN'S FERRY, O.—The Northwood Glass Co. have ready for the trade many new and strikingly handsome goods which must prove great trade promoters. Among these are two new lines: No. 183, decorated, in ruby or crystal, and No. 204 in crystal. No. 271 is a very pretty decorated wine set in crystal. No. 197 is a set done up in the new process etching. There are three new lines of flower vases in crystal, from 6 to 30 inches high. No. 197 is a tankard in crystal, decorated or etched. No. 211 is a paste mold jug with crimped top, decorated or etched. No. 500 is a new flower

vase. Nos. 502, 503 and 504 are jellies, pressed and finished in fancy shapes. No. 205 is a pint and quart jug, made in all opalescent colors. Then there are the endless variety of etchings and dec-

Mold drawing, dated "May 3rd/95" in Harry Northwood's handwriting and stamped with the firm's name and address. **Courtesy of the Fenton Museum, Williamstown, WV.**

HIPKINS' IMPROVED REAMING TOOL.

PATENTED.

NOVELTY ⋈ MOULD ⋈ WORKS,
MANUFACTURER OF
❋ All Kinds of Glass Moulds. ❋
S. HIPKINS, JR., PROP'R.
MARTIN'S FERRY, OHIO.

All Orders Strictly Private

Hipkins' business card, ca. 1895. **Courtesy of the Martins Ferry Historical Society.**

No. 205

Crystal Opal, 70c per doz.
Blue   "   70c   "
Ruby   " $1.00   "
18 doz. in a barrel
Very staple.

No. 205. HALF-GALLON PITCHER

Flint Opal, per dozen............$5.00
Blue   "   " 5.00
Ruby   "   " 6.50
1½ dozen in a barrel.
The ever popular Polka Dot Pattern

Courtesy of Nancy and Bill Sheriff.

orations on lemonade sets to suit cottage or palace. In the way of lamps No. 600 is a new one made in five sizes and hand lamp, either in plain or crystal or with decorations, all very handsome."

The "paste mold" jug noted above was produced by an interesting glassblowing procedure. The iron mould, which is very smooth inside and contains no pattern, is coated with a substance which allows the bubble of glass to take the shape of the mould without tending to adhere to it. As the glassblower expands the bubble within the mould, he simultaneously rotates it. The result is a smooth-sided article which has no mold marks. After the item is removed from the mold, the top rim can be finished in many different ways, ranging from a simple pouring lip to elaborate crimping. After a handle is applied, the pitcher would be cooled in the lehrs. Then, it could be decorated by engraving, etching or painting, as desired. At least one paste mould was made for Northwood's Ellwood City plant by the Hipkins Novelty Mould Works of Martins Ferry. This well known firm (see Kamm 7, pp. 96-99)

probably made molds for many Northwood articles produced at both Martins Ferry and Ellwood City, although only this paste mold jug can be substantiated.

The No. 205 jug mentioned above was the ubiquitous Coinspot motif, which is listed with this identical number in three Pitkin and Brooks catalogs between 1897 and 1900 (microfiche is available at the Rakow Library in the Corning Museum of Glass; see H9, p. 23). The 1897 catalog describes a "6 Pretty" assortment in which the No. 205 water set is packaged with a No. 319 water set, the latter being Swirl pattern made in a ball-shape mould. Both 205 and 319 were available in crystal opalescent, blue opalescent and ruby opalescent.

Furthermore, Northwood's No. 205 was also part of a "12 Elite" package offered by Pitkin and Brooks which included No. 319 as well as two other patterns, No. 187 and No. 447 (see H9, p. 23). No. 187, a ball-shaped pitcher which may simply be a Daisy and Fern variant (see H9, p. 83, fig. 17), was listed in crystal opalescent, blue opalescent and ruby opalescent. No. 447, which is simi-

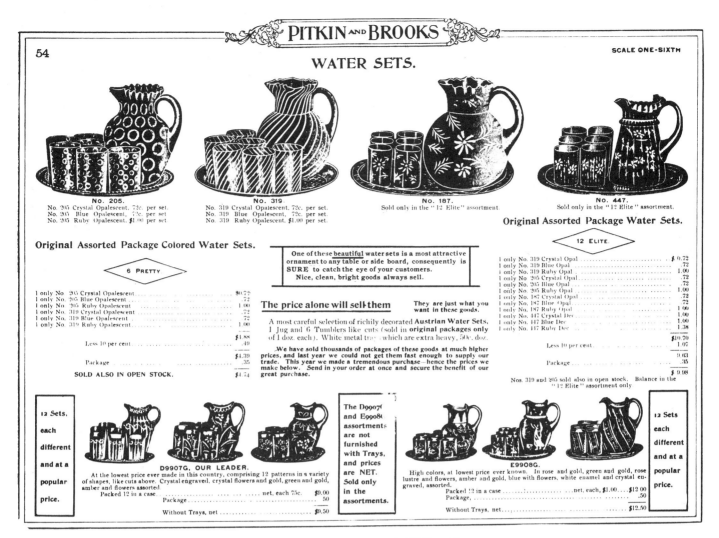

PITKIN AND BROOKS

WATER SETS.

SCALE ONE-SIXTH

NO. 205.
No. 205 Crystal Opalescent, 72c. per set.
No. 205 Blue Opalescent, 72c. per set
No. 205 Ruby Opalescent, $1.00 per set

NO. 319.
No. 319 Crystal Opalescent, 72c. per set.
No. 319 Blue Opalescent, 72c. per set.
No. 319 Ruby Opalescent, $1.00 per set.

NO. 187.
Sold only in the "12 Elite" assortment.

NO. 447.
Sold only in the "12 Elite" assortment.

Original Assorted Package Water Sets.

Original Assorted Package Colored Water Sets.

One of these **beautiful** water sets is a most attractive ornament to any table or side board, consequently is **SURE** to catch the eye of your customers.
Nice, clean, bright goods always sell.

◆ 6 PRETTY ◆

1 only No. 205 Crystal Opalescent		$0.72
1 only No. 205 Blue Opalescent		.72
1 only No. 205 Ruby Opalescent		1.00
1 only No. 319 Crystal Opalescent		.72
1 only No. 319 Blue Opalescent		.72
1 only No. 319 Ruby Opalescent		1.00
		$4.88
Less 10 per cent		.49
		$4.39
Package		.35
SOLD ALSO IN OPEN STOCK.		$4.74

The price alone will sell them

They are just what you want in these goods.

A most careful selection of richly decorated **Austrian Water Sets**, 1 Jug and 6 Tumblers like cuts (sold in **original packages only** of 1 doz. each). White metal trays which are extra heavy, 50c. doz.

We have sold thousands of packages of these goods at much higher prices, and last year we could not get them fast enough to supply our trade. This year we made a tremendous purchase—hence the prices we make below. Send in your order at once and secure the benefit of our great purchase.

◆ 12 ELITE ◆

1 only No. 319 Crystal Opal		$ 0.72
1 only No. 319 Blue Opal		.72
1 only No. 319 Ruby Opal		1.00
1 only No. 205 Crystal Opal		.72
1 only No. 205 Blue Opal		.72
1 only No. 205 Ruby Opal		1.00
1 only No. 187 Crystal Opal		.72
1 only No. 187 Blue Opal		.72
1 only No. 187 Ruby Opal		1.00
1 only No. 447 Crystal Dec		1.00
1 only No. 447 Blue Dec		1.00
1 only No. 447 Ruby Dec		1.38
		$10.70
Less 10 per cent		1.07
		9.63
Package		.35
		$ 9.98

Nos. 319 and 205 sold also in open stock. Balance in the "12 Elite" assortment only.

12 Sets, each different and at a popular price.

D9907G, OUR LEADER.
At the lowest price ever made in this country, comprising 12 patterns in a variety of shapes, like cuts above. Crystal engraved, crystal flowers and gold, green and gold, amber and flowers assorted.

Packed 12 in a case	net, each 75c.	$9.00
Package		.50
Without Trays, net		$9.50

The D9907 and E9908 assortments are not furnished with Trays, and prices are NET. Sold only in the assortments.

E9908G.
High colors, at lowest price ever known. In rose and gold, green and gold, rose lustre and flowers, amber and gold, blue with flowers, white enamel and crystal engraved, assorted.

Packed 12 in a case	net, each, $1.00	$12 00
Package		.50
Without Trays, net		$12.50

12 Sets each different and at a popular price.

lar to pitchers made in the Ring Neck mold, was a floral decorated line available in crystal, blue and ruby. Firms such as Pitkin and Brooks did not, as a rule, re-pack glassware, so these four numbered patterns are surely all Northwood products, packed into assortments at the plant. The range of catalog dates (1897 to 1900) suggests that these pitchers could have been produced at Ellwood City and, later, Indiana.

During the late summer of 1895, the Northwood Glass Co. was mentioned in just a few general notes in the trade periodicals. In various issues, *Crockery and Glass Journal* reported "thriving trade" (August 29, 1895) and a "host of new things in fancy designs and colors" (September 5 and September 12, 1895). The September 26, 1895, issue of *Crockery and Glass Journal* said the factory was "very busy" and reported that "salesman Anderson has been on the road nearly 10 months."

Trouble in Ellwood City

Despite the generally positive reports in the trade press, there are some indications that all was not well at the Northwood Glass Co. in Ellwood City. The October 3, 1895, issue of *Crockery and Glass Journal* had this to say: "A report reached Martins Ferry last week, and seemed to be confirmed by persons largely interested in the Northwood Glass Co., that that company was considering the matter of returning to the factory they left to go to Elwood [sic] Pa. There are disadvantages, it is said, that will be overcome by a return to the plant in Martins Ferry." Just a week later, however, this same publication carried a note almost contradictory to its previous remarks: "The Northwood Glass Co. of Ellwood City are gleaning good business, which they are in shape to take prompt care of, everything being in the best of working order. This town is enjoying a term of unwonted prosperity in its other industries, and there is not an idle wheel within its limits" (*Crockery and Glass Journal*, October 10, 1895).

There were other signs of problems. Two of the Northwood's salesmen, John Anderson and A. A.

"Bert" Graeser, left for jobs with the Tarentum Glass Company and A. H. Heisey and Company, respectively (*Crockery and Glass Journal*, December 5, 1895). Harry Northwood may have been having his own difficulties, too. On October 9, 1895, Harry and Clara Northwood sold their house in Martins Ferry to Thomas Mears (Belmont County Deed Records, vol. 112, p. 140). The consideration was $5200, a low figure given the reports that the home had cost $10,000 a few years earlier (*Crockery and Glass Journal*, December 4, 1890).

Furthermore, Harry Northwood's cousin, Charles O. Northwood, a designer at the plant, was sued for non-payment of rent by his landlady, Florence K. Tildesley, and Harry Northwood became a party in the lawsuit. Northwood had written to Tildesley's attorney, C. W. Wallace, in March, 1895, saying "I am guaranteeing C. O. Northwood's rent and in fact it is quite safe as the factory owes him more than will cover it. We are as you probably know back a few weeks in our pay, owing to collections being so very slow. I hardly know how to fix this up for you tomorrow, but I will try my best & yet I cannot at this writing see how to do it." Just before the lawsuit was filed, Harry Northwood contacted the attorney again, this time attempting to limit his liability: "I hereby notify you that I will not be responsible for the payment of rent for building occupied by Mr. C. O. Northwood after Dec. 31st, 1895. I trust you will use all means possible to collect back rent from him before holding me, as I have all I can do to keep my own matters straight. Respectfully yours, Harry Northwood." A Justice of the Peace, J. J. Kelley, found in favor of the landlady, holding both Charles and Harry responsible for payment. The Northwoods appealed the verdict on May 29, 1896, and a bond was posted for Harry Northwood by his cousin, Thomas E. A. Dugan, who was then in Indiana, Pa. When the case was finally tried, April 14-15, 1897, Harry Northwood was acquitted, but a judgement for $134.68 and "costs of suit" was entered against Charles O. Northwood. His motion for a new trial was refused.

Final Months in Ellwood City

If there were financial troubles beneath the surface at the Northwood Glass Co., the trade periodicals painted a generally rosy picture during the fall of 1895. The October 24, 1895, issue of *Crockery and Glass Journal* called the Northwood's new holiday lines "a revelation," and a report a month later continued the Biblical imagery: "The Northwood Glass Co., of Ellwood City, a little way out from here on the Pittsburgh & Western, are brimful of attractions that no holiday stock is perfect without. They take all kinds of shapes, have more varieties of color than Joseph's coat, and many which that garment did not possess, and are put up for use, ornament and durability. If anybody wants more than this, there is no use wasting talk on them" (*Crockery and Glass Journal*, November 28, 1895).

When the Monongahela House exhibit opened in January, 1896, both Harry and Carl Northwood were on hand to show the buyers the new lines. *China, Glass and Lamps* (January 15, 1896) carried this report:

"The most individual and artistic colored glassware on exhibit this season will be found in room 156, and consists of two new sets of tableware varied in color and artistic decoration with a breadth and finish certain to suit the widest diversity of taste. The No. 215 is a graceful set of opal tableware, decorated in blue, after the famous delft porcelain, which has enjoyed such a large run during the past year, and been favored with the patronage of the most cultured and fashionable metropolitan buyers. The characteristic feature about the set is that the hand-painted decors are originals, not mass reproductions or imitations laid on with a stencil, and which the country is to be flooded and overgorged, but no two pieces are decorated alike, and there is an individuality, distinctness, and separate artistic effort and effect in each piece of the same set, which stales not upon the eye, because of infinite variety and distinctiveness of design. The No. 217 is also a full line, very handsome in form, the pattern being a reversed central colored spot, shown throughout the casing, and comes flint, ruby and blue opalescent, making one of the finest color combinations ever turned out by the Northwood firm. The decorated, needle etched flint lemonade sets, vases and colored novelties, lamps, rose bowls, etc. make an exhibit of artistic colored glassware which delights the eye, and increases one's respect for the craft, art touch and inventive mind which fashioned and evolved these gems of the glassmakers' art."

The journal's claim of uniqueness was probably an exaggerated one, for the delft-like ware mentioned above is likely an assortment of Panelled Sprig items decorated with blue. The Venetian line made in 1899 at Indiana, however, was produced in decorated opal, and No. 215 at Ellwood City could be its predecessor.

Heacock identified No. 217 as ruby opalescent

Ruby Polka Dot covered sugar bowl made in Fancy Fans mould.

Polka Dot, and he speculated that this could be Polka Dot produced in a Fancy Fans shape mould (H9, pp. 22, 94). A decorated opal Fancy Fans sugar shaker was shown in one of his early publications (H3, p. 49). Both the colors (opal and ruby opalescent) and the shapes of these articles are consistent with other Northwood wares, although further research is needed on the Fancy Fans pattern. The 1897 Pitkin and Brooks catalog shows the Fancy Fans salt shaker, and one also appears in a November, 1896, Butler Brothers catalog.

Northwood's Sudden Departure

The January 30, 1896, issue of *Crockery and Glass Journal* carried this seemingly innocuous note: "The glass plant at Indiana, Pa., has been purchased by a Martins Ferry manufacturing company, and it expects to have the works in operation soon." A week later, the long-running Northwood ads in *Crockery and Glass Journal* and *China, Glass and Lamps* were halted in the midst of the Monongahela House exhibit, and, just a few days after the show closed, a surprising bit of news appeared in *China, Glass and Lamps* (February 19, 1896): Harry Northwood had left his position at Ellwood City and was affiliated with a new glassmaking venture at Indiana, Pa., some 60 miles to the east. This organization was destined to become the most successful enterprise of Northwood's early years.

As soon as Harry Northwood left Ellwood City, the glass plant there was shut down. One report held out "no prospects of an early resumption," but *China, Glass and Lamps* (March 11, 1896) was optimistic: "It is understood that Charles Helling and other gentlemen of Ellwood City, Pa., will organize a company and operate the Northwood Glass Works at that city. The fires were recently let out, but it is thought that the works will be put into operation 'ere long. Mr. Helling has been a member of the company for years."

The financial troubles of the Ellwood City operation were soon laid bare in a *National Glass Budget* article headlined "GONE UP THE FLUKE:"

"The Northwood Glass Company, of Ellwood City, Pa., formerly of Martin's Ferry, O., has assigned to W. F. French, of Beaver, Pa., followed shortly after by the personal assignment of William Mann, a wealthy iron founder of Martin's Ferry; Thomas Mears, proprietor of the Martin's Ferry Keg and Barrel Company, and Henry Floto, a Martin's Ferry capitalist, all stockholders of the Northwood Company, owning 75 per cent of the stock. A statement has been made by one of the interested persons that the assignments were made to wind up the affairs of the company, and to determine by judicial decision the liability of the stockholders for certain indebtedness of the company. The company's assets are placed at $150,000, and the liabilities at $75,000. Of the liabilities, $60,000 are notes endorsed by Messrs. Mann, Floto and [the] Henry Helling estate of Martin's Ferry. The Helling heirs disclaim liability for any of these notes except $10,000, or a total liability of $2,500, holding that the endorsements were irregularly made. The three gentlemen who assigned are probably good for $300,000, and their action was taken to save themselves in the windup of the company. Judgments for about $40,000 have been entered against the company, over $10,000 being taken by Martin's Ferry banks. The Northwood Company has been running till a few weeks ago, and has not been profitable for a year" (March 28, 1896).

There is evidence to support many of the particulars contained in the story from the *National Glass Budget*. The Housatonic Manufacturing company, a firm which made metal tops for salt/pepper shakers and molasses cans, successfully sued the Northwood Glass Company in March, 1896. About the same time, the stockholders from the Martins Ferry and Ellwood City enterprises were suing each other as well as the Northwood Glass Company. On February 24, 1896, two suits were brought against the Northwood Glass Company in

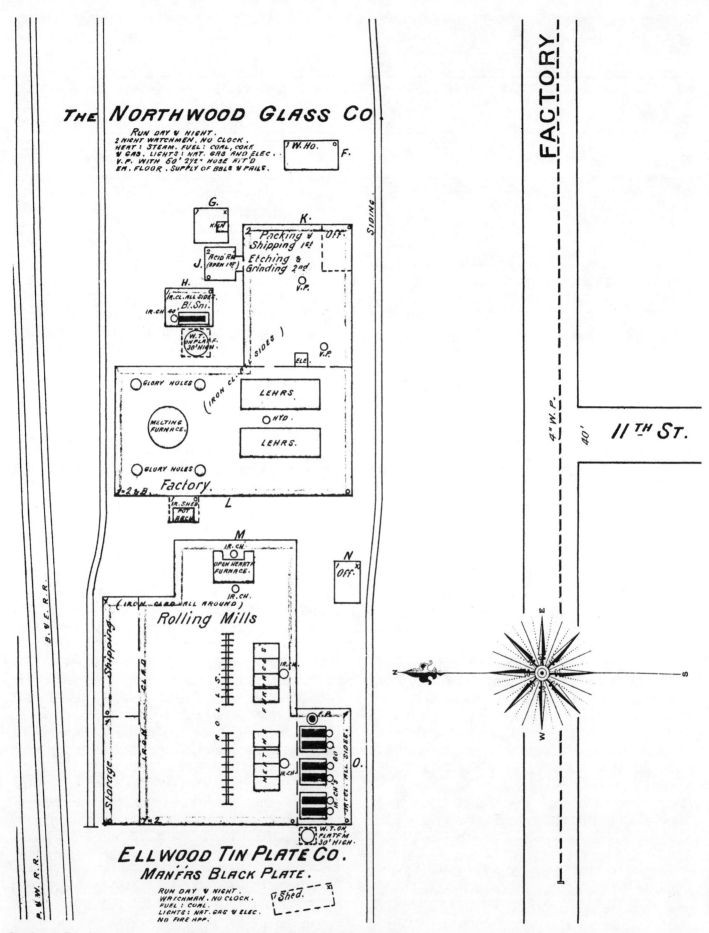

Sanborn fire insurance map of the Northwood firm and the neighboring Ellwood Tin Plate Co. (May, 1894, sheet 2).
A similar map from March, 1897, says "closed" over the Northwood plant.

Belmont County Common Pleas Court. In the first (case #8623), four plaintiffs (Charles Helling, Henry Helling, William Helling and Louis Helling) asked for $2500 plus interest from July 2, 1894. In the second (case #8624), Charles Helling sought $1500 plus interest from October 10, 1895. Case #8623 was settled on March 17, 1897, when trustee E. G. Kranter was ordered "to carry out an agreement between plaintiffs and William Mears." Case #8624 ended with a judgment against the Northwood Glass Company on May 11, 1896.

A third lawsuit in Belmont County (case #8796) was filed August 11, 1896, on behalf of the creditors of Thomas Mears, Henry Floto and William Mann, original investors in the Martins Ferry enterprise. This action was brought against Harry Northwood, Sophia Helling (executrix of Henry Helling's estate), the Northwood Glass Company and the First National Bank of Bridgeport. A series of legal maneuvers followed (including a deposition from Thomas Dugan on April 27, 1897), all of which resulted in this entry in the Appearance Docket for the Summer Term, 1899: "settled and dismissed." The Martins Ferry and the Ellwood City affairs of Harry Northwood were finally closed.

The April 8, 1897, issue of *Crockery and Glass Journal* noted that "efforts are being made to settle the affairs of the old Northwood Glass Works at Ellwood, Pa., which concern failed some time ago." These seem not to have been successful, and, after the creditors apparently became restive with trustee William C. French, a new trade publication, *Glass* (November 10, 1897), carried this story:

"About a year ago the Northwood Glass Company made an assignment for the benefit of the creditors, and William C. French was named as assignee. The creditors have entered a case in equity in the courts, asking for a citation on the assignee to appear in court at New Castle, Pa. The creditors allege that the assignee, who gave bond in the sum of $108,000 for a faithful performance, has really done nothing to promote the welfare of the plant, which is located in Ellwood, but on the other hand, has permitted it to decrease in value. The case will be heard at the December term of court. The assets of the company were quoted at something like $40,000."

French decided to sell the plant at auction, but, when only two bidders were interested, the sale was postponed (*Crockery and Glass Journal*, December 30, 1897). Shortly thereafter, a lengthy article in *Glass* (January 10, 1898) described the plant in detail:

"W. C. French, assignee of the Northwood Glass Company, offers the property of the company for sale, describing it as follows: All that certain piece of land situated in the borough of Ellwood City, county of Lawrence, the State of Pennsylvania; containing 3 69/100 acres, more or less; subject to a right of way extending across the premises for a railroad switch or siding fifteen feet in width, on which is erected a glass plant, consisting of a building 90 x 180 feet, one story, and 80 x 100 feet two story, entirely covered with corrugated iron, the two story part being first covered with boards and paper; the one story part having a fourteen-pot furnace, heated with two Murphy patent gas producers in good condition, four glory holes, one tank furnace, six lears fifty-five feet long; also mixing, selecting and sand rooms; the two-story part has on the first floor the office, sample, papering, shipping and packing rooms, with bin room for open stock; also mould shop, decorating room and elevator; the second floor contains the cutting, grinding, etching and printing rooms. The basement contains the engine room and large stock room. The building is well fitted for water and gas, and for heating with steam. There are a boiler house, smith shop, cooper shop and two kilns for decorating purposes separate from the main building; a railroad siding on the north side for fuel, and one on the south side for shipping stock; also a good water well and a 100-barrel tank for storing water. Terms of sale: One-half the purchase money to be paid on the delivery of the deed, and the balance in one year, with interest from the date of sale, the same to be secured by bond and mortgage on the premises, with scire facias and insurance clause" (*China, Glass and Lamps* for November 24, 1897, had a short notice of this sale, too).

According to *A History of Ellwood City, Pennsylvania*, the Northwood plant was idled for about two years. There were rumors (*China, Glass and Lamps*, June 22, 1898) that "the Pittsburgh Glass and Ceramic Co. will start up the old Northwood plant at Ellwood City," and *Crockery and Glass Journal* later reported (August 11, 1898) that the Empire Glass Co. "of Ellwood City ... are occupying the factory built by the Northwood Co., and are making decorated glassware." Finally, in late 1898, the building and fixtures were purchased by the American Lamp and Brass Company of Trenton, New Jersey, and the concern became known as the Clark Brothers Glass Company. The firm was reorganized as the Ellwood City Glass Company in 1905.

CHAPTER FOUR
HARRY TAKES HOLD AT INDIANA, PA.

Although Harry Northwood was not the first glassmaker in Indiana, Pa., there is little doubt that his glass plant brought both renewed excitement and some measure of economic well-being to the town. The Indiana plant was, by far, Northwood's most successful glass factory, both financially and in terms of the innovative glass products made there. Although some mould-blown glassware was made, particularly during the first year, the Northwood's reputation was built primarily upon pressed ware, especially the tableware lines made in Ivory glass and other distinctive colors.

Fortunately for collectors and glass historians, a wealth of documentation about this factory is available — trade journal quotes and advertising; wholesalers' catalogs; photographs taken in the plant; and glass fragments recovered at the site. Taken together, these materials provide a remarkably full picture of this significant American glass factory. There are a few mysteries, to be sure, but most Northwood products from this plant can be documented.

Harry Northwood was not the first glassmaker in Indiana, nor would he be the last. The full history of these other enterprises — the Indiana Glass Co., 1892-1893; the National Glass Co., 1899-1904; the Dugan Glass Co., 1904-1913; and the Diamond Glass-Ware Co., 1913-1931 — will be the subject of a later book in this series, but a brief account of the Indiana Glass Co. will be given immediately below, since its history is important background for an understanding of the Northwood plant. The rest of the chapter will discuss the Indiana, Pa., glass plant during the time it was under the managerial control of Harry Northwood.

The Indiana Glass Company

The Indiana Glass Co. had begun with high hopes in November, 1892 (*China, Glass and Lamps*, November 16, 1892; *Crockery and Glass Journal*, November 24, 1892) . The formation of a company and the construction of the plant had been an exciting project for the town, and a number of key citizens, led by Judge Harry White, participated in the effort to make the plant a reality. Unfortunately, the Indiana Glass Co. was not a success. Competition was keen, and, when the venture foundered about a year after its inception, attempts were made to secure another operator for the plant. These came to nought, and pressing debts eventually precipitated a court-ordered auction. The October 30, 1895, Indiana County *Gazette*, a local newspaper, had the details: "On next Monday afternoon Sheriff Mack will sell the property of the Indiana Glass Co. The sale will include the building and machinery, appliances for the manufacture of glass commodities, a large quantity of jars and glasses and all other articles not exempt by law. The general impression is that all will be bought in by the directors."

Within a few months, the outlook had brightened considerably. The *Gazette* carried this story (January 22, 1896) under the headline "MAY SELL THE GLASS PLANT:"

"Judge Harry White and Griffith Ellis were in

This ad appeared in Crockery and Glass Journal *for October 26, 1892.*

Pittsburgh yesterday on business relating to the Indiana Glass Co. While in the city they met with representatives of a Wheeling glass company, whose representatives visited Indiana a couple of weeks ago and inspected the local plant. The Wheeling people, it is said, were much pleased with the outlook here and carried back a good report to their home company. At the meeting in Pittsburgh yesterday arrangements were about completed for the transfer of the plants to the Wheeling company. A price was about agreed upon and the Wheeling people will visit Indiana next Saturday to complete the terms of the transfer."

The references to "Wheeling people" may have been designed to protect the identity of Harry Northwood so that arrangements could proceed without the knowledge of the Ellwood City investors from whom he was about to break. There are no other stories in the *Gazette* or in the glass trade press which refer to a Wheeling-based interest in the Indiana plant.

Northwood Comes to Indiana

Shortly after Harry Northwood made his decision to leave Ellwood City and go to Indiana, the trade publication *China, Glass and Lamps* (February 19, 1896) was first with the news:

"As we go to press, we learn that Harry Northwood has severed his active connection with the Northwood Glass Co., Ellwood City, Pa., and has purchased the finely equipped flint glass factory at Indiana, Pa., where he will be making glass within three weeks under the name and firm title of the Northwood Glass & Mfg. Co., Indiana, Pa. Mr. Northwood has long been acknowledged the foremost American manufacturer of fine blown colored and art glass products, and will continue to make in his new factory, the several lines and decorations in flint, color combinations, and opal glassware with Delft decoration, including tableware, lemonade sets, vases and novelties of all kinds. Mr. Northwood leaves for Indiana Monday next, to take personal charge of the works, designing and glass making departments, and will be ready to book orders for early delivery at once."

The sudden departure of Northwood from the Ellwood City factory was also acknowledged in the *National Glass Budget* (February 22, 1896), which ran the story under the headline "Harry Himself." The article is noteworthy for its revelations about the company and about Northwood's desire for independence:

"Mr. Harry Northwood, for years past identified with such works as the Phoenix, the Hobbs, the Northwood Glass Co., at Martin's Ferry and Ellwood, has severed his connection with the latter company, and ... purchased the finely equipped flint glass works at Indiana, Pa. ... Having heretofore been hampered for capital, or handicapped by close-fisted, over-cautious, unprogressive stock companies, Harry now proposes to be himself, and make art glass of superior quality on his own hook, and we are informed he will have associated with him several friends with ample capital, so that he will have full sway and ample opportunity to get out something worthy of himself and the glass makers' art, instead of eating away his heart in the monotony of pot boiler manufacture. Mr. Northwood stands among the foremost metal makers of our time and we shall be very disappointed if the lovers of the beautiful and artistic in glassware will not have reason to be glad of the new departure made in starting up what is to be known as the Northwood Glass and Manufacturing Co., Indiana, Pa. Mr. Northwood goes to Indiana, Pa., Monday next to personally take charge of the designing, decorating and glass making departments, and glass will be ready for shipment within three weeks. Orders from friends and the glass making trade generally will be promptly acknowledged and shipped at the earliest opportunity. The output of the works will be confined to choice and high grade blown ware in flint and colors."

Ad from China, Glass and Lamps, *March 11, 1896; a similar ad appeared in* Crockery and Glass Journal, *March 12, 1896.*

The statements regarding "close-fisted, over-cautious, unprogressive stock companies" and "pot boiler manufacture" may indeed have come from Northwood himself. As detailed in the previous chapter, the financial situation at Ellwood City and the relationships among the investors seem to have deteriorated in 1895-96. The "friends with ample capital" mentioned by the *National Glass Budget* included none of the Martins Ferry/Ellwood City stockholders, and, as will be seen later, the "friends" might have been limited to Harry Northwood's uncle, Thomas Dugan, the hotel owner from Ellwood City.

Once Northwood had left Ellwood City and relocated in Indiana, he wasted no time in preparing some creative advertising notices for his new enterprise. This ad appeared in the February 22, 1896, issue of the *National Glass Budget*:

YE
GLASS
JOBBER

Please Sir to take notice that **Mr. Harry Northwood,** that highly skilled Master Workman and fabricator of modern art glass will hereafter be established in **his own** glass factory, and that the fine **Crystal,** and fancy **Art Glass** in colors and combinations, in **Table Ware, Lemonade Sets, Lamps** and **Novelties,** known far and wide in the United States as **Northwood Art Glass** can hereafter only be secured by ordering direct from "Harry himself" as follows:

**Northwood
Glass Mf.'g
        Company.**
INDIANA, PA.

Exactly what sort of initial agreement Harry Northwood had for operating the Indiana plant is not entirely certain. He probably leased or rented the factory at a low rate and held an option to purchase it. The Indiana County *Gazette* (February 26, 1896) provides some interesting details, including the fact that Harry Northwood shipped moulds from Ellwood City to Indiana:

"Within three weeks the Indiana glass plant will again be in operation. During the past week

arrangements have been effected whereby the concern passes into the hands of Mr. Harry Northwood, a man who has had a vast experience in the glass business in various parts of the country, and under his careful guidance it is confidently expected the Indiana glass works will be placed on a paying basis. ... Negotiations for his purchase of the Indiana plant have been pending for several weeks, and last week when he met Joseph W. Clements of the Indiana Gas Company and concluded satisfactory arrangements for fuel the deal was consummated. Mr. Northwood was to have arrived in Indiana yesterday but was delayed. He is expected to arrive at noon today when he will take charge of the plant and place it in shape for operation. He writes that he has shipped to Indiana a large number of moulds and pots and hopes to have everything in full blast inside of three weeks. ... The plant will be operated on a larger scale than heretofore, and will give employment to more men than were previously on the pay roll. It is not known on just what terms Mr. Northwood secured the works."

In the course of reporting later business developments, the *Gazette* (January 12, 1898) revealed that Harry Northwood had had a contract to operate the glass works which would expire on March 1, 1898, so it seems likely that a two-year agreement (March 1, 1896, to March 1, 1898) had been struck. All of the glass trade publications heralded Northwood's arrival in Indiana. This report is typical: "The versatile 'Arry Northwood is again in a new combination that has bought a factory at Indiana, Pa., and will put it in operation on the high class artistic ware 'Arry always took such a pride in" (*Crockery and Glass Journal*, February 27, 1896).

The *Gazette* (March 4, 1896) continued its coverage of local events in a story headlined "GETTING THE PLANT IN SHAPE." Among other things, the article listed the key personnel: "Harry and Carl Northwood, Thomas Dugan, Sr. and Jr., W. Kinney and George Beaumont." The reference to the Dugans as "Sr. and Jr." is not correct, although these terms were sometimes applied to older and younger men, respectively, who shared the same name. Their relationship was that of uncle-nephew. The elder Thomas Dugan (the hotel owner from Ellwood City), who was also Harry Northwood's uncle, had no children. The younger man, who had boarded on Jacob Street with Northwood in Wheeling in the early 1880s, was Thomas Ernest Albert Dugan, Northwood's cousin and a nephew of "Uncle Tommie" from Ellwood City.

The first advertising for glassware from the Indiana plant began in mid-March, 1896, even before the factory had been made fully operational. Similar ads in *China, Glass and Lamps* (March 11, 1896) and *Crockery and Glass Journal* (March 11, 1896) listed Harry Northwood as "manager" and mentioned the numbers of five lemonade sets. No. 205 was the familiar Coinspot set. No. 319 is an opalescent swirl, and No. 187 is Daisy and Fern. The others were probably other opalescent or decorated wares similar to items made previously at Ellwood City.

An ad for the new Indiana concern in the *National Glass Budget* drew a sharp, perhaps sarcastic, contrast between Northwood's Indiana plant and the cold furnaces at Ellwood City:

LOOK YOU HERE, MR. GLASS JOBBER...

The fires in the Northwood Glass Co., Ellwood, Pa., have been drawn, and we know very well that as you are an up-to-date business man, and do not propose to allow your stock to fall below the standard by the dropping out of the eye-catchers, the beauty spots and art-gems in form and color heretofore made for you by **Mr. Harry Northwood,** you have been puzzled how to fill up the vacancy likely to occur.

But No Vacuum

Need distress you, for the pots in Harry's own factory at Indiana, Pa., are **Red Hot Now,** and the magician with the blow pipe will be blowing himself red in the face to fill your orders for fine **Colored** and **Opalescent Lemonade Sets, Art Glass Lamps,** and original Novelties, if you will only send in your orders promptly, for "Harry can take care of the trade, see?"

Northwood Glass Mf'g Company.
INDIANA, PA.

From the National Glass Budget, *March 14, 1896.*

The March 19, 1896, issue of *Crockery and Glass Journal* said that Northwood factory "expects to be making glass this week," and the *Journal* predicted a "product essentially peculiar to Mr. Harry Northwood's genius in glass making, which it will be difficult if not impossible to duplicate elsewhere." The *Journal* also mentioned "several of his favorite patterns," a clear indication that items from the previous plants at Ellwood City and Martins Ferry would be in the forthcoming Northwood lines from Indiana. *China, Glass and Lamps* (April 1, 1896) reported that the new Northwood plant "started up last week," and *Crockery and Glass Journal* (April 2, 1896) revealed that two hundred hands were employed there.

Blooming and Booming in 1896!

In mid-April, *China, Glass and Lamps* announced the first Northwood product from the Indiana plant, a decorated line in opal glass called Apple Blossom: "The factory of the Northwood Co., Indiana, is putting one of the handsomest fine blown tableware sets on the market at present that we have seen for many a day. Made in fine lead opal, graceful as artistic blown goods only can be, with an apple blossom in relief, hand painted and tinted, this line is sure to prove a leader." An ad appeared in this same publication, and, within a month, similar ads were carried in the other trade publications. The Apple Blossom line is best known in decorated opal. The shapes are similar to Parian Swirl, but both the decorations and the finely-latticed background invite comparisons with Northwood's Netted Oak, another Indiana pattern. Some collectors confuse Northwood's Apple Blossom with the well-known Cosmos pattern, which was made by several other firms (see H3, p. 21).

The Apple Blossom line includes the four-piece table set, the water and berry set, and condiment pieces: syrup jug, cruet, salt and sugar shakers, and a pickle caster (made with the spooner). A miniature lamp also exists (Smith 1, fig. 194). Some Apple Blossom shape moulds were used for opalescent Daisy and Fern pieces. The spooner, used as a pickle caster insert, is most often seen, but there are other pieces (sugar shaker, toothpick holder and cruet).

The April 22, 1896, issue of *China, Glass and Lamps* termed Northwood's workers "one of the most expert set of off hand workmen to be found in this country," and said that "Harry is just letting himself out on fine shapes, color combinations and handsome decorated glassware."

This ad appeared in China, Glass and Lamps, *April 15, 1896.*

By early May, 1896, *Crockery and Glass Journal* was calling Apple Blossom "most suitable for the season," and *China, Glass and Lamps* (May 6, 1896), in reporting on a new line of lamps, lauded the Indiana-based company: "The Northwood Co., Indiana, Pa., have prepared a new and handsome line of fine decorated opal lamps, among which there are no old hold-overs or lichen breasted, moss covered shelf squatters, for the firm are putting new lines exclusively on the market, and are engaged only on original designs and fine class goods." The May 27, 1896, issue of *China, Glass and Lamps* singled out Harry Northwood for special praise: "Harry Northwood has been making things hum in Apple Blossom tableware and artistic lamps. The Blossom is said to have proven a blooming success, and 'Arry is right in it."

The success recounted in the glass tableware trade press was reflected in the June 17, 1896, *Gazette*'s headline, "GLASS WORKS ARE BOOMING":

"Mr. Harry Northwood, proprietor of the Indiana Glass works, is more than pleased with the prospects for continued good business at the plant. The works are running almost to their capacity day and night, and if orders continue to flow in as they have been during the past month, employees of the workers are assured of steady employment during the summer and winter. Mr. Northwood does not think the works will close down this summer at all. It is customary to put out the fires for from five to six weeks every summer, but big business compels the management to disregard this old rule this season. The works are turning out some very pretty ware; just as pretty as is produced anywhere, and foreign buyers are rapidly becoming acquainted with the fact for they are snapping up the production like hot cakes. A big order received recently would alone keep the plant running for six weeks if not another order would be taken."

Even though the glass plant was extraordinarily busy, Harry and Carl Northwood and some friends found time for an energetic respite, as reported in the *Gazette* (July 29, 1896): "Messrs. Harry and Carl Northwood, Thomas and Albert Dugan, William Kinney, Joseph Moore and Harry White, Jr., all connected with the glass works, left Indiana for a week's bicycle trip on Monday morning. They first rode from here to Kittanning thence to Butler, New Castle, Ellwood City, Mercer and home by way of Pittsburgh." At the last stop,

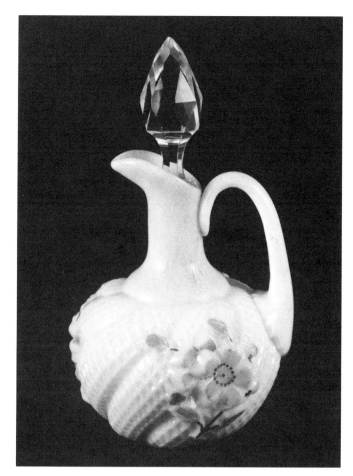

Apple Blossom opal decorated cruet (stopper not original).
Courtesy of Larry Loxterman.

Harry Northwood, "the well-known fancy glass manufacturer, ... spoke well of the trade prospects," said *Crockery and Glass Journal* (August 6, 1896).

In late August, rumors abounded that the boom was over and that the plant would be shut until November. *China, Glass and Lamps* (August 26, 1896) carried a full report of Northwood's denial: "Harry Northwood, of the Indiana, Pa., glass works, had the following to say to a reporter in answer to a rumor that the works would likely shut down till after the election: "After running right along through the dull season do you suppose we are going to quit business just when the glass trade is opening up? Our harvest is just coming, and the Indiana Co. expects to reap as large a crop of orders as the other fellows. We will be closed about four days this week pending a few necessary repairs, but the works will be running right through the fall, election or no election."

About the same time, Harry Northwood apparently made his views known on the great silver/gold question of the 1896 Presidential election, which pitted Ohio's Republican Governor William McKinley against former Congressman William Jennings Bryan of Nebraska, a Democrat who favored the silver standard. Harry Northwood, a Republican, paid the firm's workers in gold coin, and the *National Glass Budget* (August 29, 1896) had the story: "Last Saturday being the semimonthly pay day at the works of the Northwood Company at Indiana, Pa., the manager addressed the following note to the foremen of the different departments of the works:

TO OUR EMPLOYES. Gentlemen — We will this day pay all wages of $5 and upwards to our employes in gold coin, and all less than that amount in notes and silver. This money is all equal now. Our bank here, the Indiana County Deposit, at my request, has supplied us the gold without charge, as it bears no premium, but is in free circulation. If conditions were changed to free coinage of silver we could not do this, as gold would be at a premium and silver would be at a discount and much less valuable to you for wages than it is now. The Northwood Company, Harry Northwood, Manager."

The *National Glass Budget* added its own editorial comment: "This doubtless is intended as one of those object lessons in finance we hear so much about, and impels us to suggest that if the working man goes wrong this time in casting his vote, he deserves any fate that may be in store for him."

The September 1, 1896, issue of *China, Glass and Lamps*, under the headline "SOME NORTH-

Panelled Sprig opal decorated cruet and salt/pepper shakers. **Courtesy of Larry Loxterman.**

This ad appeared in China, Glass and Lamps, *May 13, 1896; a similar ad appeared in* Crockery and Glass Journal, *April 30, 1896.*

WOOD ART GLASS," had a report on glassware then in production at the Northwood plant:

"We had the pleasure of seeing several lines of fine blown art glassware made at Indiana by Mr. Harry Northwood, and are pleased to be able to note that the hand of the master of that ancient art sublime has lost none of the cunning of his youth, and that despite age, experience, and that rough and often unfair usage a gross-sensed world so often bestows on genius, our Harry's inventiveness has not weakened, nor his mind's resourcefulness decreased. The latest product of the Northwood Co. is an opal set embracing a blown lemonade set, the bottle curving in from the shoulder and flared at the lip so as to afford ample ground for choice decoration, while tumblers retain the curve outward from the center to bottom edge. The decorations are painted sprays, among which variegated pansies are delightfully handled. Barber bottles in opal, with direct photographic facsimiles of the Presidential candidates; decorated opal finger bowls; coral and opal combination berry bowls, for silver smith work, complete the set."

Although the campaign items have not been traced, the opal lemonade set may be the Panelled Sprig pattern, which had been made in rubina and as "Granite ware" (blue with white

speckles) at Ellwood City. Decorated opal items in the Panelled Sprig line are clearly visible in photos taken inside the plant in 1897-98 (see p. 122).

As the last weeks of 1896 wound down, the boom at the Northwood factory abated somewhat. The plant was closed for the first three weeks of November (*Crockery and Glass Journal,* November 19, 1896), and the *National Glass Budget* (November 21, 1896) quoted Harry Northwood to the effect that the tableware business was "slow ... because it was late in the season." Although the Northwood Company did not have any special advertising in the Holiday Number of *Crockery and Glass Journal,* there is no doubt that 1896 had been an exceptional first year for a young plant in the competitive glass tableware industry.

Tentative Times

The first six months of 1897 were not the best of times for the Northwood Company. Although the decorated wares held their own in the marketplace, a pressed pattern called Crystal Queen met with little success, and other events overshadowed glassmaking at Indiana. Nonetheless, the Northwood firm opened the year with a display at the Monongahela House in January, 1897, and *China, Glass and Lamps* had a full report:

Cruet and syrup jug in Northwood's Crystal Queen pattern.

"The Northwood Co., occupying room 155, has an excellent selection of fine blown colored ware, in the well known artistic decorations which have been the feature of Harry Northwood's handiwork for many years past. In fine ruby, blue and opal, and their combinations, many specialties are shown, as tankards, water bottles, lemonade sets, berry and fruit bowls, vases, finger bowls, tableware sets, fancy lamps — in hand, sewing and banquet styles — all of which are off hand work, the opal sets being finely decorated. In pressed crystal tableware, which is a new departure with this company, the new pattern is an imitation cut line, made in excellent metal, which is well shown by the light in-cut lines of the pattern. The Crystal Queen, as the new line has been called, has been decorated in gold, and shows off royally, as becomes her imperial majesty. The admirers of Northwood art glass will find a lot of new things awaiting their inspection, and as the exhibit is not as large as of old, it possesses no less merit, and is perhaps richer in novelty than the products shown in former years."

The Crystal Queen, an extensive pattern line containing 125 pieces, was touted with full page advertisements in three consecutive issues of *China, Glass and Lamps* (January 13, 20 and 27, 1897), and ads were carried in *Glass and Pottery World*. The February 10, 1897, issue of *China, Glass and Lamps* devoted considerable editorial space to extolling its virtues, complete with several illustrations. Despite the fanfare, this was to be the last mention of Northwood's Crystal Queen in the trade press. The pattern probably did not sell well, and the company redirected its efforts when this became apparent. Of interest to collectors today is the fact that the pattern was made by the Cambridge Glass Company several years later. It was called simply #2589 in a 1903 Cambridge catalog, where 25 different articles were shown. At this time, both the Northwood plant at Indiana and the Cambridge works were controlled by the National Glass Company, so the old Northwood moulds were probably transferred to Cambridge. There is no mention of gold decoration in the 1903 Cambridge catalog, so this may

have been an exclusive feature of Northwood's production of this short-lived pattern line.

Just when the Northwood Company's progress seemed to be tentative, the *Gazette* (February 17, 1897) carried this ominous headline: "MAY LOSE GLASS PLANT." A lengthy article revealed the particulars. A nearby Pennsylvania town, Blairsville, was courting Harry Northwood's favor. Northwood had been having some problems with the Indiana town council, and he used the Blairsville offer as leverage in obtaining municipal water service for fire protection. The article quoted Harry Northwood as follows:

"I have not yet purchased the Indiana plant ... and I am free to act in the matter. We are doing a good business here, as good as we could expect to do anywhere, but if advantageous offers were made us by any other town we would give the matter considerable thought. There has been some correspondence with Blairsville people .... I can probably save money by taking it in preference to purchasing the Indiana plant outright. We feel that we are entitled to some consideration by the people of the town, and if I can't get protection for my property here, I — well, I will go some place where I can."

Northwood made his point. The *Gazette* concluded by noting that the council had "consulted with the water company and estimates are now being made regarding the cost of laying the pipes to the necessary point. The council will request the water company to put down the pipes, which will probably be done as soon as the weather permits."

Fire protection was not the only business worry in the first months of 1897. The March 25, 1897, issue of *Crockery and Glass Journal* reported that Harry Northwood had sued the Dalzell, Gilmore and Leighton Company of Findlay, Ohio, for patent infringement. The suit alleged that the glass crimping device invented by John Northwood and assigned to Harry Northwood in 1885 (see p. 10) had been duplicated by the Findlay firm. Northwood asked for $10,000 in monetary damages as well as an injunction restraining use of his invention by others. A note in *Crockery and Glass Journal* (May 13, 1897) indicated that the Robinson Glass Company of Zanesville, Ohio, was also named a defendant in this action. This suit was not decided in Northwood's favor; Judge Ricks of the United States Circuit Court at Cincinnati, ruling in favor of the Dalzell firm, held that Northwood's device was not really an invention (*China, Glass and Lamps*, June 11, 1898).

The only mention of glassware products in the trade press during the spring of 1897 was a brief report in the April 22, 1897, issue of *China, Glass and Lamps* that New York sales agent Aleck Menzies had just received Northwood glass samples "consisting of comb and brush trays, pin trays, toilet bottles, and other fancy pieces. The new glass is opal, white with handpainted decorations." This same publication, acknowledging a visit by Harry and Carl Northwood, said only that "business is progressing favorably with them."

In late July, 1897, a severe thunderstorm caused damage at the Northwood plant when a large tree fell on an above ground gas main, breaking the pipe and interrupting the flow of natural gas to the factory's furnaces. *China, Glass and Lamps* (July 28, 1897) reported "many glass workers were made idle," and the July 29, 1897, issue of *Crockery and Glass Journal* said the pots in the furnace had cooled and broken. The first seven months of 1897 had not been kind to the Northwood concern, but these trials and tribulations would soon be forgotten as better times came with several new pattern lines.

Sometime in the summer of 1897, a young man named Frank Leslie Fenton took a job decorating glassware at the Northwood plant. He had graduated in May with academic honors from the high school in Indiana, and he considered a career as a schoolteacher before deciding to work at the glass plant. His son, Frank M. Fenton, recalls that his father's employ almost ended several weeks after it began: "My father was late in reporting for work in the decorating department, and he was told by the foreman to leave the factory. On his way out, he was seen by one of the managers, perhaps Harry or Carl Northwood. The man spoke with him for a few moments, and my father was sent back to work." Within a year, Frank L. Fenton assumed responsibility as a foreman in Northwood's decorating department. He left the firm in 1900 to go with Northwood plant manager Harry Bastow to a new plant, the Jefferson Glass Company, in Steubenville, Ohio (see Heacock's *Fenton Glass: The First Twenty-five Years*, p. 7).

The Gold Rush Patterns

During the 1897 and 1898 trade seasons, the Northwood firm enjoyed great success with two new glass tableware patterns — Klondyke and Alaska. The mid-summer exhibitions at the Monongahela House were no longer held, so the Northwood Company relied upon trade journal ads to bring the new lines to the attention of buyers.

China, Glass and Lamps (August 11, 1897) had a full account of the new Klondyke (note the spelling) line; the term "pearl" refers to glass with an opalescent edge:

"Klondyke is the name of a beautiful new line just brought out by the Northwood Co. of Indiana, Pa. They have pre-empted the name and want others to hold off from it. ... The Klondyke is well named, being of a very brilliant pattern and made

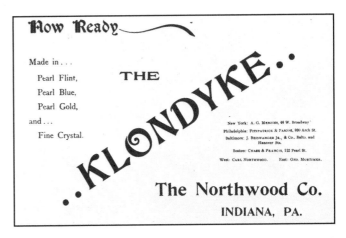

in a beautiful Klondyke gold colored glass with pearl effects. It is also made in pearl blue, pearl flint and crystal. Treated artistically with raised enamel and gold decorations, it is very rich and surpasses anything ever produced from this well known works. It is not an imitation cut pattern but is refreshingly new and original in shape and effect. The body rests on gracefully curved feet and is surmounted by a frill of great brilliancy. The whole is a beautiful shimmering effect of silky threads and prisms. We predict for it all its name would indicate."

Similarly enthusiastic statements appeared in subsequent issues of *China, Glass and Lamps*, and these excerpts are noteworthy:

"We do not now refer to the Alaskan gold region, but to the Klondyke glass made by the Northwood Co., Indiana, Pa. To get to the Klondyke mining territory a man has to confront almost insurmountable obstacles and when he reaches there must take his chances of finding the precious metal; but there is no element of doubt or uncertainty about Klondyke glass and the dealer who handles it will be a winner every time. The brilliant product is to be had in pearl blue and pearl flint, as well as in crystal, and it is decorated in a manner which makes Klondyke gold appear dim, and lustreless in comparison. He who hesitates about getting some for his fall stock is throwing away a good chance of making money on the present rising tide of advance prosperity and giving his competitor who does handle it a decided advantage over him" (August 25, 1897).

"Late reports from the Klondyke gold district of Alaska indicate that big strikes of the precious metal are at an end there and the prospective output will not be near what was expected. Much closer to home, right in Indiana, this State, is a Klondyke, which shows no signs of decadence but is in the full flush of merited popularity. This is the Klondyke tableware pattern, designed by

Harry Northwood and manufactured by the Northwood Co. of the above named place. We thought it would prove a ringer and said so from the first, but the reality has been away ahead of our surmises. Everybody who has heard of the Klondyke ware wants it, and those who have it once are satisfied to take more. The Northwood Co. are making it right along and will try to have enough to go around" (September 1, 1897).

Today's collectors also know the Klondyke pattern as Fluted Scrolls. A similar line, which seems to be an elaboration of Klondyke, is called Fluted Scrolls with Flower Band. The flowers, which resemble Forget-Me-Nots, may be decorated with gilt paint. When this pattern occurs in Ivory glass it has been called Jackson (see Brahmer's *Custard Glass*). The plain Klondyke items sometimes bear delicate painted decorations. A novelty item which is quite reminiscent of Klondyke is the Fluted Scrolls with Vine vase (H2, p. 87).

Were all of these pattern variations included in a single Northwood line? Or was Klondyke produced by Northwood and the others (Fluted Scrolls with Flower Band and Fluted Scrolls with Vine) by one or more of his successors? The Fluted Scrolls with Vine vase is shown in a Butler Brothers catalog, so this and all the other variants in the Klondyke pattern are probably Northwood-made. On the other hand, none of the Klondyke items illustrated in Northwood ads shows the additional flower band.

In any case, Northwood's Klondyke line was extensive, ranging from the four-piece table set and water and berry sets to the cruet, shakers, a small covered bowl, and an attractive epergne (H2, p. 94). Occasionally, an interesting item was created by a finisher, such as the Klondyke card receiver (see p. 134).

The commercial success of the Klondyke pattern was quickly felt in the town of Indiana. Under the headline "THE GLASS WORKS BOOMING," the

Gazette (September 1, 1897) heralded the "return of prosperity" in a long story:

"The Northwood glassworks are running full time and scarcely able to keep up with orders. Mr. Northwood got out a new line of pressed table ware, the Klondyke, last summer, which is meeting with great success. He said yesterday: 'We have a good thing in our new line of pressed ware and it is selling rapidly. Our blown goods are also as much in demand as ever. The indications are that this will be one of the most prosperous seasons we have ever had.' When asked if he attributed the large orders to the returning of good times, he said; 'Partly. People now have the money to buy with and the superior quality and design of our ware has attracted the attention of the purchasers.' The works are now turning out from 75 to 100 barrels of glassware every day. Two hundred and fifty barrels were shipped on Saturday and 150 on Monday. Five additional skilled pressed glass workers from Pittsburg went to work on Saturday."

Another article in the *Gazette* (September 29, 1897) announced that the plant would be expanded, adding two decorating lehrs. Northwood was quoted to the effect that orders for "4000 barrels" were on hand and the factory's employees were working day and night. The popularity of his Klondyke design also meant dividends for Northwood himself, of course. The Indiana County *Gazette* (September 22, 1897) reported that he "bought a handsome carriage from the firm of Shields, Painter & Sloan, of

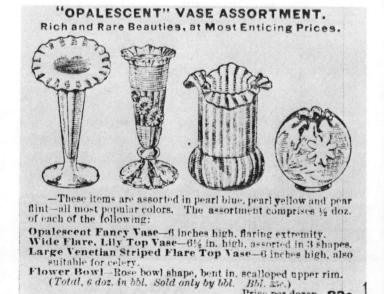

The vase is obviously Fluted Scrolls with Vine, and the "flower bowl" seems to be Daisy and Fern. From Butler Brothers catalog, 1899.

Greensburg.... Mr. Northwood ordered the carriage shipped to his parents, who reside in England."

The success of the Klondyke line was soon paralleled by the next pattern introduced by the Northwood firm. Called Alaska, it was mentioned briefly in *China, Glass and Lamps* (October 13, 1897), which confidently predicted that the Alaska line would "sustain the Northwood reputation for preeminence in ornamental glassware...."

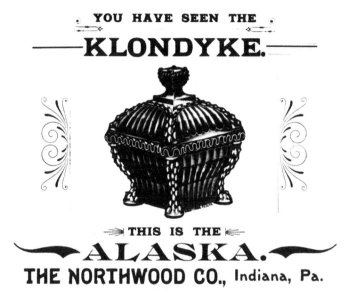

Ad from Crockery and Glass Journal.

Advertising began in earnest with the December 15, 1897, issue of *China, Glass and Lamps* and continued throughout the first three months of 1898. *China, Glass and Lamps* (December 15, 1897) said the Alaska pattern was "up to the regular Northwood standard," and, less than a month later, quoted Northwood workers who related that Klondyke was "a wonderful seller" and Alaska "is a beauty, and will sell just as well." The January 12, 1898, issue of *China, Glass and Lamps* discussed the Northwood's display at the Monongahela House:

"Last week Harry Northwood had the assistance of George Mortimer and Carl Northwood in showing his elegant wares to interested visitors, but this week he is holding the fort alone, as his confreres have started out on the road to give people who may not come here a chance of seeing the numerous fine things they have provided for the delectation of the trade and consumers this season. As our readers are already aware, the Alaska is the newest pattern got out by this firm. There is a full line of table goods in this line. The shape is square and the colors are pearl blue, pearl gold, green and crystal, all in gold and

enamel decorations. The goods are got up in the true Northwood style and that is saying about enough. There are none others in the country or out of the country in the same line that can beat them and few that come any way near them. The other new pattern, got out only a little while before the Alaska is the Klondike [sic]. They have this in pearl blue, pearl gold and canary. It also comprises a full line. This is a round, footed shape and is altogether new in conception."

The Alaska line apparently offered more articles than the Klondyke, and Alaska is known in flint opalescent, blue opalescent, canary opalescent or "yellow," and green (rather dark, without opalescence). These Alaska articles are known to exist: four-piece table set, water set, berry set, cruet, salt/pepper shakers, and several sizes of rectangular bowls, including some with out-turned edges (H2, p. 38). Heacock believed that the salt/pepper shakers and the tumblers were common to both the Klondyke and the Alaska lines. Klondyke and Alaska were mentioned prominently in Northwood's ads in a new trade publication — *China, Glass and Pottery Review* — during March, 1898, and the factory was said to be "very busy" (see next page).

About the time that Klondyke and Alaska were enjoying great popularity and sales, a photographer visited the Northwood plant. Some of the photos taken in various areas of the plant are remarkably sharp (see pp. 120-125). Many specific glassware articles can be identified, and words stencilled in various places can be read with a powerful magnifying glass. These photos provide an extraordinary visual record of Northwood's products, ca. 1897-98, all of which contributed to the firm's success during the Gold Rush.

Some other Northwood products deserve mention here even though they seem to have achieved little recognition in their own time, probably because the success of Klondyke and

A catalog issued by the Falker and Stern Company in the spring of 1898 shows Northwood's Alaska table set. Only blue opalescent was offered, and there is no mention of decorations.

Klondyke and Alaska

KLONDYKE.

ALASKA.

In Crystal, Green,
Pearl Yellow and
Pearl Blue.

Opalescent and Decorated
Lemonade Sets IN LARGE VARIETY AND AT RIGHT PRICES.

THE NORTHWOOD CO.,

INDIANA, PA.

NEW YORK,
Frank M. Miller,
76 Park Place.

PHILADELPHIA,
Fitzpatrick & Pascoe,
930 Arch Street.

BALTIMORE,
Andrew J. George.

WEST, Carl Northwood.   EAST, George Mortimer.

Klondyke and Alaska were advertised together in China, Glass and Pottery Review *in 1898* (see next page).

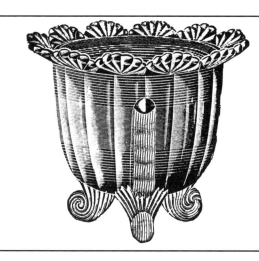
Alaska overshadowed them. The January 12, 1898, issue of *China, Glass and Lamps* mentioned "a line of new water sets alongside of which any imported will pale the ineffectual fires — these are in crystal, blue, green and ruby." A later trade notice (*China, Glass and Pottery Review*, April 1, 1898) said that "The Northwood Co. ... are coming prominently to the fore as producers of opalescent and decorated lemonade sets." This reference to "opalescent" might be to Daisy and Fern or to the No. 205 (Coinspot) set, but the "deco-rated" lemonade sets remain elusive pending research on the characteristics of Northwood's pitchers and decorations. The No. 205 set was made at Ellwood City (see p. 100), and it continued in production at Indiana. The other sets shown in the previous chapter (see p. 101) could be either Ellwood City or Indiana products, of course, but similar sets were likely made at both locations, especially since Northwood secured the moulds from Ellwood City and moved them to Indiana.

More importantly, the same issue of *China,*

The barrels in the left foreground are marked "Alaska assortment" and at least one of them says "packed by Bert Wichs." The packer in the center holds a decorated opal Panelled Sprig pitcher. Courtesy of Ernest R. Dugan.

Glass and Lamps (January 12, 1898) mentioned "a new fine of opal tableware, decorated in green and pink, and an assortment of novelties and small wares which will be found very interesting to department [store] people and caterers to the general notion trade." The term opal usually designated opaque white (milk glass) ware, and this brief note might refer to Netted Oak, a pattern shown in the photographs taken inside the plant. Netted Oak is usually found in opal glass, decorated in various ways, but it is also known in two transparent colors, amethyst and pale green, although these were probably made after Northwood's time in Indiana and appear in Butler Brothers catalogs in 1903. A decorated Netted Oak sugar shaker, (called Acorn) and a Panelled Sprig sugar shaker (called Melon) were advertised in Falker and Stern's catalog for spring, 1898.

In early March, 1898, the Northwood Company continued to advertise its Klondyke and Alaska

The square sauce dishes in the left foreground are Alaska pattern in an opalescent color, and the men and women are busy grinding the tops of opalescent Daisy and Fern tumblers. Daisy and Fern was made previously at Ellwood City, of course, and the water or lemonade set was probably a staple item in the line for a number of years. **Courtesy of Ernest R. Dugan.**

patterns together in several publications, and an ad in *China, Glass and Lamps* called them "the two great winners of the season." These two patterns, named in association with the Gold Rush, were, by all accounts, the "largest sellers this season" (*China, Glass and Lamps*, April 20, 1898). The Gold Rush — in glass rather than precious metal — had come to Indiana, Pa.

Important Business Decisions

In the midst of the prosperity engendered by the sales of Klondyke and Alaska, rumors surfaced once more regarding the possible relocation of the Northwood plant. On November 17, 1897, the *Gazette* reported that Steubenville, an Ohio town which had been the locale of many glass factories, was attempting to attract the Northwood firm and that an offer was "under careful consideration." *China, Glass and Lamps* (November 24,

1897) carried the story, too, noting that the Northwood plant at Indiana "is entirely too small for their vastly increased business." The December 2, 1897, issue of *Crockery and Glass Journal* intimated that Harry Northwood might run both the Indiana plant and the one at Steubenville.

At first, the overture to Northwood from Steubenville caused some alarm in Indiana. The *Gazette* (January 5, 1898) had a front page story, "MAY LOSE GLASS WORKS," in which an important meeting of Indiana's influential citizens was reported:

"Last night a meeting was held in the Court House, at which a number of the business men of this town met to decide whether or not they would grant the inducements asked for by the Northwood Glass Company to have them continue the operation of the plant at this place. The

The men are holding Panelled Sprig items which have just come through the decorating lehr. More Panelled Sprig items are visible in the left foreground, and there is an Alaska butter dish base near the corner of the photo. Four rather plain tumblers, apparently ruby-stained and decorated with a floral motif, are also present. Just to the right of center is an Alaska pitcher, along with more opal decorated Panelled Sprig and two pieces of decorated Netted Oak in opal. Lamp parts or bases are at the extreme right. Courtesy of Ernest R. Dugan.

proposition was that the citizens of Indiana buy the local plant and give it to the Northwood Company free of cost. Then they will enter into a contract to operate it permanently. The meeting was presided over by H. M. Lowry, and Edward Rowe acted as secretary. Judge White stated the prime object of the meeting and offered such explanation as was necessary to the better understanding of the facts in the case. Recently Mr. Northwood received a communication from the Board of Trade of Steubenville, Ohio, in which he was offered splendid inducements to go to that place and operate a plant. The facilities are better there than here. Mr. Northwood, liking Indiana as a location, but being awake to his own interests in the consideration of the Steubenville offer, brought the matter before the Board of Trade to see what Indiana could do to keep him here. That

the operation of the plant has been a benefit to Indiana, is evident. Judge White said that many persons, who would otherwise have to live off the charity of the town, are now able to make a good living by the employment they receive from the glass factory. The payment of labor every two weeks never amounts to less than $1,000, and for the two weeks preceding Christmas $4,800 was paid to the employes. Of course, this means circulation of money in Indiana, a strong feature to be considered in its favor. Many families have moved to this place attracted here by this industry.

"While the requests of the glass company were not complied with at the meeting, it is thought the start was made by which they will. It would be a long story to detail how the plant was erected by local enterprise, at a cost of $28,000, unsuccessfully operated for awhile, and finally the whole affair being purchased for $11,000. It is now owned by Judge White, Thomas Sutton, the Wilson estate, W. R. Loughry, Delos Hetrick, Griffith Ellis and John Hastings, who offer to sell it to the citizens for $8,000. Off this amount, as their share of the bonus, the owners agree to deduct $1,000. Several suggestions were offered, but the one which seemed most practical was the mention made by W. S. Daugherty that the Indiana Board of Trade prepare a subscription, payable quarterly, and that such subscription paper be submitted to a meeting of the citizens of town at the Court House tomorrow evening, at 8 o'clock. This motion was carried. Several men offered subscriptions ranging from $500 to $1000, and it is thought the amount will be raised. A canvass will be made of the town and Indiana will hardly lose her glass works."

A week later, the *Gazette* (January 12, 1898) reported on the progress of the fund-raising effort:

"The committee appointed at the citizens' meeting, consisting of J. A. Scott, J. M. Stewart, Joseph W. Clements, W. S. Daugherty and A. S. Cunningham to solicit subscriptions to a fund for the purchase of the glass factory, with the view of having the Northwood Company remain here, have made a canvass of the town with fairly good results. The amount to be raised is $7,500, but the subscriptions thus far have not reached that amount. Many of the citizens have already invested considerable money in the works and feel they are unable to give any more. An earnest endeavor is being made by both the committee and the citizens at large to raise the required amount, but so far only about $2,800 has been subscribed, with a possible $1,000 still in sight. It is hoped with a little more attention on the part of the people during the week, enough money can be raised to retain the Northwood Company here under arrangements satisfactory both to the citizens, who have contributed, and to the Northwood Company.

"It is urged by the Board of Trade that the public see it to their best interests to keep the works here, as they employ over 200 of Indiana's people, most of whom otherwise would have no employment. If satisfactory arrangements can be made, Mr. Northwood proposes to double the capacity of the plant at his own expense, an outlay of about $8,000 in addition to the cost of the works as they now stand. He also proposes to bring 25 additional families here, who will become citizens of the town.

"The matter will likely be decided on Monday evening, as Mr. Northwood's contract expires on March first. The Steubenville offer is open at any time so that whatever is to be done must be done immediately."

By mid-February, 1898, the matter was settled. The February 16, 1898, *Gazette* headline, "NORTHWOOD COMPANY STAYS," tells much of the story:

"The indications are that the Northwood Glass Company will remain in Indiana. The committee appointed by the Board of Trade has made a thorough canvass of the town and has secured between $4,500 and $5,000. The amount asked for was $8,000 but it was impossible to raise that much. Mr. Northwood in appreciation of the efforts of the citizens will himself give the remaining $3,000 towards the purchasing of the plant, provided the amount on the subscription papers is brought up to $5,000.

"In all probability the amount will be raised this week and the papers drawn up for the transfer. The deed will not be made until after the incorporation of the Board of Trade on March 1. Mr. Northwood expects to remain here indefinitely, but the terms of the contract between him and the Board of Trade will be that he remain here and operate the plant from three to five years, and until these requirements are fulfilled by Mr. Northwood a clear deed will not be made. This has been jointly agreed upon. It is Mr. Northwood's intention to enlarge the plant as soon as possible and put in some of the latest improved machinery. He has for some time been cramped for working room, especially in the packing and decorating departments. Several improvements will also be made out in the factory. The company is still enjoying the large trade with which it began last fall's business. The new ware, the Alaska, has proven a favorite and the famous Klondike [sic] is as much in demand as ever. The entire plant is being operated both day and night giving employment to about 225 hands." (this account in the *Gazette* was the basis for a similar story in the March 2, 1898, issue of *China, Glass and Lamps*).

Some developments escaped the public eye, however. When the subscriptions had been raised and the transaction completed, the deed, dated March 30, 1898, listed the purchasers as Thomas Dugan and Clara Northwood (Indiana County Deeds, B64, p. 295). The consideration was $8000. The *Gazette*'s article mentioned a total price of $8000, and the implication was that Harry Northwood personally contributed about $3000 after the subscription campaign had raised about $5000. Thomas Dugan, Northwood's uncle from

Courtesy of Ernest R. Dugan.

The storage bins have labels, and articles are visible, as noted.

125

Ellwood City, probably provided a substantial portion of the $3000; thus, his name is on the deed, albeit as a very "silent" partner. The appearance of Clara Northwood's name, rather than Harry's, may reflect a wish to keep assets out of Harry Northwood's name, just as the couple had done during the Martins Ferry era.

The promise to enlarge the Northwood plant was quickly realized. According to the *Gazette* (May 4, 1898), an addition was constructed during a shutdown: "In order to enlarge the shipping capacity the Northwood company is erecting an addition of 60 by 40 feet to the glass works. The office and sample rooms will occupy the addition, and the former office and sample rooms will be used as extra shipping and packing rooms. The works are closed down awaiting repairs on the boiler. The tubes were badly out of repairs and new ones were sent for, but when they came they were half an inch too short. Mr. Northwood secured a traction engine, which partly filled the bill, but the owner took it away on Saturday. Mr. Northwood hopes to have the works running by the middle of the week." About the time of this respite, *China, Glass and Lamps* (May 11, 1898) summarized the plant's fortunes: "The unique ware of the Northwood has had an exceptional run all last year and thus far during the present year an increase over the previous year is reported."

Other Northwood Products

Some glassware patterns and/or colors cannot be linked to Northwood's Indiana plant through original ads or trade journal notes. Nonetheless, there is no doubt that these articles were made there, for fragments have been unearthed in several areas at the factory site. William Heacock used these fragments in a series of extensive research reports which documented both Northwood and Dugan glass.

These glass fragments were not recovered through systematic archaeological digs, however. Del Helman of Indiana (the person who sent fragments to Heacock) acquired them at various times when Indiana University of Pennsylvania, which now occupies the factory site, made excavations. One such occasion was the installation of a road sign near the football stadium. Heacock sorted the fragments by pattern and color, and he placed them in manila envelopes which sometimes bear notes in his handwriting. In the early 1980s, Heacock shared many fragments with carnival glass researchers (see Edwards' *Standard Encyclopedia of Carnival Glass*, p. 5).

A few lines, such as Daisy and Fern, seem to have been continuations of patterns first made in Martins Ferry and/or Ellwood City. One must remember that the entire Northwood operation, moulds included, was moved from Martins Ferry to Ellwood City in 1893, and also that Harry Northwood shipped moulds from the plant in Ellwood City to Indiana in 1896. Of course, the Northwood moulds remained in Indiana after Harry Northwood returned to England in late 1899. The National Glass Company had both the opportunity to use them at Indiana and the ability to move them to other factories. A catalog issued by the National's McKee and Brothers Works, ca. 1900, contains illustrations of Croesus, a pattern first introduced in 1898 by the Riverside Glass Co. Apparently, Croesus was also made later at McKee. A similar situation may have existed for Northwood's Geneva (see pp. 141-144), which also appears in this National/McKee catalog.

These Northwood-era pattern lines can be linked to the Indiana plant through fragments: Apple Blossom; Argonaut Shell; Chrysanthemum Sprig; Crocodile Tears; Daisy and Fern; Grape and Leaf; Inverted Fan and Feather; Louis XV; Maple Leaf; Opaline Brocade; Panelled Sprig; Swirl and Leaf; Quilted Phlox; and Wild Bouquet. Shards of many, many National- and Dugan-era patterns and items have also been found, and these will be important evidence in later publications.

Crocodile Tears appeared as a sketch in Heacock's first book (Hl, pp. 50-51), and it has been the subject of much further research. In addition to the toothpick holder, collectors have

Quilted Phlox cruet.

Quilted Phlox syrup jug. **Courtesy of Larry Loxterman.**

reported salt/pepper shakers and a larger sugar shaker as well as an interesting miniature lamp with matching shade. These articles may come in several opaque colors (opal; yellow-custard; pink; and blue) and in transparent light yellow green and amethyst. Unfortunately, the only item for which definite attribution is possible is the miniature lamp, since it appears in a Dugan Glass Company catalog issued between 1904 and 1910 (this catalog was reprinted by Jennings). Whether the other items are Dugan products or items which could have been made by both Northwood and Dugan remains a mystery.

Swirl and Leaf was discussed in the previous chapter. Like Grape and Leaf, it is perhaps best known in opaque green with crystal overlay, although items are also found in opaque pink and opaque blue as well as opal. Heacock also noted items in a yellow custard that seems quite similar to the color used for Crocodile Tears, and he also reported an opaque gray piece (this might be similar to the opaque gray Wild Bouquet creamer noted elsewhere in this chapter). A Swirl and Leaf shaker is shown in Pitkin and Brooks 1900 catalog, revealing that it was known as pattern No. 101 at Indiana.

In the previous chapter, the characteristic opaque green of Northwood's Cactus (a design first made at Ellwood City) was mentioned. This color matches shakers in the Quilted Phlox pattern and is similar to shakers in Beaded Crosstie, which raises the possibility that the latter pattern is also a Northwood product. A number of different Quilted Phlox items are known: salt/pepper shaker; cruet; toothpick holder; sugar shaker; syrup jug; rose bowl and miniature lamp (Smith 1, fig. 388). The opaque green pieces usually have an outer layer of crystal, as do a few known pieces in opaque blue, opaque pink, opaque yellow and opal glass. The clear outer layer is reminiscent of the Leaf Umbrella articles from Northwood's Martins Ferry plant. Other colors mentioned by Heacock are crystal, apple green, blue and amethyst, the latter three almost surely made by Northwood's successors at Indiana.

Using the same principle of color similarity with Quilted Phlox, Heacock suggested that a cased green syrup jug in Grape & Leaf (H3, p. 26; H6, p. 29) might be Northwood-made. The salt shaker in Grape and Leaf is known in both opaque green and decorated opal, and the latter's decoration resembles Netted Oak items made at Indiana. A number of fragments of Grape and Leaf in carnival glass (called "Vineyard" in references on carnival) have been found at Indiana, so it is likely that Grape and Leaf was made there in opaque green and opal by Northwood and the line was continued by his successors.

In July, 1898, some significant factory improvements were under way. The Indiana County *Gazette* (July 13, 1898), in reporting that a new tile floor was being laid in the factory, added this line:

Grape and Leaf cruet. **Courtesy of Larry Loxterman.**

127

"A tank is being erected which is necessary in the making of ivory glass, a new product the factory will make when it resumes work." The term "Ivory" denoted what collectors know today as "custard" glass, and this ware was destined to become yet another Northwood success story.

Mixed Emotions

Although the Northwoods had been to England a number of times during the late 1880s and through the 1890s, no journey contained the range of emotions occasioned by the crossing in 1898. The trip began with a letter from John Northwood calling his sons home. *China, Glass and Lamps* (May 18, 1898) had the details: "Harry Northwood, ... accompanied by his brother Carl, started on a sad trip to England last week. Their father, Mr. John Northwood, the most expert and renowned artist and master workman identified with the glass industry of England during the present century, who now has fame and honor by his splendid reproduction of the Portland vase, has written his sons that, in view of approaching blindness, which specialists declare will totally obscure his sight in a few months, he desires to look upon their faces as soon as possible." As it turned out, John Northwood did not lose his sight entirely, although there is no doubt that years of work at glass carving under harsh lighting conditions left his vision impaired.

On June 25, 1898, Carl Northwood married Rose Overton in Wall Heath, Staffordshire, England. The news was reported in the July 13, 1898, Indiana County *Gazette*, which announced that the newlyweds "will make their future home [in Indiana]." The Northwoods planned to return to the United States "about the first of August," and the July 1, 1898, issue of *China, Glass and Pottery Review* further noted that Carl and Harry's cousin, Thomas E. A. Dugan, "has general charge of the business ... and is handling the factory in good shape."

Shortly after the Northwoods returned from England, the trade journal *China, Glass and Lamps*, quoting the Indiana County *Gazette*, carried this interesting story:

"Harry Northwood, the well known glassmaker, whose works in Indiana, Pa., is turning out as fine ware of its class as is made anywhere, is doing what he can to fraternize the two greatest nations on earth, as will be seen by the following clip from the Indiana *Gazette*: "When Harry Northwood, manager of the Northwood Glass Co., returned from England last week, he brought with him a gift for the factory in the shape of an English flag, which he prizes very highly. The flag was presented to the Northwood Co. and its employes by some of Mr. Northwood's English friends. They sent a letter along with the flag stating that they had sent it in appreciation of the friendly feeling existing between England and the United States, and asked that the Union Jack be floated on a staff beneath the Stars and Stripes. This will be done as soon as a pole suitable for holding both flags can be erected. The ceremony may take place on Saturday but more definite information will be given. Judge White will make the presentation speech. In speaking of the flag, Mr. Northwood said, 'I feel quite certain that this is the first flag sent over from England with the request that it be hung with the American flag, or in fact the first English flag sent over to any American manufactory.' When asked about English friendship for us during the war, he replied that he thought the mere request to hang their flag underneath ours should be sufficient answer. He said that this friendly feeling existed all over England and that every time the United States army or navy won a victory the English hurrahs were mixed with ours" (August 17, 1898).

About a month later, the flagpole had been erected, and a flag-raising ceremony was held at the plant. The *Gazette* (September 7, 1898) had all the splendid details of the occasion:

"An event of unusual occurrence in this country was celebrated down at the glass works when the Union Jack of Old England was floated on the fine 110 foot flagstaff under the American flag last Friday afternoon. The brass band and glee club were present to enliven the occasion with music and a big crowd of people gathered on the scene. After Dr. Walter had offered prayer, Judge Harry White, who was to make the presentation speech, read the following letter sent by English donors of the flag: "To the Northwood Glass Co. and its Employes: Having read of your recent festival on the occasion of raising aloft the flag of your nation it has seemed fitting to a number of residents in this glass district of old England to demonstrate in some practical form the sympathy we have for your ideals and the fellow-feeling we have in your enthusiasm. The visit of Mr. Northwood to his native district had presented a fit opportunity of securing an honored bearer of our gift, which though trifling in cost, is the most precious gift an Englishman can make, namely: The Union Jack of this country. We thereby wish you to feel that in the triumphs, which have always followed your wake, we join with gladness and mingle our hurrahs with yours; while in the sorrows from which no nation is free we would have you feel that you are not alone. There is a patriotism higher than that of nations, namely, the patriotism of race, which by your courage and high purpose in these present days makes everyone of Anglo-Saxon blood thrill and glow with the proud boast of kinship. We express to you all honor for your noble dead, now sleeping 'til the bugle sounds the reveille once more, and all sympathy for the strong, straight march which your nation is now going on for the sake of civilization. We venture to hope that you will raise our flag on the same mast as yours in token on our brotherhood, and we have requested Mr. Northwood to secure the services of his honor, Judge White, to present it to you in our name. Signed:

David Campbell	John H. Bradley
Will Meredith	W. Northwood
Fred Northwood	Leonard Guy
C. M. Attwood	Albert Glaze

"After reading the letter, the judge proceeded with his address. On behalf of the Northwood Company and its employes, John A. Scott, Esq., received the flag and the Stars and Stripes and Union Jack were raised amid great cheering. The English flag is a beauty and the raising of it on the staff with the banner of American liberty furnished occasion for fitting expositions of the relations and destinies of the two great Anglo-Saxon nations."

The eight Englishmen who signed the letter of presentation were related to Harry and Carl Northwood. W. [Will] Northwood was an uncle, and Fred Northwood was a brother. The other six were brothers-in-law, each having married one of the Northwood sisters. Many of these gentlemen and their spouses are pictured later in this book (see p. 145). Thus, a trip begun in sadness with the news of John Northwood's deteriorating sight later marked by two happy occasions — Carl Northwood's marriage and a great patriotic outburst in Indiana upon the Northwoods' return.

The trip to England was a clear indication of the strong ties between the Northwood brothers and the rest of their family. An undated photo, perhaps from Christmas, 1898, shows the six Northwood sisters, posing playfully with a barrel from the Northwood firm.

Success in Ivory Ware: Louis XV et al.

In July, 1898, while Harry and Carl Northwood were in England, the company introduced its new Louis XV line with notices in the trade publications. The July, 1898, issue of *China, Glass and Pottery Review* (*Housefurnisher* was later added to the title of this publication) had the first ad for the Northwood's new line, but the other trade journals were not far behind.

The August 24, 1898, issue of *China, Glass and Lamps* carried a full report of Northwood products past and present, complete with a vivid description of the Louis XV line:

"The Northwood Co., Indiana, Pa., presided over by that resourceful and original glass master, Harry Northwood, always succeeds in giving the trade something different from the old conventional glass patterns. Last year the Alaska and Klondike [sic] patterns led all the rest, and for a time jobbers couldn't be promptly supplied, so

This Northwood family photo (probably by George Woodall; see p. 3) shows Harry and Carl Northwood's sisters. Ina Northwood is at the far left, and Eva Northwood, who had visited the United States in 1890-91, is just above Winifred Northwood, who is at the center of the photo. Amy Northwood is at the upper right, and Mabel Northwood (l.) and Ethel Northwood (r.) are standing in the barrel. Note the writing on the barrel (BRIMFUL OF XMAS GREETINGS) as well as the address on the barrel-head behind the women (see p. 3 for another photo which shows five of the six sisters). **Courtesy of the Fenton Museum, Williamstown, WV.**

great was the demand. This year the productive facilities have been enlarged, and every arrangement has been made to supply the trade promptly. The special pattern this year is one of the richest things ever put on the market in pressed glassware. It is called Louis XV, after the luxurious and courtly king of France, and is made in ivory and gold. The ivory of Harry Northwood is no cheap cryolite or spar mixture, without gloss or polish, but the bright, white and lustrous metal, which in color and polish rivals the genuine ivory of the billiard ball. There is a low relief figure, just a breath, being a combination of Hogarth's graceful lines of beauty, into which a spray of color is thrown, which greatly increases the artistic effect. The edges are gracefully scalloped, and tipped with bright gold. The tiny curved feet, in imitation of sea shells, are in the style of the best English castor place laid on work, and are in gold decoration. The set is a happy combination of the best features of pressed and blown ware, has swing and curvature and is elegantly touched with gold by the decorator's art. The set embraces the spoon, cream, covered butter and sugar, individual salt and pepper, 9 1/2 inch bowl, 5 1/2 inch nappy, tumbler, oil bottle with violet cut stopper, and half gallon jug. Louis XV will prove a leader."

Extensive promotions were undertaken for the new Louis XV pattern line. A full page ad appeared on the front page of *China, Glass and Lamps* for four consecutive issues (September 1, 8, 15 and 22, 1898), and *China, Glass and Pottery Review* (September 1, 1898) said that the Northwood firm "issued a sheet showing their Louis XV pattern in ivory and gold, done in the three-color process, by means of which the article is shown in its exact natural colors." Small

This ad appeared in China, Glass and Lamps *from July 27 to October 17, 1898.*

notices in the September 29, 1898, issue of *China, Glass and Lamps* mention Louis XV in both Ivory and gold and green and gold, so production of the latter can also be linked to this time period at the Northwood plant.

By late November, 1898, *China, Glass and Lamps* (November 24, 1898) reported the Northwood firm was hurriedly "filling orders for 'Friscos holiday trade." *China, Glass and Pottery Review* (December 1, 1898) quoted Harry Northwood. "We are and have been, very busy. Our Louis XV line has been a success. The trouble has been to fill orders in time for the jobbers to distribute the goods for holiday trade."

Although the Louis XV line may have been the most successful Northwood line in decorated Ivory, mention should be made of other patterns. Northwood's Wild Bouquet is a pattern whose dates of origin are not known for certain. Ivory items in Wild Bouquet are rather scarce, but vir-

Ad from China, Glass and Pottery Review, *July, 1898.*

Ad from China, Glass and Pottery Review, *September, 1898.*

tually all are found decorated with a very attractive pink flower and pale green foliage as well as gold rims. The flower has given the pattern name Iris some currency among collectors, but its original manufacturer's name, if any, remains unknown. Heacock was quite interested in some rare Wild Bouquet items in an opaque gray/blue color, which he took pains to explain was not the so-called "blue custard" (H4, p. 29 and PGP, pp. 19-20). The opalescent items in Wild Bouquet (flint, blue, green and, rarely, canary) should probably be credited to Northwood's successors at Indiana, for flint and blue opalescent items are pictured in Butler Brothers catalogs for 1902, indicating a somewhat later time of production. Green opalescent was mentioned in an early 1900 reference to the Northwood's products, however, so this color could date from Northwood's time at the plant.

A few Fluted Scrolls with Flower Band articles

appear in Ivory glass (some collectors call them Jackson). The relationship of these Ivory items to the Klondyke pattern is not known for certain. Fragments from the Indiana site make possible the attribution of these likely Northwood patterns which were made in Ivory: Chrysanthemum Sprig (original name Pagoda; see p. 137); Inverted Fan and Feather (see p. 138); Maple Leaf; and Argonaut Shell (original name Nautilus, see pp. 140-141). The attributions of both Maple Leaf and Inverted Fan and Feather are admittedly speculative, since neither was advertised in the trade press.

Ivory fragments of several other patterns have been unearthed at Indiana: Beaded Circle; Fan; and yet another Maple Leaf line. Although Heacock associated Beaded Circle and "Northwood's" Maple Leaf with the Indiana plant prior to 1900, continuing research indicates that some (if not all) of these patterns should proba-

Photo of Northwood's Louis XV from China, Glass and Pottery Review, *September, 1898.*

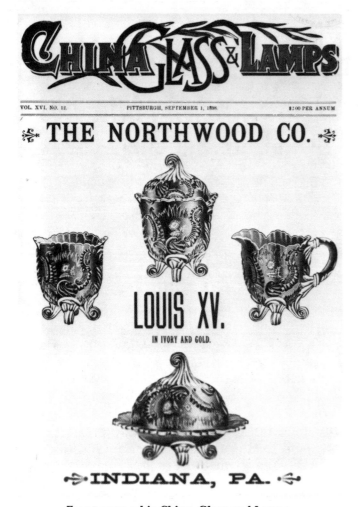

VOL. XVI. NO. 12.   PITTSBURGH, SEPTEMBER 1, 1898. $2.00 PER ANNUM

❧ THE NORTHWOOD CO. ❧

LOUIS XV.

IN IVORY AND GOLD.

❧ INDIANA, PA. ❧

Front page ad in **China, Glass and Lamps.**

bly be credited to Harry Northwood's successors at Indiana: the National Glass Company, 1900-1904, and the Dugan Glass Company, 1904-1913.

Three New Lines for 1899

The November 24, 1898, issue of *China, Glass and Lamps* said that the Northwood plant "is now preparing a set of eye burners for the trade after the holidays," and a modest ad mentioned two new lines, Intaglio and Opaline Brocade. In the December 1, 1898, issue of *China, Glass and Pottery Review*, Harry Northwood was quoted as follows: "We are working away on our new line of pressed ware, which will be called Intaglio, and a new line of blown ware which will be called Opaline Brocade. We think we can promise a better display of glassware than we have ever made for the January exhibit. The Intaglio line will be made in new effects of color, decorated richly with gold .... We shall add to our already large line of lemonade sets and opal novelties, and feel sure we can stop the importations of many goods of this character."

A full page ad in the January 12, 1899, issue of

China, Glass and Lamps mentioned all three new lines — Intaglio, Opaline Brocade and Venetian. The ad, which contained no illustrations, ran for eight consecutive issues, from January 12 through March 2, 1899. A similar ad then appeared on the front page of *China, Glass and Lamps* (March 9, 1899). A small ad in *China, Glass and Pottery Review* mentioned all three lines and illustrated the Intaglio creamer and covered sugar bowl .

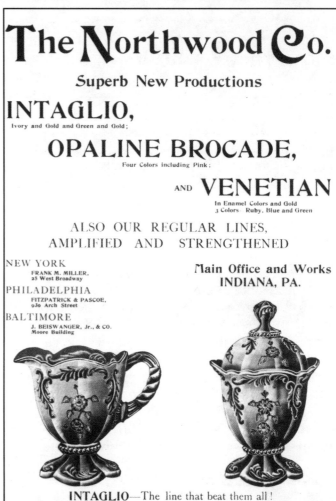

At the outset of this advertising campaign, a writer for *China, Glass and Lamps* (January 12, 1899) visited the Northwood exhibit at the Monongahela House and penned this report:

"Harry Northwood, the glassmaster, is present himself in Room 62, and assisted by a staff of salesmen, has been kept busy showing buyers his handsome new lines. The trade has annually come to look to Northwood for blown and pressed lines of glassware which, in design, finish and conception, are of a higher artistic merit than the ordinary or general run of glassware pattern, and Harry has never disappointed the trade in this respect, and this year is no exception to the rule. This year three original lines are shown, each distinct from the other, which are briefly described as Intaglio, in ivory and gold, and green and gold; Opaline Brocade, in four colors, including pink, and Venetian in enamel colors and gold, and in three colors, ruby, blue and green. As always, these lines are handsomely modeled, and designed especially for light decorative effects. Besides the above new lines, the Northwood is showing the best, most artistic and greatest variety of blown novelties, in colors and color combinations, made by any American firm, and buyers in search of fine goods will make no mistake in looking into Room 62."

By early March, 1899, the three new lines were well-established in the glass tableware trade. The Ivory Intaglio articles differ slightly from Northwood's earlier production of this pressed opaque color, for Intaglio is generally lighter and somewhat thinner than Louis XV. Ivory Intaglio can be found with either green/gold or blue/gold decoration, both of which were offered in an 1899 Pitkin and Brooks catalog. Northwood also advertised Intaglio in "green and gold," and these attractive items are found today in transparent emerald green. Intaglio articles are also known in blue opalescent, but these may well have been made somewhat later, under the auspices of the National Glass Company and/or the Dugan Glass Company, after Harry Northwood was no longer associated with the firm. Intaglio items appear in Pitkin and Brooks catalogs from both 1899 and 1900, along with articles in Opaline Brocade and Venetian.

Opaline Brocade, which is popularly known today as Spanish Lace, is an extensive blown line, judging from articles in collections today. Opaline Brocade opalescent items are known in crystal, blue, canary, cranberry and green, but Northwood's advertising mentioned only "four

Ad from China, Glass and Pottery Review, *December, 1898.*

colors" and identified just one, "pink," the usual term for cranberry or ruby opalescent. A Pitkin and Brooks catalog from 1899 lists "Brocade Pattern" in four opalescent colors (crystal, blue, canary and ruby), so the green opalescent production may not be from the Northwood era in Indiana (no fragments in green opalescent have come from the factory site).

Photo of Northwood's display at the January, 1899, exhibit at the Monongahela House. Intaglio items are clearly visible on the right, and some Louis XV articles are on the left.

TEN AND FIFTEEN CENT COUNTER GOODS.

Original Assortment.

◇ **10 and 15.** ◇

Sell three dozen at 10c each, three dozen at 15c each; you receive $9.00 for the assortment which we sell you at $6.00

½ doz. 563 Card Receivers Asst.
½ doz. 563 Vases Asst.
½ doz. 562 Rose Bowls Asst.
½ doz. 565 Candlesticks Asst.
½ doz. 562 Vases Asst.
½ doz. 566 Pumps Asst.
½ doz. 567 Troughs Asst.
½ doz. 521 Vases Asst.
½ doz. 561 Vases Asst.
½ doz. Klondyke Card Receivers Asst.
½ doz. Brocade Rose Bowls Asst.
½ doz. Brocade Celeries Asst.

6 doz. for 83⅓c doz., $5.00 net.

Sold only in this assortment. Each item assorted ⅙ doz. each, of three colors: Flint Opal, Blue Opal and Canary Opal.

SCALE ONE-THIRD

NO. 565. CANDLESTICK.
Height 6¾ inches.

NO. 562. ROSE BOWL
Height 5½ inches.

BROCADE ROSE BOWL.
Width 4½ inches.

The three pieces not shown we guarantee to be equal to ones illustrated.

NO. 562. VASE.
Height, 6¾ inches.

NO. 566. PUMP.
Height 6½ inches.

NO. 567. TROUCH.
Length 5 inches.

KLONDYKE CARD RECEIVER
Width 7¾ inches.

BROCADE TALL CELERY.
Height 6½ inches.

NO. 563. CARD RECEIVER.
Width 6¾ inches.

31

Courtesy of Nancy and Bill Sheriff.

Two Opaline Brocade items are pictured as part of the "10 and 15" assortment in Pitkin and Brooks 1900 catalog, and the other articles shown there are also Northwood products. Each was offered in "Flint Opal, Blue Opal and Canary Opal." The Klondyke card receiver is a novelty made from the spooner mould of the popular pattern which had been introduced several years earlier. The No. 562 rose bowl (called Opal Open in H2) is familiar to collectors of opalescent glass, but it seems curious that the plain vase with ruffled top bears the same 562 designation. The No. 562 rose bowl may also be cupped into an hourglass shape, making an attractive vase. The No. 562 vase, which Heacock once called Lorna (H2, p. 87) may have the top finished as shown in the catalog or in a triangle-shaped crimped edge; a similar article was made at the Model Flint Glass Co. The Dolphin candlestick and the similar card receiver are well-known (see H2, p. 79), and the No. 566 and 567 Pump and Trough combination is already famous. The listing of these opalescent

items in a 1900 catalog, particularly with the Opaline Brocade and Klondyke patterns, is strong evidence that all were in production during Harry Northwood's tenure at the Indiana plant.

The Venetian line, earlier called Utopia Optic by Heacock (H6, p. 11), features delicate enamel floral and geometric decorations as well as gold bands on some pieces. Items can be found in three transparent colors — blue, green and ruby — although the latter is quite hard to find. Only green and ruby are mentioned in a 1900 Pitkin and Brooks catalog, so the blue could be later production by Northwood's successors.

The four-piece table set and a few other pieces are also known in decorated opal, featuring gold bands and a scenic decoration. The outdoor scene, which is done mostly in brown tones, includes a lake and sailboat as well as trees and birds. An assortment of these pieces, dubbed "Landscape Glass Assortment," appeared in Montgomery Ward's catalog No. 62 (Fall-Winter, 1897-98). This pre-dates the introduction of

Venetian by over a year, so the decorated opal pieces may have proven unsuccessful, although the moulds were later used for the characteristic transparent colors in the Venetian line.

Landscape Glass Assortment.

55137 Made of white opal glass decorated with gold lines and each piece with a beautiful landscape scene executed artistically in bright effective colors. All the pieces are very shapely and full size. The price is at least one-half less than we have ever offered similar value; sold only in the well selected assortment. We can not break packages under any consideration. Set consists of the following pieces: One covered butter dish, one covered sugar bowl, one cream pitcher, one spoon holder, one ½ gallon water pitcher, twelve ½ pint tumblers, one syrup pitcher, one vinegar bottle, three salt shakers, three pepper shakers, one tall celery holder. Price securely packed for shipment... $4.95

Courtesy of the University of Wyoming's American Heritage Center.

The unusual twig finial on the sugar bowl and butterdish is similar to that used on the Opaline Brocade pattern, and the shapes of Venetian articles generally resemble their counterparts in Opaline Brocade. Apparently, the Venetian line

may have been known also as pattern No. 225, for it is so designated in a 1900 Pitkin and Brooks catalog. In this same catalog, the Venetian syrup is shown in "Decorated 57" and offered in crystal, blue and green. This indicates that more than one decorating motif may have been available on this pattern.

Thus, by early 1899, the Northwood's reputation for high-quality, readily-salable glass tableware was even more firmly established. The Indiana County *Gazette* (March 1, 1899), under the headline "A GREAT GLASS INDUSTRY," reported on the status quo at the local plant:

"Without doubt the busiest place in Indiana county is down at the Northwood glass works. The growth of the company's business during the last two years has been marvelous, and it has been necessary to enlarge the plant frequently, so that now the buildings cover at least a third more ground, besides the addition of two tanks in the factory proper for the making of glass.

"The goods made by the Northwood company are of such quality and so unique in design that they are in great demand all over the country. The orders come in so fast since the beginning of the year, that it has been necessary to call in one of the travelling salesmen. During the annual display by the different manufacturers at Pittsburg in January the display of the Northwood company was generally conceded to be the best. While, of course, there were displays of higher priced glass, none on exhibition so satisfied the wants of the people in general as the wares made by the Northwood company. This has been demonstrated by the large orders taken at the exhibition. Over 300 people are employed at the factory, and every two weeks the payroll amounts to about $4,500. Most of the labor comes from Indiana, only the heads of the different departments and the expert glass makers having come from other places.

"Since the first of January the daily shipments have averaged about 125 barrels. Monday's mail alone brought in orders for 350 barrels" (a report based on this *Gazette* story appeared in the March 16, 1899, issue of *China, Glass and Lamps*).

In early March, 1899, Carl Northwood became an American citizen. He had made his declaration of intention some five years earlier, when he was associated with the Northwood firm at Ellwood City (see p. 92). On March 9, 1899, Northwood and his two witnesses, Franklin Sansom and J. C. McGregor, appeared before the Indiana County Prothonotary, and Carl Northwood took the oath of citizenship.

PITKIN AND BROOKS

18

SCALE ONE-THIRD

INTAGLIO PATTERN

ASSORTMENT

INTAGLIO GREEN, REG.

Body is of ivory color, light, something new and very handsome. The rococo raised work is decorated in a beautiful shade of green, with cluster of flowers and leaves decorated in coin gold. Gold decoration is also put on upper and lower edges and all handles, knobs, etc.

ASSORTMENT

INTAGLIO BLUE, REG.

Same description as remarks to left, only raised work is decorated in a delicate shade of blue

Shapes are EXQUISITE

INTAGLIO SUGAR

INTAGLIO CREAM

INTAGLIO SPOON

INTAGLIO COVERED BUTTER

INTAGLIO FOUR-PIECE SET

INTAGLIO GREEN, REG.

INTAGLIO, IVORY, GREEN AND GOLD DECORATED

1/3 Doz.	Set	$17.00	$5.67
1/4 "	Jugs, 1/2 gallon	8.50	2.13
1 1/2 "	Tumblers	1.65	2.48
1-12 "	Berry Comports, 7 inch	7.00	.58
1-12 "	" " 8 inch	8.00	.68
1 "	" Nappies, 5 inch, Footed	2.25	2.25
1-6 "	Oil Bottles	3.00	.50
1/2 "	Shaker Salts, S. P. T	1.50	.75
1/2 "	" Peppers, S. P. T	1.50	.75
1-6 "	Footed Jellies	3.75	.63
			$16.42
	Less 10 per cent		1.64
			$14.78

INTAGLIO BLUE, REG.

INTAGLIO, IVORY, BLUE AND GOLD DECORATED

1/3 Doz.	Set	$17.00	$5.67
1/4 "	Jugs, 1/2 gallon	8.50	2.13
1 1/2 "	Tumblers	1.65	2.48
1-12 "	Berry Comports, 7 inch	7.00	.58
1-12 "	" " 8 inch	8.00	.68
1 "	" Nappies, 5 inch, Footed	2.25	2.25
1-6 "	Oil Bottles	3.00	.50
1-2 "	Shaker Salts, S. P. T	1.50	.75
1-2 "	" Peppers, S. P. T	1.50	.75
1-6 "	Footed Jellies	3.75	.65
			$16.42
	Less 10 per cent		1.64
			$14.78

ASSORTMENT

INTAGLIO GREEN BODY

Body is of green glass, with flowers, leaves, upper and lower edges decorated in coin gold

INTAGLIO GREEN BODY

INTAGLIO, GREEN BODY, GOLD DECORATED

1/3 Doz.	Sets	$14.00	$4.67
1/4 "	Jugs, 1-2 gallon	7.25	1.81
1 1/2 "	Tumblers	1.50	2.25
1-12 "	Berry Comports, 7 inch	6.75	.56
1/6 "	" " 8 inch	7.50	1.25
1 1/2 "	" " 5 inch	2.00	3.00
1/6 "	Oil Bottles	2.75	.46
1-2 "	Salts, S. P. T	1.35	.67
1-2 "	Peppers, S. P. T.	1.35	.66
1/6 "	Footed Jellies, 5 inch	3.25	.54
			$15.87
	Less 10 per cent		1.59
			$14.28

Courtesy of Nancy and Bill Sheriff.

PITKIN AND BROOKS

SCALE ONE-THIRD

17

BROCADE PATTERN

Body of Glass is either Crystal, Blue, Canary or Ruby, with raised figure work in opalescent. Medium weight.

BROCADE COVERED BUTTER

BROCADE CREAM

BROCADE SPOON

BROCADE SUGAR

Brocade Four-Piece Set

Original Assortment — BROCADE — Package Glassware

CRYSTAL OPAL

1/2 Doz.	Sets	$10.00	$0.83
1/2 "	Jugs, 1/2 Gallon	5.00	.42
1/2 "	Tumblers	.85	.43
1/2 "	Large Berry Nappies	3.75	.31
1/2 "	Small Berry Nappies	1.35	.67
1/2 "	Oil Bottles	2.25	.19
1/2 "	Molasses Cans	2.00	.17
1/4 "	Shaker Salts	.75	.19
1/4 "	" Peppers	.75	.19
1/2 "	Rose Bowls	1.25	.10

BLUE OPAL

1/2 Doz.	Sets	$10.00	$0.83
1/2 "	Jugs, 1/2 Gallon	5.00	.42
1/2 "	Tumblers	.85	.43
1/2 "	Large Berry Nappies	3.75	.31
1/2 "	Small Berry Nappies	1.35	.67
1/2 "	Oil Bottles	2.25	.19
1/2 "	Molasses Cans	2.00	.17
1/4 "	Shaker Salts	.75	.19
1/4 "	" Peppers	.75	.19
1/2 "	Rose Bowls	1.25	.10
1/2 "	Celeries	1.35	.11

CANARY OPAL

1/2 Doz.	Sets	$12.00	$1.00
1/2 "	Jugs, 1/2 Gallon	6.00	.50
1/2 "	Tumblers	1.00	.50

RUBY OPAL

1/2 Doz.	Sets	$13.50	$1.13
1/2 "	Jugs, 1/2 Gallon	6.50	.54
1/2 "	Tumblers	1.25	.63
1/2 "	Large Berry Nappies	5.00	.42
1/2 "	Small Berry Nappies	2.00	1.00
1/2 "	Oil Bottles	3.50	.29
1/2 "	Molasses Cans	3.50	.29
1/4 "	Shaker Salts	1.00	.25
1/4 "	" Peppers	1.00	.25
1/2 "	Rose Bowls	1.75	.15
1/2 "	Celeries	2.00	.17
			$14.23
	Less 10 per cent		1.42
			$12.81

SOLD ONLY IN THIS ASSORTMENT

NOTICE PRICES ARE LOW, COST OF PACKAGE VERY LITTLE AND ASSORTMENT VERY GREAT.

BROCADE TUMBLER

BROCADE OIL

BROCADE SMALL NAPPY

BROCADE MOLASSES CAN

Courtesy of Nancy and Bill Sheriff.

VENETIAN PATTERN

Body of glass, either Green or Ruby, richly decorated with flowers, leaves, etc. in bright colors. Also with gold bands as shown in cuts.

SCALE ONE-THIRD

VENETIAN COVERED BUTTER

VENETIAN SPOON

VENETIAN CREAM

VENETIAN SUGAR

VENETIAN TUMBLER

Pieces not Illustrated we Guarantee will be Satisfactory in every way

VENETIAN SMALL NAPPY

VENETIAN LARGE NAPPY

HIGH-GRADE GOODS AT A VERY LOW PRICE

VENETIAN MOLASSES CAN

Venetian Four-Piece Set

ORIGINAL ASSORTED PACKAGE — VENETIAN — FANCY GLASSWARE

GREEN

RUBY

Less 10 per cent.

Sold only in this assortment.........

Courtesy of Nancy and Bill Sheriff.

Harry's Last Hurrah: Pagoda

In late June, 1899, the Northwood plant added yet another line to its already impressive array of Ivory glassware. The new line was called Pagoda, but collectors today will be surprised to learn that this is the now familiar Chrysanthemum Sprig pattern. The June 29, 1899, issue of *China, Glass and Lamps* said the glassware "is attracting general attention and is being welcomed as one of the most artistic creations in tableware offered for years." A month or so later, incoming orders for the decorated Ivory ware necessitated enlarging the decorating department at the Northwood plant (*China, Glass and Lamps*, July 20, 1899). No illustrated ads for Pagoda appeared.

Near the focal point of the Pagoda ads is a stylized, cursive Northwood signature, identical to that used on the outside base of many pieces in the Chrysanthemum Sprig pattern (and, later, on the Nautilus line). At least some record of Pagoda's success in the glassware market exists, albeit an exaggerated one. *China, Glass and Lamps* (August 3, 1899) carried this report: "Frank M.

Miller, the well known New York glass salesman, reports that all the glass men on Manhattan Island, regardless of creed or religious views, are bowing down in hatless admiration of Harry Northwood's new Pagoda line."

The most important bit of evidence regarding Northwood's Pagoda comes from the Bawo and Dotter *Bulletin* for September 1, 1899, well within Harry Northwood's time at the Indiana plant: "Frank M. Miller, the New York representative of this firm, showed us a new line of table glassware this week that is handsome as well as novel. The general appearance, shape and decoration is Chinese and the term Pagoda is aptly applied. The whole gamut of table requisites in glass is run except stem ware, and is shown in two colors, ivory and turquoise, with raised gold decorations. It is the best line the Northwood people have ever produced" (this quote from the *Bulletin* was first found in the files of J. Stanley Brothers, Jr., at the Rakow Library in the Corning Museum of Glass).

The use of the Northwood script signature in advertising, coupled with the above information

Ad from July 27, 1899 issue of China, Glass and Lamps.

about the colors Ivory and turquoise, makes clear that Pagoda is indeed Chrysanthemum Sprig. This Ivory (custard) pattern is very well-known by collectors, and the turquoise items (often, but mistakenly, called blue custard) are much sought after.

At some point in his research, William Heacock thought that Pagoda might be the pattern called Inverted Fan and Feather (see H9, p. 12). The Inverted Fan and Feather pieces are not marked with the Northwood script signature, however, although some salt shakers have been seen with "Northwood" in reverse block letters on the underside (see p. 85). A blue opalescent Coinspot syrup jug made in the Nine Panel mould bears this same block letter mark (CG3, p. 41). The Ivory glass Inverted Fan and Feather line was, in all likelihood, made while Harry Northwood was still at Indiana, for the general design elements, the Ivory color and the gold decor are typically Northwood. There is no doubt that the Inverted Fan and Feather pattern was made at Indiana, of course, for many fragments have been unearthed. Heacock's delight in a single fragment in opaque green (H4, p. 17) was heightened in December, 1987, when a collector provided a photo of an

Inverted Fan and Feather salt shaker.

138

opaque green Inverted Fan and Feather covered sugar bowl.

Opalescent blue Inverted Fan and Feather items are shown in Butler Brothers catalogs during 1907, so they were likely made about that time, well after the National Glass Company had sold the plant to the Dugan interests in 1904. The so-called "pink slag" items in Inverted Fan and Feather are not as easy to date. There is no clear record that Harry Northwood made this unique opaque ware while he was at Indiana. As later research will show, this color was probably produced while the Northwood plant was under the control of the National Glass Company and Northwood's cousin, Thomas E. A. Dugan, was manager.

Northwood Joins the National Glass Company

The formation of the United States Glass Company in 1891 brought together many of the major glass tableware manufacturers in America. In spite of the decision to run the plants with non-union labor, which precipitated a lengthy strike by AFGWU members, the United States Glass Company was able to compete successfully with other glass tableware plants, all of which were independently owned. From time to time, rumors surfaced that some important firms, including Harry Northwood's, would join forces via agreements or mergers. One such coalition, comprised of glass tableware plants in the Wheeling area, was proposed in 1892, but the independent entrepreneurs preferred to go their separate ways.

In the late 1890s, competitive pressures and a lessening of demand for glass tableware created hard times for many plants. Talk of combines and mergers began anew, and a meeting of many tableware manufacturers took place in Pittsburgh in late August, 1898. In a long story, *Crockery and Glass Journal* (September 1, 1898) mentioned the need to advance selling prices as well as "petty jealousies, price cutting, and a general want of harmonious relations among the manufacturers [which] had completely demoralized the market and their industry." Over the next several months, the glass tableware manufacturers considered the formation of a giant combine or cartel which would have embraced most of the plants then in operation, including all of the factories controlled by the United States Glass Company. This plan collapsed, but nineteen factories joined together in November, 1899, to form the National Glass Company, which had its headquarters in Pittsburgh.

In August, 1899, the citizens of Indiana, Pa., were greatly concerned about the fate of the Northwood plant when that firm contemplated joining the National Glass Company. The *Gazette* (August 23, 1899) sought to allay fears in a story which quoted Harry Northwood frequently:

"Though the matter is not as yet settled, there is no question but that the transfer will be made by the middle of September" was the statement made by Harry Northwood yesterday, to a *GAZETTE* reporter in answer to a question regarding the rumor that the Northwood company was considering the advisability of selling out its big glass works, at this place, to a trust, controlling the manufacture of table glass ware. The rumor has gained wide circulation and is the subject of much comment and speculation.

"When approached about the matter Mr. Northwood stated that the advisability of selling to the National Glass Company had been under consideration for some time, and that four different committees had already been to Indiana to look over the plant, but he had given no option.

"Mr. Northwood claims that the National Glass Company could scarcely be called a trust, but is rather a corporation of glass manufacturers having in view the bettering of the general condition of tableware makers. The corporation at present consists of several of the leading table ware factories in Pennsylvania, Ohio and Indiana, but their object is to get a combination of 85 per cent. of the factories engaged in making table ware, so as to control the prices.

"Mr. Northwood claims that the National Glass Co. has no intention to close any of the works over which it gains control, or to make any change in the management, except where incompetency is manifested. Under an agreement which Mr. Northwood made with the Indiana Board of Trade, it will be necessary to run the plant for the next two years, in order that a clear title can be made for the property. In the event of the National Company buying the plant, the conditions of this agreement must be fulfilled, or it will be impossible for the corporation to get a title for the plant, as the agreement is in the form of a mortgage, which does not run out until the contract has been complied with."

Several of the reports regarding the absorption of the Northwood plant into the National Glass Company predicted that Harry Northwood would soon return to England. The *Gazette*'s (August 23, 1899) first report was straightforward: "Should the Northwood Co. merge into the National Glass Co. in all probability the Northwoods will return to England and engage in the business there." In a later article, the *Gazette* was more cautious: "... dame rumor has it that Mr. Northwood will be given charge of the London office." The trade publication *China, Glass and Lamps* (September 14, 1899) also said that "Harry Northwood, the well known Indiana glass master, whose works have been absorbed by the National Glass Co., is likely to accept the London, Eng., sales agency of the company."

On September 6, 1899, the *Gazette* reported that the Northwood firm had decided to join the National Glass Company and that "the plant will be run, as at present, for the next two years." These time constraints probably reflect an earlier agreement under which Northwood acquired the plant in 1898, pledging to run it for several years. There is no agreement to be found in the Indiana County records, but the deed transferring the Northwood plant's real estate to the National Glass Company from Thomas Dugan and his wife Anne and Harry and Clara Northwood was executed on September 4, 1899, although it was not filed at the recorder's office until November 7, 1899 (Indiana County Deeds, vol. B82, p. 354).

By mid-October, 1899, it was clear that Northwood would return to England. According to the October 19, 1899, issue of *China, Glass and Lamps*, the Northwoods booked passage on the steamship Shamrock. Just before they left Indiana, a surprise party was held to honor them. The *Gazette* (November 29, 1899) had the details: "On Saturday the employes of the Northwood glass factory presented Harry Northwood, their former employer, with a fine silver loving cup. Carl Northwood was also presented with a fine gold-headed cane. The presentation speech was made by George Pownall. Both of the Northwoods were kept in ignorance regarding the presents and their surprise was complete. The Northwoods will leave with their families on Thursday evening, and will sail for England from New York on Saturday" (a similar report also appeared in *China, Glass and Lamps*, November 30, 1899).

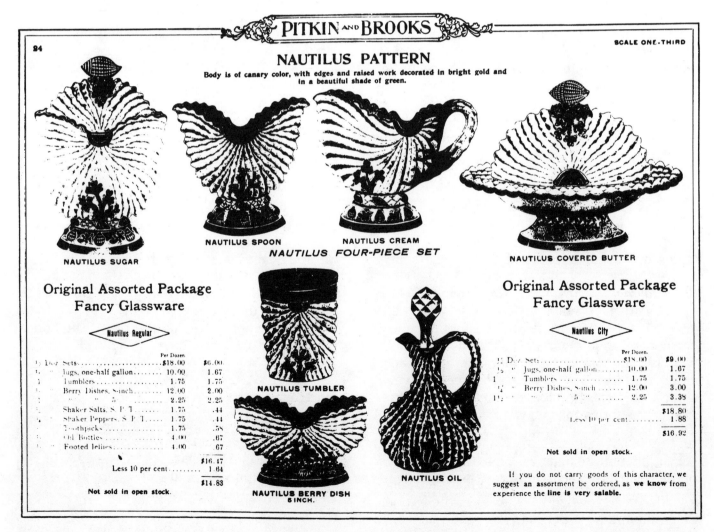

Courtesy of Nancy and Bill Sheriff.

The National's Northwood Lines

The November 8, 1899, issue of the Indiana County *Gazette* said that the "business of the plant will be conducted as heretofore, there being no change except in the ownership." A new manager, Harry Bastow, was mentioned, and the *Gazette* noted that "George Mortimer will be retained as the traveling salesman...." Although Harry Northwood was not connected with the National's manufacturing operation at Indiana, Pa., the plant was officially called the Northwood Glass Works of the National Glass Company. During the summer and fall of 1899, before it was certain that the plant would be sold to the National, Harry Northwood and his colleagues were working on new pattern lines for the 1899-1900 season. The Pagoda line, which had been introduced in June, 1899, was a Northwood creation, of course, and it probably continued to sell under the aegis of the National Glass Company. In January, 1900, a full-page ad for the National which extolled the virtues of the individual factories contained this line: "Ivory ware, fancy water and table sets — the production of the Northwood works is unequalled" (*Crockery and Glass Journal*, January 4, 1900). A week later, *Crockery and Glass Journal* mentioned "Northwood's new decorated opal" at the National Glass Company's showroom.

Instead of mounting a separate exhibit at the January, 1900, Monongahela House show, the National Glass Company conducted business from its showroom at Liberty Avenue and Eighth Street in Pittsburgh. In a long article, *Crockery and Glass Journal* (January 18, 1900) detailed some 18 new lines offered by the National's factories, including the Indiana, Pa., plant: "The Northwood has one new line and several new creations in pieces and sets. This factory's ware is all opalescent and opal, and is very artistic, dainty, delicate and ornamental. The opalescent is in a number of elegant tints — pink, canary, green, blue, etc. — and is more or less engraved. The "Nautilus" opal possesses striking beauty in its shapes and decorations."

The Nautilus pattern is known today as Argonaut Shell (H4, pp. 16-17, 27), and most Ivory pieces bear the distinctive Northwood script signature. A 1900 Pitkin and Brooks catalog illustrates seven different items and offers two assortments of this relatively expensive glassware. Although the pattern was first marketed shortly after Harry Northwood left the plant, there is little doubt that he was responsible for it. The Ivory color, the design and the added green and gold decoration were inspired by a large Worcester china vase which remains in the Northwood family today.

Miss Elizabeth Robb remembers her grandmother relating that Harry Northwood returned from England with the Worcester vase, vowing that he would re-create it in glass. A "Z" in the mark on the underside dates it to 1888 (see *Kovel's New Dictionary of Marks*, p. 254). Exactly when Northwood brought the vase to the United States is uncertain, since he made numerous trips. The opalescent Nautilus articles, which will also be discussed in the forthcoming Dugan/Diamond book, may date from 1900 or shortly thereafter, but the carnival glass items made later are definitely beyond the Northwood era at the Indiana plant.

Another pattern shown in the 1900 Pitkin and Brooks catalog warrants discussion here, because there has been considerable controversy over its place of manufacture. Heacock first attributed the Geneva pattern to Northwood (H3, p. 25), but later had doubts (H4, p. 32) and finally concluded that McKee made it (H6, pp. 28, 66), based upon a 1901 National Glass Company catalog from the McKee Works. Geneva is also shown in a 1900 Pitkin and Brooks catalog, including one page where it appears with Intaglio, a Northwood pattern introduced early in 1899. Interestingly, Intaglio is described as "ivory," while "canary" is used for Geneva. The term canary also appeared in a 1901 Montgomery Ward catalog (Kamm 6, plate 6), but there is no doubt that it referred to an opaque glass. Many collectors have noted that Geneva is not the same color as Northwood's other Ivory lines — Louis XV, Intaglio, Pagoda, or Nautilus — but the separate terms ivory and canary may be an acknowledgment of this difference at the time the glassware was being produced.

The illustrations of Geneva in two separate catalogs from 1900-1901, each with a somewhat different description as noted below, suggests at least the possibility that Northwood could have made the pattern first. The difficulty involved in moving moulds from Northwood to the McKee plant at Jeannette, making and decorating the glass at McKee, and getting the wares distributed to two independent wholesalers who were able to prepare their own catalogs with illustrations — all after Northwood's Indiana plant was sold to the National late in 1899 and in time for early 1900 catalogs to be issued — would have been considerable.

In the 1900 Pitkin and Brooks catalog, Geneva is described as "Fans decorated in Shaded Green

Worcester china vase and Ivory glass Nautilus spooner. **Courtesy of Miss Robb and the Ogelbay Institute, Wheeling, WV.**

and Knobs and Feet in Bright Gold." Most Geneva in collections today has red and green decor on the fans and lacks gold on the feet and knobs (see page 87; compare the tumblers in the top row). These differences, and the placement of Geneva on the same catalog page with Northwood's Intaglio, suggest the possibility that Geneva was made first at Northwood ca. 1899, as well as somewhat later at McKee. The lack of any advertising or trade journal notes for the pattern is a mystery, to be sure, but the absorption of the Northwood plant into the National Glass Company may account for this.

Geneva certainly bears at least some resemblance to other Northwood patterns. The feet bring to mind both Klondyke and Louis XV, and the scroll-like designs on the body of the pieces are reminiscent of Louis XV. Perhaps Northwood initiated the Geneva pattern with the green/gold decoration described by Pitkin and Brooks; Heacock mentions that Geneva with "fire[d] on green with gold" is "quite hard to find" (H4, p. 32).

Geneva cruet with green and gold decoration (compare with p. 87). **Courtesy of Larry Loxterman.**

142

Courtesy of Nancy and Bill Sheriff.

Courtesy of Nancy and Bill Sheriff.

After both the Northwood and McKee firms had become members of the National Glass Company, Geneva moulds could have been moved from the Northwood works to McKee in Jeannette, Pa. When they revived the pattern, McKee's approach to decoration was somewhat different, using the red/green and dropping the gold. The same National Glass Company/McKee Works catalog which shows Geneva also illustrates Croesus, a pattern definitely initiated by the Riverside Glass Company of Wellsburg, West Virginia, in 1898. The 1901 Montgomery Ward catalogue (Kamm 6, plate 6) shows Geneva with red/green decor, and McKee's new Prize pattern, which was introduced in early 1901, appears on the same page.

The London Office

The National Glass Company's London office was, in reality, a showroom-sales outlet through which the company sought to expand its export trade. The idea was simple enough: have a permanent representative in London who functioned like the manufacturers' representatives in the United States, displaying the various lines and novelties, as well as taking orders for fulfillment by the factories. A key difference, of course, was that the showroom was managed by a National Glass Company employee, Harry Northwood, rather than by an independent businessman who reaped a percentage of sales from all the factories represented in his showroom and might, consequently, give preference to one firm's wares at the expense of another's. The National Glass Company may have felt that Harry Northwood's English birth was an asset, but the company's creation of the London post was probably on the order of a sinecure, for it would both keep Northwood out of the glass manufacturing business and garner whatever overseas trade could be had through the London showroom.

Despite the earlier reports of Northwood's eagerness to return to England, there is some evidence to suggest that Harry Northwood was a bit restive after about three months in England. *China, Glass and Lamps* (May 3, 1900) carried this report: "We are in receipt of a letter from our old friend Harry Northwood under date of April 2. He is, as our readers know, general agent for the sales of the National Glass Co.'s wares in London. He is getting along all right there, but still, though an Englishman and "to the manor born," would prefer to live in this country and draws a comparison between it and his native land not at all flattering to the latter. He desires to be remembered to all the "boys" in the glass trade and thinks it

not impossible that he may pay a short visit to Pittsburgh during the ensuing summer." The May 1, 1900, issue of a British trade publication, The *Pottery Gazette and Glass Trade Review*, carried a lengthy article devoted to the National Glass Company's London office. The writer's description of the glassware is punctuated by editorializing on a number of trade-related issues:

"The National Glass Company, Pittsburgh, Pa., U.S.A., have established a London agency at Bath House, 57, Holborn-viaduct, E. C., where they are represented by Mr. H. Northwood, assisted by his brother. The name of Northwood is familiar to most people in the glass trade on both sides of the Atlantic. The brothers were the founders of the Northwood Glass Works, Indiana, Pa. (one of the companies taken over by the National Glass Company), and are well known in the American trade, while their father, Mr. John Northwood, who now has the direction of the artistic work of Messrs. Stevens & Williams, Brierley Hill, is known the world over as the man "who reproduced the Portland vase in glass." The National Glass Company have extensive and well-arranged showrooms on Holborn-viaduct, and we confess to a feeling of considerable regret when we saw the really fine display of good pressed and blown table glassware they are making. Our regret was occasioned by the knowledge, which we happen to have, that the influx of foreign (American and Continental) pressed glassware on our home market has been encouraged by, if it is not the direct result of, the stupid policy of our glass workers. United action of workers, when wisely directed on sound lines, is not only advantageous, but has been necessary. Labourers have obtained many just concessions by concerted action which would long have been refused to individual effort. But when a few men make a mistake, and thousands of men "unite" to support them in it, the evil is intensified. At one time we had the moulded and pressed glass trade practically in our own hands. The men were doing well, and wanted to do better. There was no harm in that. But when they sought to improve their individual takings at the expense of the trade from which they derived them, they emulated the Greek countryman who "killed the goose that laid the golden eggs." When the men's unions insisted upon restrictions that were detrimental to the interests of the trade, and demanded, and obtained, wages that were not justified by the market, they certainly secured better wages for their members, but they diverted to other countries the demand for the goods from the production of which those

This photo of the Northwood Family was taken at the home of John Northwood I in Brierley Hill in 1900. Courtesy of Miss Robb.

All rows, read left to right.

back row: Charles Attwood; Clarence Northwood (son of Clara Elizabeth and Harry Northwood); Jack Bradley; Dave Campbell.

3rd row: Louise "Louie" Northwood (Fred Northwood's wife); Fred Northwood; Carl Northwood; Rose Overton Northwood (wife of Carl); Winifred Northwood Meredith; Mabel "May" Northwood Bradley; John Northwood I; Will Meredith; Lennie Guy (later married Ethel Northwood).

2nd row: Ina Northwood Attwood; Clara Elizabeth Beaumont Northwood; Elizabeth Duggin Northwood; Eva Northwood Campbell; Ethel Northwood; Harry Northwood.

front row: Elsie Northwood (daughter of Fred and Louise Northwood); Allie Northwood (daughter of Fred and Louise Northwood); Mabel Virginia Northwood (daughter of Clara Elizabeth and Harry Northwood); Marie Northwood (daughter of Fred and Louise Northwood).

wages were derived. We do not like this importation of foreign goods in the place of goods that could be made here, but it is impossible to prevent it, and it would not be desirable if it was possible. We have more glass consumers than glass makers, and the majority must be considered. Perhaps it is not too late to hope that the competition of foreign manufacturers will revive the intelligence of our workmen, so that, with the improved facilities now available, a strong effort may yet be made to restore our pressed-glass trade to something like its former position. The National Glass Company, however, have given them something to do. It is no experimental business that Mr. Northwood is exploiting in this country. The National Glass Company is a combination of nineteen of the largest factories in America, producing pressed and blown table ware (decanters, tumblers, and wines), licensed victuallers' supplies, lamps, founts, and chimneys, confectioners' novelties, stationers' sundries, and, in fact, moulded and blown glass for all purposes. We do not remember to have ever before seen such an extensive display of pressed glass goods. In one room we have specimens of the leading specialties of nineteen factories that until recently were operated independently, so that to have seen such a variety, we should have had to visit nineteen separate showrooms. It must, however, be mentioned that Mr. Northwood is not representing nineteen firms now. Each factory continues to produce its own goods, as heretofore, but they are distributed together from the company's central depot at Pittsburgh. Importers can therefore have an assortment from each of the factories in one consignment. Every grade of pressed glass is represented in this collection from the very cheapest to the very best."

Harry Northwood in Repose

Thus, Harry Northwood seemed resolved to represent the National Glass Company in his native land. One fine day in 1900, many members of the Northwood clan and their spouses gathered in the home of John and Elizabeth Northwood at Brierley Hill. Later, they assembled outside, and, after a photographer arranged them with some semblance of symmetry, a group portrait was taken. The seated Harry Northwood, now about 40, looks relaxed and at ease, but, less than a year after this photo was taken, he would once again be making his presence felt in American glassmaking circles. (To be continued in *Harry Northwood: The Wheeling Years*).

BIBLIOGRAPHY

American Flint Glass Workers Union, archives and photos, Toledo, OH.

American Glass Worker, various issues, 1885-1886.

Baker, Gary Everett. "Hobbs, Brockunier & Co.'s Glass Factory Burned," *The Glass Club Bulletin*, Fall, 1987, pp. 14-16.

Belmont County, OH. Public records, including deeds, leases/agreements, lawsuits in Common Pleas and appellate courts, birth records, and records of naturalized citizens.

Boultinghouse, Mark. *Art and Colored Glass Toothpick Holders*. N.p.: n.d.

Brahmer, Bonnie J. *Custard Glass*, second ed. N. p.: by author, 1967.

Bruce, Carole and Bob. "The Other "Cactus" Pattern," *The Pioneer* (published by the Antique and Art Glass Salt Shaker Collector's Society), June, 1988, pp. 2-3.

Callin's Wheeling Directory, various issues, 1881-1888.

Cambridge Glass Co., *1903 Catalog of Pressed and Blown Glass Ware*. (reprinted by NCC, Inc., 1976).

Charleston, R. J. *English Glass*. London: Allen and Unwin, 1984.

China, Glass and Lamps, various issues, 1890-1901.

Crockery and Glass Journal, various issues, 1882-1901.

DiBartolomeo, Robert E. "19th Century Eastern, Ohio Glass Factories," *Spinning Wheel*, October, 1971, pp. 16-19; November, 1971, pp. 24-28; March, 1972, pp. 22-26, 62.

Dugan, Blanche Mock [Marshall]. "Samuel Dugan family history" (handwritten, 1960).

Dugan, Blanche Mock [Marshall]. Interview with Jabe Tarter (recorded in August, 1978, at Indiana, PA).

Dugan, Ernest R. Correspondence and interview with James Measell (August 1, 1989).

Dugan, Frances (daughter-in-law of Thomas E. A. Dugan). Interview with James Measell, August 29, 1989.

Eige, Eason. *A Century of Glassmaking in West Virginia*. Huntington: Huntington Galleries, 1980.

Ellwood City Historical Association. *A History of Ellwood City, Pennsylvania*. Ellwood City: privately printed, 1942.

Fenton Museum, archives and photos, Williamstown, WV.

Ferson, Regis and Mary. *Yesterday's Milk Glass Today*. Pittsburgh: privately printed, 1981.

Freeman, Larry. *Iridescent Glass*, enlarged second edition. Watkins Glen, NY: Century House, 1964.

Gazette, Indiana County (newspaper), various issues, 1892-1899.

Goldstein, Sidney M. and Leonard S. and Juliette K. Rakow. *Cameo Glass: Masterpieces from 2000 Years of Glassmaking*. Corning: Corning Museum of Glass, 1982.

Gilleland, Mildred Northwood. Interview with Jabe Tarter (recorded in August, 1978, at Indiana, PA).

Grover, Ray and Lee Grover. *English Cameo Glass*. New York: Crown, 1980.

Harden, Donald B. *Glass of the Caesars*. Milan: Ollivetti, 1987.

Harrison, Sam. B. *Front! or Ten Years with the Travelling Men*. New York: American News Co., 1889.

Hartung, Marion T. *Northwood Pattern Glass: Clear, Colored, Custard and Carnival*. Emporia, KS: by author, 1969.

Hartung, Marion T. *Opalescent Pattern Glass*. Des Moines: Wallace-Homestead, 1971.

Hayes, F. L. *Illustrated Atlas of the Upper Ohio River Valley*. Philadelphia, 1877.

Heacock, William. *Pattern Glass Preview* (abbreviated PGP).

Heacock, William. *The Glass Collector* (abbreviated GC).

Heacock, William. *Collecting Glass* (abbreviated CG).

Heacock, William. *Toothpick Holders from A to Z*. Marietta: Antique Publications, 1974; second edition 1976.

Heacock, William. *Opalescent Glass from A to Z*. Marietta: Antique Publications, 1975; second edition, 1977.

Heacock, William. *Custard Glass from A to Z*. Marietta: Antique Publications, 1976.

Heacock, William. *Syrups, Sugar Shakers & Cruets from A to Z*. Marietta: Antique Publications, 1976.

Heacock, William. *1000 Toothpick Holders*. Marietta: Antique Publications, 1977.

Heacock, William and Bickenheuser, Fred. *U. S. Glass from A to Z*. Marietta: Antique Publications, 1978.

Heacock, William. *Oil Cruets from A to Z*. Marietta: Antique Publications, 1981.

Heacock, William. *Old Pattern Glass According to Heacock*. Marietta: Antique Publications, 1981.

Heacock, William. "Carnival Glass by Dugan and Diamond," *The Antique Trader Weekly*, February 25, 1981, pp. 78-81.

Heacock, William and Gamble, William. *Cranberry Opalescent Glass from A to Z*. Marietta: Antique Publications, 1987.

History of Beaver County, Pennsylvania. Philadelphia: A. Warner and Co., 1888.

Housefurnisher: China, Glass and Pottery Review, various issues, 1898-1900.

Indiana County, PA. Public records, including deeds, births, and deaths.

"John & Harry Northwood: A Family Tradition," exhibition catalog for the Mansion Museum prepared by Holly L. Hoover. Wheeling: Oglebay Institute, 1982.

Kamm, Minnie Watson. *Pattern Glass Pitchers*. Vols. I-VIII. Grosse Pointe, MI: by author, 1939-1954.

Klein, Dan and Lloyd, Ward. *The History of Glass*. London: Orbis, 1984.

Lagerberg, Ted and Vi. *Collectible Glass, Books 1-4*. New Port Richey, FL, privately printed, 1963-1968.

Lawrence County, PA. Public records, including deeds, leases/agreements, lawsuits in Common Pleas and appellate courts, births, deaths, and wills.

Lechner, Mildred and Ralph. *The World of Salt Shakers*. Paducah: Collector Books, 1976.

Lee, Ruth Webb. *Nineteenth-Century Art Glass*. New York: Barrows, 1952.

Manley, Cyril. *Decorative Victorian Glass*. New York: Van Nostrand Reinhold, 1981.

McDonald, Ann Gilbert. "Milk Glass Lamps and the Northwood-Dugan Connection," *The Antique Trader Weekly*, February 27, 1985.

Measell, James and Smith, Don E. *Findlay Glass: The Glass Tableware Manufacturers, 1886-1902*. Marietta: Antique Publications, 1986.

Morgantown Post (newspaper), May 3, 1947.

Morris, Barbara. *Victorian Table Glass and Ornaments*. London: Barrie and Jenkins, 1978.

Murray, Melvin L. *History of Fostoria, Ohio Glass, 1887-1920*. Fostoria: by author, 1972.

National Glass Budget, various issues, 1896-1900.

New Castle Official City Directory 1895-96 Akron, Ohio: Burch Directory Co., 1895.

Northwood, John II. *John Northwood: His Contribution to the Stourbridge Glass Industry, 1850-1902*. Stourbridge: Mark and Moody, 1958.

Northwood, Ken. Correspondence with James Measell (1989).

Ohio County, WV. Public records, including deeds, births, deaths, and wills.

Peterson, Arthur G. *Glass Salt Shakers*, second printing. Des Moines: Wallace-Homestead, 1970.

Peterson, Arthur G. *Glass Patents and Patterns*. Sanford, FL: by author, 1973.

Pottery and Glassware Reporter, various issues, 1884-1892.

Pressed Glass, 1825-1925. Corning: Corning Museum of Glass, 1983.

Revi, Albert Christian. *American Pressed Glass and Figure Bottles*. New York: Nelson, 1964.

Revi, Albert Christian. *American Art Nouveau Glass*. Exton, PA: Schiffer, 1968.

Revi, Albert Christian. *Nineteenth Century Glass: Its Genesis and Development*, revised edition. New York: Galahad Books, 1967

Richards, Bart. *Lawrence County*. New Castle: New Castle Area School District, 1968.

Robb, Elizabeth Northwood. Correspondence and interviews (May-August, 1989) with James Measell.

Shenker, Israel. "A celebrated Roman vase has become a 20th-century phoenix," *Smithsonian*, July, 1989, pp. 52-63.

Smith, Frank R. and Ruth E. *Miniature Lamps*. New York: Nelson, 1968.

Spillman, Jane Shadel. *American and European Pressed Glass in the Corning Museum of Glass*. Corning: Corning Museum of Glass, 1981.

Spillman, Jane Shadel. *Glass Tableware, Bowls & Vases*. New York: Knopf, 1982.

State of Ohio, *Annual Report ... Of Workshops and Factories* (title varies), 1887-1900.

Taylor, Ardelle L. *Colored Glass Sugar Shakers and Syrup Pitchers*. N.p.: n. d.

United States Patent Office, various records pertaining to U. S. Patents and Designs.

Warman, Edwin G. *Milk Glass Addenda*, third edition. Uniontown PA: Warman Publishing, 1966.

Welker, John and Elizabeth. *Pressed Glass in America: Encyclopedia of the First Hundred Years*, 1825-1925. Ivyland, PA: Antique Acres Press, 1985.

Whitehouse, David. *Glass of the Roman Empire*. Corning: Corning Museum of Glass, 1988.

Wingerter, Charles A. *History of Greater Wheeling and Vicinity*. Chicago: Lewis Publishing, 1912.

INDEX OF PATTERNS AND ITEMS